The King and I

The King and I

HANGING OUT IN MANCHESTER WITH ERIC CANTONA

Claude Boli

Translated from the French by Peter Cossins

**SIMON &
SCHUSTER**

London · New York · Sydney · Toronto · New Delhi

First published in Great Britain by Simon & Schuster UK Ltd, 2022

Copyright © Claude Boli, 2022

English translation copyright © Peter Cossins, 2022

1 3 5 7 9 10 8 6 4 2

Simon & Schuster UK Ltd
1st Floor
222 Gray's Inn Road
London WC1X 8HB

www.simonandschuster.co.uk

Simon & Schuster Australia, Sydney
Simon & Schuster India, New Delhi

A CIP catalogue record for this book
is available from the British Library

Hardback ISBN: 978-1-4711-9916-5
Trade paperback ISBN: 978-1-3985-1906-0
eBook ISBN: 978-1-4711-9917-2

Typeset in Bembo by M Rules
Printed and bound by CPI Group (UK) Ltd, Croydon, CR0 4YY

To the Cantona family

CONTENTS

CHAPTER 1

Teenagers in Auxerre

As with the beginning of many a great friendship, my first encounter with Eric Cantona came about by chance. The memory makes me smile. It was 9 November 1981, and the football team my brothers Roger and Basile were playing for, CA (Club Athlétique) Romainville, had a match in the Championnat des Cadets (the Junior Championship). It was against l'Association de la Jeunesse Auxerroise, generally known as AJ Auxerre, whose team featured a 15-year-old Eric Cantona. The match was tight, intense, some of the play fabulous. Ultimately, Romainville won it by two goals to nil, with Roger scoring both goals – hence my smile. The yellow-and-blues of Romainville battled magnificently with the blue-and-whites from Auxerre. Yes, the first time I saw Eric, he was playing for a team that was wearing Manchester *City's* colours. Life can bring all kinds of surprises . . .

My name is Claude Boli. I come from the Ivory Coast, a former French colony, and at the age of nine I moved from

Abidjan, the capital, to France to continue my education. According to the Boli family, academic success was the only way to climb the social ladder. My father and mother came from families that had no material assets: no land or money. Both of them lost their parents when they were babies, so I never knew my grandparents. Orphaned at such an early age, my parents had to work hard to escape the spectre of a miserable life, both starting work young and having several jobs. In due course my father opted to join the army, and my mother became a small market trader selling fabrics imported from Holland and England (including Manchester).

My father, Jean, who could hardly read and write, was a former 'French Empire' soldier who fought in the Second World War in France, where he was one of the African soldiers called *tirailleurs sénégalais* – Senegal was where these soldiers, infantrymen in the main, were initially recruited from. He was a keen sportsman and especially enjoyed boxing, which he learned in the army, and football, which was imported to Abidjan by French nationals in the 1930s and '40s. For her part, my mother, Clémentine, married very young and never went to school. Her father had also been a soldier, who had fought with the French during the First World War.

When I arrived in France I lived with one of my elder sisters, Elisabeth, who had the difficult task of looking after the whole Boli family, which included my two footballing brothers, Basile and Roger, and me, the youngest member. Elisabeth was an executive secretary at the Ivory Coast embassy in Paris, and living with her was a big change for me compared to our extremely modest home life in Abidjan, where, for example, we didn't have running water in the house and couldn't eat meat every day. In Paris I discovered bathrooms, hot water, lifts, shoes that were my size, super-markets, the Métro … We lived in a middle-class building in Paris's 19th arrondissement, at the Porte des Lilas.

Like many kids born in Africa, and particularly in Ivory Coast, football was the main focus of our leisure time. My older brothers both wanted to take this passion for football further than just kicking a ball around in the streets, and so they joined a club not too far from the Porte des Lilas. That club was CA Romainville, which was located in the capital's suburbs. Although the name might not be familiar to most fans, Romainville had a reputation as one of the best junior clubs in France and played in the French Championship at that level. This meant that Roger, Basile and their teammates came up against almost all the most promising players in France at that time, including playing France's best club at that level: AJ Auxerre.

During this period, Roger and Basile were contacted by representatives of several clubs – FC Nantes, FC Sochaux-Montbéliard, Paris Saint-Germain and others. But in the end they decided to sign with Auxerre, partly because the town was comparatively close to Paris, lying about 150 kilometres away to the south-east. But the main reason my two brothers signed for Auxerre was the presence of one particular person: Guy Roux, a former player for the club who had taken over as player-manager in 1961 when they were in the Burgundy and Central Area regional league, four levels below France's top division. In 1980, with Roux still at the helm, Auxerre had been promoted to Ligue 1, joining France's biggest teams.

A major factor in that rise through the divisions was the strength of Auxerre's academy and junior teams. They had players from all over France – from Paris, like my brothers, from Marseille, from Nîmes, from Strasbourg. It was heartbreaking for Eric Cantona to leave his family in southern France and travel a thousand kilometres to the north, to a small town where it was much colder and the character of the people quite different from the Latin temperament in Marseille. What's more, Auxerre had a population of around 35,000-40,000, nothing like the big city environment that Eric was used to as a kid.

AJ Auxerre was created in 1905, an important date in France because it was the year the state and the church were split apart from each other under the terms of the Loi de la Laïcité. It was what was known in France as *un club de patronage*, that patronage coming from local Catholics, which also explains why the ground is called Le Stade de l'Abbé Deschamps, because he was the priest who founded AJ Auxerre as a sports club, initially embracing all kinds of activities in addition to football, including gymnastics and tennis.

There was definitely a sense of Catholic rigour within the club when Eric was playing there. Before the training centre was set up, the young players used to live in an establishment called Le Patronage, the name offering another reminder of its roots. The club was a bit like a YMCA or even the Catholic clubs established in England, often known as lads' clubs, where the approach to the youngsters was quite Victorian in manner, although not as strict: there were no punishments or sermons and church attendance wasn't compulsory. The people who ran it viewed sport not only as a way of bringing young people together, but also as a means of moralising. There was very much a social side to it, just as there was in some clubs in England, such as Manchester City, which had similar beginnings as Gorton AFC, and Birmingham City, clubs that emerged thanks to the church or to men linked closely to the church.

Auxerre was also remarkably well placed from a geographical perspective. There was no other club nearby that played in the first division. The towns that were relatively close – Bourges, Troyes, Dijon, Orléans – didn't have a team in the first division, and so within Burgundy and the Centre region all the attention was concentrated on that little club that had been forged by Guy Roux.

It was Roux who managed to convince my brothers that it would be the best club for them. It wasn't too difficult a task, as AJ Auxerre had established an excellent reputation for helping young players blossom. So at the end of the summer of 1982 my two brothers moved to Burgundy and into the accommodation at Auxerre's training centre.

I stayed in Paris and carried on going to the local lycée. I used to go down to Burgundy quite often to see them and would see Eric Cantona when I did, but we only used to say 'Bonjour' to each other. Gradually, though, my personal circumstances in the capital became more difficult and the environment I was living in was deteriorating. Finding myself a long way from the discipline my parents would have imposed, I was hanging around in neighbourhoods that weren't suitable for a kid of my age. I became a bit of a lout. Realising how bad things were getting, my two brothers decided, with the full agreement of my sister, that I should join them in Auxerre.

Like many of the footballers who had made the pilgrimage

to Burgundy hoping that Guy Roux's magical ability to bring through young players would rub off on them, when I arrived in Auxerre I was rather overwhelmed by the culture shock. Everything seemed tiny and the pace of life was very slow. In Paris I could travel quickly from one arrondissement to another using the Métro, and the shops weren't concentrated in one place. In Auxerre, everything you needed was in the town centre. If you wanted to be seen, you had to go to the town centre. The heart of the town, and its greatest pride, was AJ Auxerre. The club's success meant a huge amount to this small town in the Yonne. For many *Auxerrois*, the highlight of the week was the Saturday night football match at the Stade de l'Abbé Deschamps on Route de Vaux. Those who played for AJ Auxerre were local stars. For me, an urbanite, this was totally new. As I settled into life in Auxerre, I found myself enveloped in the atmosphere of a country town, with its rites, its habits, its charms.

Best known for the local wines, and particularly Chablis, Auxerre had also become renowned as a conveyor belt of French footballing talent, with an organisational set-up that was well in advance of its rivals at that time and probably among the best in Europe.

Guy Roux had established a scouting system that reached into every French region, and enabled them to spot and then court the best young players across the country. Not a single young prospect slipped beneath the radar of Roux and his scouts. Their first-team players came from every corner of France: north, south, east and west. Guy Roux was more than a coach for his players. He was their mentor, and for some certainly a father figure. He was completely dedicated to these young players, a number of whom in some cases had left their families at the age of thirteen or fourteen in order to try to become professional footballers. Some managed it, but the majority failed to take the big step up to this level. It was very hard for kids of that age to leave their parents and travel hundreds of kilometres to Auxerre and then find themselves competing for places in the team with the best young players in France.

Eric had made the long trip from the south, from Marseille and the SO Caillolais club that had produced several other big names, most notably Jean Tigana, and would later produce Christophe Galtier, who would go on to become a successful manager at Saint-Etienne and, more recently, LOSC Lille, France's Ligue 1 champions in 2020/21.

In 1982 Auxerre won the Coupe Gambardella, which features the best under-18 teams in France. Eric was an important member of the under-18 team at that time and a very good player, but he didn't stand out as extraordinary. There were other players in the team who looked as if they were going to make more of an impact on the game than him. Yes, he was good, but he wasn't shaping up to be in the class of Diego Maradona, Pelé or Lionel Messi, who were exceptional when they were teenagers. He was maturing much more steadily, a bit like Zinedine Zidane did, or Michel Platini. By the time they were twenty-four, twenty-five, twenty-six, they were recognised as being among the world's best, but not when they were in their mid-teenage years.

I started to get to know Eric a bit better early in 1983. Right from the off there was a special something between us: a smile to start with, a look of mutual regard, a degree of complicity. In short, we clicked. As we began to talk more, we realised we both loved Ajax of Amsterdam and the Dutch national team that featured Johan Cruyff and Johan Neeskens in the 1974 World Cup. We liked the Brazil team of the 1970s too that featured Pelé, Tostao and Jairzinho. We also talked about and revered Garrincha and other Brazilian players from the previous era, and the likes of Sócrates and Zico from the 1980s, players that personified the kind of beautiful football we both appreciated.

Music was another pillar of our friendship. We listened to lots of different types of music, from the Doors to the French singer-songwriter Christophe to jazz, and also lots of British music as well. We loved the new stuff from Britain – groups like Eurythmics, Simple Minds, Orchestral Manœuvres in the Dark, Tears for Fears, Talk Talk – but also other musical genres – Supertramp and Dire Straits, for instance. One group we both particularly liked was Genesis, and especially the vocalist, Peter Gabriel. We were big fans of the guitarist Carlos Santana too. Talking about these passions for Holland, Brazil and music brought us closer together, and made us realise we had a lot in common, that we enjoyed many of the same things.

That we became very good friends was down to one incident, though. Like all of the other members of the academy team, Eric lived in the accommodation provided for young players. After he'd been at Auxerre for a couple of seasons, Eric decided for reasons that weren't all that clear that he wanted to leave the training centre where the fifteen or so academy players were based. His mood had changed, and he wanted to live away from the other players. So he went to see Guy Roux, who was the head of the academy as well as the first-team coach. Eric told him that he would like to move out on his own – remember, this is a 17-year-old kid. Guy Roux wasn't happy, but he'd got to know Eric well, and so he decided to help him find an apartment. As a result, Eric become one of the first players, if not the first, to leave the training centre where my two brothers and the rest of the young players lived.

He got his own place, and the next time I saw him he said, 'Would you like to share the apartment with me?' That was when our joint story really began. I found out later that he'd already been to see Basile and politely asked if he could find out if his little brother would share with him. We were both very young. Eric was seventeen and I was just fifteen. Initially we were only together in the flat at weekends, because I was a boarder at a school in Avallon, a small town about 50 kilometres from Auxerre. I would board there during the week and return to Auxerre every weekend, and the two of us would then spend a good deal of that time together.

We lived in two different places in Auxerre. The first was in what in France they call the ZAC, the *zone d'activité commerciale*: a small district just outside the town centre where a lot of workers lived. It was a pretty basic apartment, a small place with two bedrooms, what in France is known as an HLM, in other words a council-owned property. It was quite rare to see youngsters like the two of us living there, unless they were young couples who had just set up home together. It was almost unheard of to find two teenage boys sharing a place in that part of town. It was pretty close to the training centre, however, and Eric would travel there and back on a motorbike, sometimes with me as his passenger. It was a pretty simple life. The second place we shared was a two-room apartment that had the advantage of being nearer to the Stade de l'Abbé Deschamps. We were close to the River Yonne and a beautiful park, the Parc de l'Arbre Sec.

While it was a little peculiar for two adolescents to be living like that, one of the things about football at that level is that players join the set-up when they're very young and become quite mature pretty quickly. Without their parents close at hand they have to become responsible for themselves and their actions, and figure out how to get by. It's a hard life, and not normal at all for a kid of thirteen, fourteen or fifteen. It's a paradoxical situation: on the one hand, you're a footballer who is still only hoping to turn professional; on the other, you're already effectively living the life of a professional footballer. The bottom line is, you have to behave like an adult.

Although I wasn't a footballer myself, because I was very close to several promising players I stuck to the same regime as them, or at least I tried to. I attempted to make that switch from child to adult. Being with Eric made this easier. Our relationship was based on an extremely simple approach to life. I used to do the cooking, and Eric really liked the food I dished up, which was based on the meals I'd seen being prepared when I was a kid back in Ivory Coast. My usual meal, called *maffé,* was a stew made with peanut sauce that was served with rice.

Eric was privileged, I suppose you could say. He was already doing things in his own way and not following the routine laid down for the other players. But I don't want to give the wrong idea. We were two kids living what was really quite an innocent life. At the same time, we had to behave responsibly. Although Eric hadn't yet signed a full professional contract with AJ Auxerre, he still lived in a disciplined manner. We didn't have any alcohol in the flat, for instance. There was no hint of the lad culture that was the norm among young English players at that time. We were quite serious, by which I mean we were comparatively mature, not that we were straitlaced. Our life was very much organised around our passion for culture, as well as football, of course. Those were the things that really mattered to us, that stimulated and excited us.

What I remember more than anything about that time is the match days. At that time, Eric was playing for Auxerre's reserves in the third division. I'd attend most of the home games, and every time the B-team was playing away I used to listen to the game on the radio. It was a bit like being in the 1950s, listening in on my little transistor radio, just as I had back in the Ivory Coast. When we went to the stadium to watch a football match, we would take our transistor radios and listen to the enthusiastic commentary while we watched the game. I can remember being very happy when I heard that my brothers and Eric had played well or scored, which they generally did.

If AJ Auxerre had been playing away, Eric would usually get back to our apartment very late in the evening, towards midnight or even half-past. I'd always have a meal waiting for him and he'd tell me how the game had gone. He didn't talk a great deal about it, but he'd pick out the most significant moments. Beyond that he wouldn't go into much detail, and quickly forgot what had happened – he was always looking ahead to the next game rather than dwelling on the last one.

At that time Eric really liked Olympique de Marseille, but also some Italian players, such as Giancarlo Antognoni and

Paolo Rossi, and the Argentinian genius Diego Maradona. He used to talk about his parents and family a lot, about his life growing up in Marseille. His father worked as a nurse in a psychiatric hospital, and his younger brother Joël was also on the road to becoming a professional footballer as a member of the academy set-up at Olympique de Marseille. I would be captivated by his stories about his home city, because Marseille was multicultural, and also where my father had arrived in France during the Second World War, which gave it real resonance for me.

Eric was very close to my two older brothers, but over time the two of us become closer still, despite our difference in age, which was quite significant given we were still so young. Our bond did stem, of course, from our mutual love of football, but there were other aspects to it as well beyond the sporting – literature, painting and, above all, music were the cement in our relationship, were at the very heart of it. We were also both just naturally very curious about things.

Early on, Eric told me about his passion for African art and for African masks. Their mystical nature really fascinated him. He also talked to me about his desire to travel in Africa – not the Africa that tourists see, but the enchanted and unreal side of the continent. He loved talking about it, finding out all he could, exchanging ideas. He wanted to meet people who lived in little villages, people who knew about the plants in their local countryside, people who handed down their culture in the stories they told, and the memories that we in turn passed on.

Eric loved painting, and would devote every Sunday to it. His father used to love painting as well, which is where Eric had picked up his passion. It shaped him in a significant way, as he could express himself through art. Looking at his paintings, I could see he'd got inspiration from all kinds of artists. There was one that was mainly red with a dollar symbol and really resembled pop art. He also liked the Expressionists and Post-impressionists. He painted landscapes in a style quite similar to Cézanne, and abstract works that were like Kandinsky's. He spoke to me with real empathy about Vincent van Gogh. He knew a lot not only about van Gogh's paintings but also about his life, and would talk a great deal about him being an artist who had lived in total penury and only really become famous after his death. Eric was truly fascinated by the Dutch painter. He also bought a lot of works by both well-known and less renowned artists: Pierre Ambrogiani, Antoine Ferrari, Auguste Chabaud . . .

While Eric was painting and I was engrossed in my school-books, there would always be music playing – Miles Davis, Pink Floyd, Yes, Santana, Peter Gabriel. During these periods, Eric would be very introspective. I guess this time we spent together was a major contribution to the philosophical side to Eric that everyone readily associates him with now, as was his father's artistic bent, of course. Eric was still only seventeen and had finished his formal education a year or two earlier, so he was exploring all kinds of ideas.

He wasn't an extrovert who would chat to anyone. He was more reserved, as I was, but when we were together we could and did talk about anything. People used to think he was quite distant, but that was only because they didn't know him. It wasn't like that at all between him and me. We really got on well and understood one another.

I don't want to give the impression that we were totally focused on culture and the arts to the exclusion of everything else. Our friendship was also forged via others in our peer group. AJ Auxerre wasn't simply a football club: it was a family, drawn together by so many different ties. Away from the football pitch, we also had a variety of extra-curricular activities to distract and engage us. Being teenagers, we were interested in girls and would talk about the ones we'd met and fancied. Romance offered the chance to escape from the pressures of being an apprentice in professional football. They were magical moments, quite innocent rites of passage that all youngsters go through: first date, first kiss, first love, first disappointment, first musical souvenir . . .

Eric rarely spoke about his girlfriends, but I remember there was one he was quite scared of. 'Your friend doesn't say very much,' I remember her saying to me one day. 'Is he shy?' But most of the girls who were part of our social group we knew either because they were friends with other players, or because their parents came to see AJ Auxerre play. Some of the parents were very proud to see their daughters going out with a footballer – Auxerre was, after all, a small town, and the football club was at the very centre of life there. The local paper, *L'Yonne Républicaine*, was almost obliged to cover it because of the attention it brought the town, and so the footballers were extremely well known.

Eric met the first big love of his life while he was at Auxerre. Her name was Isabelle Ferrer, and she was the sister of his teammate, Bernard 'Nino' Ferrer, who also went on to play for Marseille. They met in 1985 at Bernard's wedding. Eric was nineteen and Isabelle twenty-two. She was studying psychology at the University of Aix-en-Provence, near Marseille. As soon as he saw her, it was love at first sight. I remember the first thing he said to me about her: 'Claudio,

I've met a real woman. She's Nino's sister. She's beautiful, intelligent, composed, gentle. She's at the University of Aix. You'll see, she's absolutely nothing like the girls here. She's so charming! I liked her from the very first moment. It's really serious between her and me. Her eyes shone with happiness.' I couldn't wait to meet this 'extraordinary' woman. He fell for her in a big way, and within three years they were married.

When Eric got back to our flat on Saturday night after he'd played, we'd go out to nightclubs. There was a particular one we'd go to about 25 kilometres from Auxerre, and all our friends would be there as well. But, as I've already mentioned, the big difference between France and England was the attitude towards alcohol. In England at that time, players would go out and have a lot of beers, but in France that simply didn't happen. That's not to say that the players didn't drink: they would have spirits in moderation – vodka, gin and tonic – but they didn't take it to excess. They'd sip at their drinks rather than go out with the aim of having a skinful.

Because the team wouldn't get back from away games until midnight or one in the morning, we'd go out very late and stay out until the early hours, until half five in the morning, knowing we could sleep in and chill out on the Sunday. Thinking back, I can't ever remember Eric the worse for wear as a result of drinking too much. All we were interested in was having a good time with the other players and our friends. We really enjoyed those nights out with Roger, Basile, Daniel Dutuel, William Prunier, Jean-Marc Arena, Ferhat Khirat, Franco Vignola, Jocelyn Monate, Gaetan Laclef and others.

As I got to know these young players so well, what stood out for me were the sacrifices they'd made in coming to

Auxerre from all over France. They had such passion for football, but they were still very young men who had to deal with all kinds of unforeseen issues and difficulties, and above all the knowledge that one stroke of bad luck – most probably an injury – could mean the end of a playing career.

Consequently, they had to be psychologically very strong. They couldn't let themselves become downhearted by one bad performance, because there was so much competition for places. Auxerre's extensive scouting system meant that new players, the latest crop of France's best talent, would be arriving regularly. During the mid-1980s the team had a reputation for winning everything, for competing at a higher level than their rivals, and this was why. Burgundy would always win the French Regional Championship, but Auxerre were always favourites to win the championship at youth level. Like several of his teammates, Eric also showed his talent in the French national side at junior level.

They had some great young players at Auxerre then: the likes of Patrice Monier and Eric Villa – some of them, indeed, more highly regarded as future talents than Eric. My brother Basile was certainly more precocious as a player than him. He made his first-team debut at sixteen, on 29 April 1983, lining up in central defence away at Monaco. Eric found it a little harder to break through because he was in direct competition with Patrice Garande and, in particular, a very good Polish centre-forward, Andrzej Szarmach. He'd played in the 1974 World Cup when Poland had finished third, and in the 1978 finals too. Although he was very much a veteran compared to the youngsters in the Auxerre team, he was still the main striker and a regular goal-scorer. He'd joined Auxerre in 1980 as the French realised that, coming from the Eastern Bloc, he wasn't going to cost them that much. He turned out to be an absolute bargain. Szarmach gave Eric a lot of advice about the game, about the positions he needed to take up as a striker, the runs he needed to make.

The other player who really stood out, much more than Eric, was Jean-Marc Ferreri, who was four years older. The team leaned on him in a big way. As he was their number 10, he was dubbed the next Michel Platini. He was a member of the French team that won the European Championship in 1984 and is remembered for the likes of Platini, Alain Giresse and Jean Tigana. Ferreri was also in the squad for the 1986 World Cup in Mexico, where France finished third.

The relationship between Eric and Guy Roux was a special one, because the Auxerre coach knew Eric had a lot of potential. It wasn't what you'd call a father–son relationship, as was the case between Roux and my brother Basile. The two of them really were close, while Jean-Marc Ferreri was probably even closer to the coach, not least because he lived in Roux's house. With Eric it was different, but they still had a lot of respect and time for each other. Guy Roux also realised that Eric perhaps needed to be treated slightly differently. Allowing him to live outside the training centre was proof of that: Roux could see that Eric wasn't happy, needed his own space, and that it would probably be better for both player and club if they could work out a different arrangement.

Within the group of young people we hung around with, there were the highs that came from playing in the first team but also plenty of lows: injuries, setbacks on the pitch, the fear of never signing that all-important first contract as a *stagiaire* (a triallist) and, of course, the biggest fear of all, of never signing a professional contract. These thoughts obsessed a lot of the players – with good reason, because many of the players who were part of the academy set-up in 1982/83 didn't end up signing pro forms. But Eric was one of those few players who signed a pro contract and made it into the first team.

Witnessing them achieve these landmarks made this period particularly special. Not only did I see my brothers excelling at Auxerre, but I also saw my best friend doing so, and as a result earning his first caps as a junior international. I used to watch him playing for the youth and B-teams, and also remember his occasional games for the first team – even some of the goals that he scored, including his first for Auxerre's first team. It was on 14 May 1985, in an away game at Rouen. He scored a superb goal that proved to be the winner in a 2-1 victory. Two weeks later, he scored again in what was a vital game for Auxerre. They were playing away again, this time at Racing Club Strasbourg. It was an intense game that eventually finished as a 1-1 draw, Eric scoring from 25 or 30 metres out with a tremendous shot. That result meant Auxerre qualified for the UEFA Cup in the following season.

I recall another game quite clearly. It was also in 1985, the final of the Coupe Gambardella, the youth cup final. That year Auxerre were playing Montpellier l'Hérault, whose team featured Laurent Blanc, who would become one of Eric's best friends as well as a future Manchester United player (2001-3). The match took place in Bourges, about 150 kilometres from Auxerre, and the first half was fiercely contested. Gradually, though, AJ Auxerre took control of the game. In the team were my brother Roger and two other players who would go on to have great careers at the top level: striker Pascal Vahirua and goalkeeper Lionel Charbonnier, who was the team's captain and later featured in the French squad that won the 1998 World Cup. Auxerre won the game 3-0, with Eric scoring all three goals.

When the 1985/86 season got under way, Eric got a few more opportunities in the first team as Andrej Szarmach had moved on. But he still wasn't a regular starter, and at the end of 1985 he was loaned out to Martigues, who played in the second division. Naturally, I continued to follow his career very closely. It was very hard for a young kid like him to make an impression at a team in the second division: it's a tough league to play in, and he only got a dozen or so games, but nevertheless it was a turning point. After six months he returned to Auxerre and over the next couple of seasons became a first-team regular. In the 1986/87 season he was Auxerre's top scorer in the league with thirteen goals, as the team finished fourth and qualified for the UEFA Cup again.

By then, my brothers had both signed professional contracts with Auxerre and had moved into a new place together, and that was when I started living with them. When Eric came back from Martigues we were soon as thick as thieves again, but circumstances were changing for both of us and our lives were about to go in different directions, with radical consequences for our relationship. Eric started living with Isabelle, and in 1987 they got married. Two years later they had their first child, Raphaël. Then, following another good season for Eric in 1987/88, we were destined to drift a little further apart. Several teams expressed an interest in signing him. He had a choice between AC Milan, Monaco, Paris Saint-Germain, Racing Matra de Paris – a big club then, which doesn't exist any more – and l'OM (Olympique de Marseille). He decided, not too surprisingly given that he is from Marseille, to join the club that had always been close to his heart. It's difficult for any player who comes from Marseille to resist the lure of OM; it's such a big club, with a huge and very fervent following.

In 1990, my brother Basile left Auxerre to join Eric at Olympique de Marseille. I was doubly satisfied: Basile was going to play in one of the best teams of the time, and I was going to see Eric more often. That same year, I passed my baccalaureate and decided to stay on in the south of France at the University of Montpellier, studying sociology. That season, I went to the Stade Vélodrome a few times and met up with Eric. He seemed happy and had the confidence of a coach he liked and respected a lot – 'the Kaiser', Franz Beckenbauer. During the matches, I would sit and talk with Isabelle and notice how Raphaël was growing up. Although it wasn't often, Eric and I were always pleased to see each other whenever the opportunity arose.

During his final two years at Olympique de Marseille (1989-91) Eric had his ups and downs. He suffered a serious injury that sidelined him from playing for several months, and he was suspended by the club after ripping off and throwing away his shirt when he was substituted during a friendly. Following this incident, he was loaned out to Bordeaux and then to Montpellier, where he contributed significantly to the club's first French Cup win in 1990.

While I was studying, I kept up with Eric's progress through the press and my brother Basile. In 1991, he signed for Nîmes, which was only thirty minutes away from Montpellier. Although the team didn't have the stellar reputation of Auxerre, Marseille or Bordeaux, and despite the fact that he'd also had offers from Paris Saint-Germain and Olympique Lyonnais, his choice of a smaller club like this was certainly linked to the esteem in which he held the club's president, Michel Mézy. The other factor was beautiful Nîmes itself and its surroundings, especially the Camargue, with its tracts of empty wilderness and expansive plains where magnificent white horses galloped, and the Roman city's amphitheatre where bullfights were held during its famous Feria des Vendanges festival.

Unfortunately, Eric didn't stay long at Nîmes, and we only managed to see each other once when he was playing for them. We didn't have time to talk much, but he told me he was enjoying his new life. On a sporting level, the club was doing well, and Eric was also performing very nicely in the French team. However, as was getting to be the case with Eric, a beautiful relationship with his team sometimes came to an unexpectedly abrupt end. This time it was a league match between Nîmes and Saint-Etienne: Eric protested about a decision the referee had made and, in a fit of pique, threw the ball at him. He was sent off, and subsequently given a long ban.

The sanction made Eric decide to retire from professional football. However, thanks to the prompting of Gérard Houllier and, particularly, Michel Platini, who both told him he was too young to end his career, he decided to reverse his decision. Houllier and Platini used their contacts to help him find a new club, where he could show that he was a great footballer. England, they decided, would be best suited to welcoming Eric Cantona. So his move to England came about by accident, but it was one of those marvellous twists of fortune life can bring about.

My friendship with Eric had developed gradually and was cemented by those two years living together in Auxerre. That sealed our friendship, our loyalty, our bond, and it was what enabled us to rekindle our friendship when our paths crossed once more in Manchester. We'd got to know each other when we were very young, which was crucial, because it's such a significant part of anyone's life. It's transformative. When we became close friends again, it was largely because he already knew me, and I already knew him. That's often the way with friends you make when you're young: despite all that life throws at you they stand the test of time. This second time round I was a PhD student and he was married with a child, both of us young men well set on our career paths.

CHAPTER 2

Two *Frenchies* in Manchester

In November 1993, I left Montpellier and the south of France for Manchester in the north of England. My new home was in the Victoria Park area in the south of the city, in a small but attractive Victorian house a short walk away from Rusholme with its famous Curry Mile, where some of the best Indian, Pakistani and Sri Lankan restaurants can be found. I found myself fully immersed in multicultural England, its population testament to the reach of the country's former empire.

The different communities intermingled, the result a mixing of the flavours of Asia and of England. Rather than being a barrier, food brought them together. It was perfectly acceptable, for instance, to buy beer in an off-licence and take it into a Pakistani restaurant where the sale of alcohol was prohibited for religious reasons. There were plenty of pubs in among the restaurants. Every Thursday at the Clarence, one of the preferred drinking establishments for Manchester City fans, there was an Irish music night. The club's ground was not too far away from Rusholme.

I was sharing the house on Conyngham Road with my girlfriend, Anne, an anthropology student specialising in African textiles, also known as wax prints. It was, in fact, down to her that I decided to continue my studies, and specifically here in Manchester. When, after three years at the University of Montpellier, I discussed my desire to continue my studies in England with her, she said she was happy to go with me on the condition that we went to Manchester. Perhaps there was a sense of destiny too, stemming from a political science lecture I attended in Montpellier when I found myself captivated by the work of the English historian Eric Hobsbawm, which dealt with the economic and social history of Great Britain. The Victorian era and the Industrial Revolution started to become an obsession, and drew me from one lecture to the next. I wanted to find out all I could about Victorian England. Although it didn't matter to me where I ended up, it was entirely fitting that I was able to immerse myself in the place at the very heart of this global upheaval: Manchester, the embodiment of the modern industrial city, according to Karl Marx in his classic 1845 work *The Condition of the Working Class in England.* Consequently, I left France for the land of the Beatles and UB40, hoping to understand how the Industrial Revolution had come about.

Why did Anne choose this city? She knew a lot about its industrial history, and told me that the city once known as Cottonopolis still played an important role in the textile world. Indeed, Manchester was one of the two places, along with Helmond in the Netherlands, where wax fabrics were still manufactured for the African market. I knew these products very well as they'd been familiar to me since childhood.

My mother was a wax seller at the Abidjan market in Ivory Coast. So Manchester Cottonopolis it was to be.

As well as what I'd read about the city's industrial past, I also knew that Manchester had long been a hugely influential place when it came to football, thanks to the exploits of both Manchester United and Manchester City. I knew the Red Devils better, though. In 1991, they had knocked Montpellier out of the European Cup Winners' Cup in the quarter-finals and gone on to win the title following the lifting of the five-year ban on English clubs from European competitions. And of course Eric, one of the stars of the Montpellier team along with Laurent Blanc and the Colombian Carlos Valderrama, had been the architect of the French Cup victory in 1990 that enabled them to qualify for Europe.

The city was also well known to me for other reasons too, especially music. Among the bands I enjoyed were Simply Red, with their fantastic singer Mick Hucknall, who would later become an acquaintance, thanks to Eric. Then of course there were the Smiths. I had begged the English assistant at my high school in Burgundy to lend me her cassette of their album *The Queen is Dead*. Then there was Joy Division and, later on, New Order, plus the mythical Hacienda club. I knew Manchester too for the Umbro sports brand based there. Consequently, moving to Manchester seemed like the obvious thing to do.

Another decisive reason was, of course, Eric being there. Through various contacts, Eric had initially spent a very short spell with Sheffield Wednesday, but quickly signed for Leeds United, on loan to start with. But, as the Yorkshire team marched towards the title, the move was made permanent. He played a significant role in that championship success. He featured more regularly in the team the following season, but put in a transfer request after being dropped for a game against Arsenal. Realising that he was available, Manchester United put in an offer and the transfer was rapidly completed.

We'd lost touch a bit, but I got news about him from time to time via my brother Basile – they both played regularly for the French team. The physical distance between Eric and me and, to a certain extent, his family life had limited our friendship to occasional messages. In April 1993, a few days before the France vs. Sweden World Cup qualifying match, I called him at the Clairefontaine training centre near Paris where *Les Bleus* meet before each game. I started telling him about my idea of coming to England, and he interrupted me. 'Come to Manchester,' he said – 'you're going to enjoy it. It's a footballing city, a real cultural city, with a big student population, and I'm sure you'll like it.' He finished by saying that we would meet again soon, and gave me his two phone numbers, one for the Novotel West hotel, where he was living temporarily, and the other for Manchester United's training centre, the Cliff.

Our reunion took place in October 1993. After several days of acclimatising to our new English life, I decided to call Eric at the Cliff. He wasn't surprised to hear from me, and even seemed relieved that I'd called. We talked for barely a minute. 'Okay, Claudio,' he said, the nickname taking us back to the moments we shared in Auxerre. 'I'll see you this evening. Do you know the centre of Manchester at all?' I told him I did – since my arrival I had been walking almost everywhere to get to know my new home town. I had rediscovered a fundamental part of my native Africa.

Anne and I walked to the bus stop near our house and took the first Stagecoach bus into the city centre. It was about five in the evening, and we were still not used to the fact that by that hour it was effectively night-time. As strangers in any city tend to do, we went upstairs to the top deck.

I'd arranged to meet Eric at six at J. W. Johnson's, a chic bar on one of Manchester's busiest and trendiest streets, Deansgate. The memory of our meeting has stuck with me ever since. We sat at the back of the room, facing the entrance, so I could see him as soon as he came in. Barely ten minutes passed and Eric arrived. In seconds the atmosphere in the bar was transformed, becoming thick with murmuring and unconcealed excitement. I looked around, stunned to see that everyone was following his every step. At the same time, it was also clear that everyone was wondering who the lucky person was who was going to meet the city's new star. Suddenly every head turned towards Anne and me. Eric sat down and greeted Anne in the typical French style with a kiss on each cheek. Then we embraced each other.

I hadn't told Anne we were planning to meet an old friend, and she was surprised and a little shaken to see him, to meet the man she could remember holding up the Coupe de France trophy in Montpellier's Place de la Comédie in 1990. As is generally the case when he's with people he knows well, Eric was very chatty. He talked and talked, asked us if we'd settled in okay, about the area we were living in, about our plans at the university. I asked him for news of his family, about Isabelle and his son, Raphaël, his parents, his two brothers, Jean-Marie and, especially, Joël, with whom I've spent a lot of time and always got on really well with since we first met in

Auxerre. Joël was the second member of the Cantona family to become a professional soccer player, and came through the ranks at Olympique de Marseille.

The conversation turned back to Manchester. 'You'll soon see I'm fine here,' Eric said, 'and the people love me. You can feel the passion for football everywhere. The stadiums are full, in the stands the fans sing and enjoy themselves. They're always behind their team, no matter what the result is. Home and away, they are there.' He kept repeating, 'I'm fine here.' He was full of praise for the city, for all the possibilities it offered. 'As someone who loves music, you're going to enjoy it here. You remember Simply Red, Joy Division? Those guys are all from here. Manchester is a special kind of city, one that has no need to envy London. It's like it is in France, where there's Paris and then the rest of the country. But Manchester is just as important as London in every aspect, whether it's sport, culture, music, literature,' he explained.

Naturally, we spent some time recalling our memories of Auxerre. We discussed the friends we'd had among the players there – William Prunier, Daniel Dutuel, Miguel Pineda, Franco Vignola, Ferhat Khirat, Stéphane Drici, Jocelyn Monate – and the places we used to go to in the city centre, such as the l'Arbre Sec park. We reminisced about the training centre, the apartment we'd shared in the ZAC, teenage romances, the nightclubs we used to go to – the Mini Cumba, Le Paradisier, Le Number One. We couldn't stop ourselves from laughing at some of the ridiculous things we'd got up to. Seeing us crying with laughter, the other customers in the bar glanced across, our mirth eliciting little smiles of understanding.

When Anne excused herself to go to the ladies', Eric asked

me about my relationship with her. He wanted to know about her personality, where she came from, whether she had a career or was a student, how we'd come to be living together – everything a friend wants to know about the person you're sharing your life with: 'Where did you meet her? Have you known her for a long time? Does she like football? Who does the cooking – you or her?'

When Anne returned to our table, the conversation turned back to Manchester. I explained to Eric what had driven me to go there. It didn't take long for us to decide we were going to do all we could to get the best out of this great city. As a result, Eric and I would become inseparable all over again. We stayed in the bar for less than an hour, then Eric invited us to go to another place, a bar on Oldham Street. As we left J. W. Johnson's, all eyes were on him. I was surprised to see that there was no hint of animosity towards him at all, just lots of smiles and looks of fascination as other customers realised who he was. As soon as we walked in the door of the next bar, three people, including two women in their thirties, rushed to ask for his autograph. A taxi driver shouted, 'Eric, you're the best!' Another fan actually crossed the road to greet Manchester United's number 7. Within minutes, I'd realised how popular Eric had become. I'd never seen this kind of response to him before. I was aware, too, of his charisma. I turned to him. 'You're right,' I said. 'You're loved here.' He gave me a little smile and we walked on.

Sometimes Anne would join us, but most of the time it would just be me and Eric who would wander along the city's most renowned streets: King Street with its fashion boutiques, Oxford Street and Whitworth Street, the artistic centre that was also one of the hubs of the music and dance scene, including the Hacienda club, and the area around Bridgewater Hall. Oxford Road would become another of our hangouts, close to the University of Manchester and Manchester Metropolitan University, where the pubs selling alcohol at unbelievably low prices were at the heart of student life.

Sometimes consciously, sometimes not, we went to places steeped in history, in business or politics, or even followed in the footsteps of the Romans. We'd go to the Royal Exchange, the Corn Exchange, the Reform Club, Free Trade Hall, Castlefield Roman Fort. Because we were foreigners, we didn't have pre-conceived prejudices about anywhere. Our status as 'outsiders' was a pass, a kind of licence to access all areas, and our desire to get to know the city was a strong motivation for these strolls. We decided to make Manchester our land of discovery and insight into an England that we appreciated more and more each day.

This freedom resulted in us stumbling into some strange and funny situations. One day, between Whitworth Street and Portland Street, on a glorious afternoon when the sun was breaking through after a brief shower, we discovered a wonderful spot with the Rochdale Canal running through, and decided to stop for a drink. We could see that everyone in the bar was a little surprised to see us there, but they welcomed us with complicit smiles. By that point we weren't surprised at all by the warm welcome: we were getting used to the fact that Eric was recognised and appreciated even by people who weren't United supporters or football fans, simply because he was a footballer who was regularly in the press, and a little different from the norm.

But as we sipped our beers, we noticed on the walls a

series of pictures of the bodies of beautiful boys. We started laughing. Bloody hell! The bar was called Manto, and was one of the focal points for Manchester's gay community. Our roaming had carried us into the middle of the gay village, allowing us to see another vibrant part of the city's life. We carried on chatting without any feeling of embarrassment.

During these walks, I sometimes turned my gaze upwards, a little like Eric used to on the football pitch. I often observed buildings in this way, prompted apparently by some historical reflex hidden in a corner of my mind. When we passed buildings dating from the Victorian and Edwardian eras I'd be on high alert. I quickly got to know and love the Free Trade Hall on Peter Street that was designed by Edward Walters in 1856, the Britannia Hotel on Portland Street, designed by Travis and Mangnall in 1858, the Barton Arcade on Deansgate, a sumptuous shopping arcade built by Corbett, Raby and Sawyer in 1871, Lancaster House and India House on Whitworth Street, designed by Henry S. Fairhurst in 1906, and the Midland Hotel on Peter Street, where Charles Rolls and Frederick Royce had met in 1904.

When I got home, I'd get out my notebook and write down the names of the streets, the buildings, and the people linked to them, a history of the city of Manchester that has never left me. In Eric, I had found an accomplice in the present with whom I could venture into the past.

CHAPTER 3

Past and Present

At the University of Manchester I was enrolled in the Department of Sociology under a brilliant professor, Rodney Watson, a Francophile who gave Anne and me a great deal of help in getting used to university life in England. He taught ethnomethodology, a radical but very important approach to urban sociology that examines the ways in which individuals negotiate interpersonal relationships in everyday life.

I relished discovering the work of eminent British and American sociologists such as Norbert Elias, Anthony Giddens, Howard Becker, Erving Goffman and Harold Garfinkel. However, I was more drawn to the writings of historians, especially those from Oxford and Cambridge, and consequently I decided on a new direction for my studies, closer to social history. English history from the mid–nineteenth century to the present became my new area of investigation.

I devoted myself to the works of both classical historians and emerging figures among the new generation of academics who were adopting a fresh approach to the subject, giving particular attention to those who concentrated on Manchester and sport. As a result, I was captivated by the work of A. J. P. Taylor, Eric Hobsbawm, Asa Briggs, J. F. C. Harrison, David Cannadine, James Walvin, Arthur Marwick and Dave Russell.

One crucial event influenced my transformation from sociologist to historian. During a conference on European football at the London School of Economics, I met two French lecturers: Pierre Lanfranchi, Professor of History at the International Centre for Sport, History and Culture at De Montfort University in Leicester, and Christian Bromberger, an ethnologist at the University of Aix-Marseille, a renowned specialist in the behaviour of supporters of clubs in Marseille, Turin and Naples.

Our exchanges proved constructive, as Pierre Lanfranchi told me he was looking for students with my profile as a sociologist–historian and invited me to join the team of researchers investigating the links between football and society in European countries. He suggested I look at English football and use Manchester United as a case study. The idea appealed to me, and things started to fall into place. A collaboration agreement was signed between De Montfort University, where I was continuing my studies after leaving Manchester University, and the sociology department at the University of Nantes, headed by Jean-Michel Faure and Charles Suaud, who had initiated the exploration of the sociology of football in France. A research grant from the French National Centre for Scientific Research (CNRS) was also made available to me at the University of Nantes, effectively making me a student at De Montfort and Nantes.

Two of us had been chosen to look at sport in England and France. At De Montfort University, there was a 'dream team' of British sports specialists: Tony Mason, Richard Holt, Chuck Korr, Wray Vamplew, Jeff Hill, Matt Taylor and Jean Williams. They had produced some of the best football books and articles around. The university was also the first research centre to look at sport from an international perspective, which gave the institution global recognition.

This presented me with a major challenge: how could I meet these enormous expectations? I set out with a single goal in mind: analysing English society as it was and had become, using Manchester United as a point of reference.

Before delving into newspaper archives, searching out press articles and other journalistic works, and reading the biographies and autobiographies of Manchester United's managers and players, I set out to identify the facets of modern sport from its beginnings in the 1870s and 1880s, focusing initially on the works of the pioneers in this domain: James Walvin, Tony Mason, Richard Holt, Peter Bailey, Derek Birley, Dennis Brailsford, T. J. L. Chandler, J. A. Mangan, Neil Tranter, John Williams and Eric Dunning (sociologists of the University of Leicester).

Then I started to research sport in Manchester and the surrounding areas, which led me to visit archives in all kinds of places. I became 'addicted' to the Manchester Central Library, the John Rylands Library, the Working-Class Movement Library, Cheetham's Library, Portico Library and all the libraries around the city and in Bolton, Stockport, Oldham, Bury, Rochdale and Wigan. Armed with a large, orange-striped notebook, a four-colour pen, a yellow and black pencil and a Staedtler rubber, I roamed around any institution I could find with reference books and archives. To get to grips with the history of English sport and fully understand what I was reading, I bought a lot of new and used books around the Manchester University campus, at Blackwell's, Dillon's, Haigh and Hochland, the Portland Bookshop and Waterstone's.

As I travelled around by bus, tram and train, I made a surprising and exciting discovery. Unlike in France, these libraries were full of books that could be purchased at extremely low prices. Every visit to a library therefore became an opportunity to obtain 'the best bargain ever'. I found other places too where the price of books was surprisingly low: charity shops. Gradually, I became an expert on the best places to find books; on where to pick up contemporary history books (Oxfam in Didsbury), books on local sport (Sale or Macclesfield Library), and on Manchester United (Oldham Library). I knew where all the charity shops were across Greater Manchester and the particular niches they specialised in, and faithfully traipsed round them.

My tours of these sometimes quite unusual places in my quest to lift the lid on the past saw Eric nickname me 'Mister Bargain'. It was an odd feeling for my mind to be wandering down all manner of paths into the past at the same time as my being in close contact with one of Manchester United's key players. Two or three times a week, in between studies and searching out books and archives, I would organise a get-together with Eric.

I'd often take the bus to the Cliff on the edge of Salford, and right from the start, October 1993, I was allowed into this inner sanctum. The first time I went, I was amazed at the dilapidation of this place where so many glorious names had trained and been nurtured in the past: Charlie Mitten, the Busby Babes, Denis Law, George Best, Alex Stepney, Martin Buchan, Ray Wilkins, Norman Whiteside ... It looked rather shambolic: a football pitch with a tired old stand overlooking it to provide a touch of antiquated charm.

Once inside the main building, I used to sit down on the benches near the changing rooms where the players took their showers. I'd hear singing and shouting, and chat to scantily clad players who were already established stars – the likes of Bryan Robson, Steve Bruce, Gary Pallister, Peter Schmeichel, Denis Irwin and Brian McClair – as well as to the upcoming generation of young conquerors – Lee Sharpe, Roy Keane, Ryan Giggs, David Beckham, Paul Scholes, Phil Neville. I would also see the United manager Alex Ferguson and his staff, including his assistant, Brian Kidd.

The atmosphere was always upbeat. I was accepted. Everyone who came by paid me special attention: there'd be a gesture, a smile, a kind word. Occasionally someone would say hello in French. I was always particularly pleased to see Alex Ferguson, who'd ask, 'Are you all right, son?' in his thick Glaswegian accent.

When Eric came out of the changing room, we'd walk out to the car the club had lent him. At the time, the car park wasn't full of luxury cars owned by the players: the vehicles were more modest. Then, just beyond the exit gate, there'd be a line of supporters waiting for him in the hope of getting an autograph, a photo, a touch, a smile. The time these encounters with the supporters took varied, but it was generally more than half an hour. On certain occasions – when Eric had had a great match, or when the fans felt he needed support after he'd been sent off and was under attack in the press – I'd be sitting in the passenger seat next to him for as long as an hour.

Then we'd head off into town for lunch, chatting about current affairs, about books and art, television shows and matches we'd seen, movies we wanted to see. Depending on the mood of the moment, we'd be listening to the Gypsy Kings, perhaps, or one of my favourite bands – Prefab Sprout, Everything But the Girl, the Style Council, the Brand New Heavies, Omar, Simply Red – the music accompanying us as we made our way into Manchester. We used to talk a lot about comedy shows on BBC 1, and particularly *Harry Enfield's Television Programme* and *The Fast Show*, the two of us often re-enacting the skits we'd seen – 'Suits You, Sir', 'Ted and Ralph', 'Ron Manager' and 'Channel 9'.

And we would, of course, talk a lot about football. During the 1993/94 season, I started to write down my impressions of the world of football, in which naturally Eric occupied an important place. That season was particularly rich in detail and anecdotes. On the Wednesday evening of 20 October 1993, I attended my first game at Old Trafford, along with Anne. On that initial visit I sat in the North Stand, now the Sir Alex Ferguson Stand, but that was the only time: after that I was always in the area reserved for the players' families, the Family Stand, near the Stretford End.

It was a European Cup match in which United were playing the Turkish side Galatasaray, and it unfolded in a strange way. United had a 2-0 lead with less than a quarter of an hour played. Yet, in the sixty-third minute, the Turks scored to take a 3-2 lead! Eric's equaliser with just minutes remaining saved the Reds from a humiliating defeat as the match ended 3–3. 'I don't understand why we didn't win this game,' Eric said as we drove into Manchester later that evening. 'You can see, Claudio, that we still lack experience in the European Cup. We should have won this match easily. But here in England, we don't know how to play like they do in Italy, by "shutting up shop" after we've scored two goals. It's not in our playing philosophy. We want to attack, attack, to please the crowd, to put on a show. A draw is not that bad a result, and I think we'll win at their ground. I'm not worried. We've got experienced players – Hughes, Robson, Bruce, Schmeichel.'

As we made our way to dinner, I listened to Eric's analysis without saying anything for a while. When I did reply, I said that the Turks had surprised me, that they had played with a lot of confidence. 'I think you scored too fast,' I said, and then I asked, 'Why was Lee Sharpe playing at full-back?'

'The manager wanted an attacking team,' said Eric. 'You'll have noticed that Lee tried to attack a lot. It's a risk because he can't defend very well. But his form meant it was difficult to take him out of the starting eleven. He's a hell of a striker. And did you see our attack tonight? Up front we had young Giggs. He's a phenomenon, he can do anything.'

I awaited the return leg in Turkey eagerly. I don't know why, but I was dreading it a little bit too. As it turned out, it was a disaster for United, and Eric ended up on the end of a great deal of media attention. United went out of the competition on away goals when the game ended in a 0–0 draw, and Eric was given a red card *after* the game.

A few days later, we were talking about this 'fucked-up' game, this scandalous match. Unusually, our conversation had taken on a very serious tone; there was no hint of the humour almost always there. 'It was an ambush,' fumed Eric. 'I can still picture the referee's face, and he wasn't calm at all. At some points he was clearly afraid of blowing for fouls against the home team. I complained to the referee and what he did was cowardly: he gave me a red card because I dared to tell him the game was fixed. Worst of all was what happened in the tunnel. There, in the dark, I was struck from behind by a policeman. Imagine – policemen in uniform who were supposed to protect us! The supporters were also mistreated: we heard some were beaten up and couldn't make it to the match.'

On 9 November, Alex Ferguson expressed his outrage at UEFA's decision to sanction Eric and overlook the plight of United's fans. 'It's unbelievable,' he told the press. 'Horrific things happened to our supporters inside and outside the ground, and our players were assaulted in the tunnel by the police, yet UEFA are only concerned about hauling Eric Cantona over the coals.' The affair took a diplomatic turn when the Foreign Office announced that it had been beset by complaints from United supporters who had suffered mistreatment at the hands of the Turkish police. On 1 December, following pressure from the British government, six supporters held in prison in Turkey were released without charge. A few months afterwards the same referee was suspended for corrupt practices during another game he handled.

Four days after the game in Istanbul, the focus was back on the Premier League, and specifically on the Manchester derby at Maine Road. Eric had invited me to see this game, which is unlike any other. He talked about it with real passion. 'I like this kind of game. They've got amazing supporters. And, of course, you're at home.'

His words put me in an excited mood. I was really looking forward to this game, the first derby I'd attended: the 117th between the two clubs. For me the match had a special flavour: I lived a short walk from Maine Road, and the club had become my team, bringing out my 'Poulidor' side. It's a very French thing, this love for 'magnificent losers', epitomised by the French cycling legend Raymond Poulidor, who finished on the Tour de France podium eight times but never won it.

For the first time, I felt like a neutral; despite leaning towards the Blues, I still wanted my friend to shine: I was a fan of Eric *and* the Blues. I was sitting with the United supporters. The match was sensational, the pace incredibly intense. At half-time City led two-nil. But at the start of the second half, United were transformed. 'Alex Ferguson had a real go at us,' Eric told me afterwards. 'I could already see in the guys' eyes that his words had the right effect, and I knew the second half was going to be terrible for City. As soon as I scored, I told myself that the real United had returned.'

Two goals from Eric put the Reds back in the game. Finally, a third goal from Roy Keane confirmed their dominance. I returned home happy with Eric's performance, but a little disappointed to see City cave in completely under United's pressure. Since that match, Eric has known that underneath I've got blue blood in me.

By this time, I'd started researching both the city's historical figures and those associated with the Red Devils. Partly as a result, I was terribly affected by the death of Sir Matt Busby in January 1994. I'd been trying to set up an interview with him. I bought all the newspapers for the tributes to him and went to Old Trafford to see his funeral cortege pass by, watching as hundreds of people lined the road near the clock commemorating the Munich Disaster of February 1958 (when eight players died in a plane crash as the team returned from a European Cup match), some laying flowers, others scarves in United's colours or some other personal memento.

When I talked to Eric about him he said: 'I only met Matt Busby a few times, but every time I saw him he felt like a very strong, almost mystical presence. He was a wise old man, who had accomplished so much for the club that all the players had great respect for him and didn't even dare talk to him out of modesty. I was told he was very emotional when we won the title after twenty-six years of waiting. He's someone I really liked.'

By now I was attending all Manchester United's home matches, and becoming a regular in the Family Stand. After every game we'd meet for dinner in a trendy restaurant in the centre or at the Novotel West, where Eric had a room between February 1992 and November 1993, preferring a life of solitude at the hotel to uprooting his family, who were still living in Leeds. Our mood was always cheerful and positive. Laughter and self-deprecation were our weapons against any form of sadness, even in the most difficult times.

I remember, for instance, March 1994. What a terrible month! The Manchester United winning machine seemed to be running out of steam. On Saturday, 5 March, playing Chelsea in front of 44,745 spectators at Old Trafford, United lost 1-0. The London club put an end to seventeen months without defeat for the Red Devils at Old Trafford and also a run of thirty-four games unbeaten in all competitions. Eric missed the game owing to injury and, very often, when they were without their number 7 the team lacked inspiration. Eric was the one who could make the most of the speed of Andrei Kanchelskis, the guile of Mark Hughes or the acceleration and power of the young Roy Keane.

Almost a fortnight later, Eric hit the headlines during two league games. On 19 March, he was sent off while playing against Swindon Town at the County Ground for stamping on John Moncur. Three days later at Highbury, Eric picked up another red card against Arsenal after receiving two yellows. Roy Keane, Brian McClair and Steve Bruce were angry with the referee, who they felt had yielded to pressure from the home fans. As a result, Eric became the first United player to receive a red card in two consecutive games.

The press once again seized on these incidents to underline the Frenchman's volatile character. On each occasion, the broadsheets and the tabloids highlighted Eric's complexity, comparing the genius and the thug, the virtuoso and the madman, the aesthete and the hooligan. By depicting him in this way, the press suggested that the so-called French spirit was characterised by ambivalent and contradictory qualities. For them, Eric Cantona embodied the idea of 'the real Frenchman'.

Eric wasn't particularly upset by the two dismissals. But I would say that he was fairly convinced that the treatment he received from referees was different from that given to other players. On an afternoon of watery sunlight we settled down in a bar opposite the facade of Town Hall, in Albert Square, where Manchester United players had gathered to celebrate the anniversary of the team's first FA Cup in 1909, and started talking about the two referees' decisions. 'Showing me a red card has become a "trophy" for some referees,' Eric mused. 'When you watch the moment when I came into contact with Tony Adams [the Arsenal defender and captain], I'm running flat out and trying to avoid him. But if you look at what happened, the referee doesn't even try to figure it out. He simply has the red card in mind. Next time,' he continued in a jokey tone, 'I'll put the red cards in my pocket. If the referee hesitates, I'll apologise to him and say, "Sorry, sir, are you looking for this biscuit?"'

Even though he could joke about it, Eric was still annoyed by the relentlessness of some of the officials. The other players always took his side: they were sometimes shocked by how few of the referees' decisions went in Eric's favour. Some of them used to say that the fact he was a player from the 'continent' and, what's more, French, partly explained such injustices. Nevertheless, the club decided to sanction him by fining him two weeks' wages, around £16,000.

For some time now I had been recording *Match of the Day*, the Saturday night show treasured by all football fans. On Sundays, I would watch the highlights of the games I hadn't been able to see because I'd been at Old Trafford the previous night. When United were playing, I'd watch their games closely and focus particularly on Eric's performance. When we got together again, we'd talk about these games, but also about other sports: about cricket and chess, about our fascination with snooker and darts, both hugely popular on television in those days.

Despite the setbacks in March, the end of the season turned out well. On 10 April, Eric received the Player of the Year trophy, which was awarded by professional footballers. It might not have been apparent, but he was delighted to receive the award. 'This means a lot to me, Claudio. It comes from the players' votes, from those who know football best.' It was the first time it has been won by a foreign player: an historic moment – and by a French player at that. English football was changing, and Eric was partly responsible.

A month later, Manchester United won the FA Cup, crushing Chelsea 4-0 in the final. Eric scored two goals from the penalty spot, each time sending the keeper the wrong way. It made him the first French player to achieve the double of the Premier League and the Cup, and the first to score two goals in the Cup Final. It was also the first time in its history that Manchester United had achieved the double. Eric was transforming not only the image of this club from the north of England, but, moreover, also that of English football as a whole, especially abroad.

CHAPTER 4

Saturday is Match Day

My time in England hinged on one day in the week. Saturday. Saturdays, and particularly 3 p.m. sharp, are still match days to me, Premier League match days. My years in Manchester were inextricably wrapped up with that sense of excitement and anticipation millions of fans feel ahead of a game. When I'm feeling nostalgic for England, two phrases instantly come back to me: *When Saturday Comes* and the *match day*.

In the early 1990s, attending Manchester United games regularly was a privilege. For some it was a sign of upward mobility, for others a sacrifice that could result in poor families being broken apart. Some fans, especially the more fervent ones from working-class backgrounds, had been forced out of stadiums because the price of match-day and season tickets had got so high. As a consequence of government legislation, particularly the Taylor Report of 1989, the footballing authorities and the clubs' boards had opted to increase ticket prices in order to stem the menace of hooliganism. The result was that watching matches live became a real middle-class treat.

I felt lucky being able to go to games. It gave me the chance to analyse English society while enjoying all of Manchester United's matches at Old Trafford, and also to see them play in other legendary stadiums. For me it was the perfect amalgam of academic work and my passion for football. I went to Anfield and heard Liverpool fans singing 'You'll Never Walk Alone', felt the love for Newcastle United manager Kevin Keegan at St James' Park, was enthralled by the atmosphere at West Ham's bubbling Upton Park in East London, witnessed the distress of relegation in the eyes of fans at Manchester City's Maine Road, was dizzied by the charm of Arsenal's Highbury stadium, where the first ever live broadcast of a match was made on the radio in 1922, and was bowled over by the architecture of Everton's Goodison Park, one of the stadiums built in the Victorian era. What an immense pleasure it was. I knew I was the envy of millions of fans in the 'Red Army' in every corner of the world.

Match day at Old Trafford featured all kinds of rituals, some large, others small. Pieced together, they could have filled a notebook. In the early days, I always carried an umbrella that complemented a rather distinguished outfit I'd bought during the January sales. Yet, the almost constant wind and never-failing ability of the Manchester rain to penetrate my clothing, despite the protection I'd expected the umbrella to provide, pretty quickly forced me to give it up for good. Instead, I usually wore a flat cap to keep the elements at bay. I always carried a bag in which I kept the match programme, my ticket, notebook and any fanzines I bought.

Match-day afternoons would begin with me catching the bus at the Whitworth Park stop in Rusholme. I'd get off at

Manchester Central Library station, then take the tram towards Sale. When it arrived at the Old Trafford station that's overlooked by Lancashire's famous cricket ground, I'd get off and join the army of Man United supporters walking down Talbot Road. We all had Old Trafford in our sights, heading along Stretford Road. As I walked, I'd be looking left and right at the makeshift stalls selling unofficial Manchester United merchandise. Among the myriad products on sale, there were many hailing Eric: a flag featuring his image on a blue, white and red background, a stall where you could have 'Eric the King' face paint applied, scarves in Manchester United colours adorned with his portrait, 'Eric The King' T-shirts, 'King Eric' jumpers and other more unusual items such as plates, beer glasses, bottles, key chains, bags, paintings and caricatures.

Local and foreign supporters of the Reds intermingled, the atmosphere thick with the scent of fried onions, hot dogs and mustard, burgers and ketchup, fat-cooked chips sprinkled with vinegar and, of course, fish and chips. I also loved to diagnose the mood of the day: hearing the supporters' comments on the players' performances in the last match, who was on form and who wasn't, which of the opposition's players they felt were the biggest threat, the tactics the Reds had to adopt to win the match.

When it came to Cantona, I would often eavesdrop on what was being said. Attending my first few games, I had a very hard time understanding a conversation between Mancunians for more than a short length of time because I wasn't at all attuned to the accent. However, the more I listened, immersed myself in Manchester life and became able to exploit the talent for mimicry I'd been renowned for since secondary school, the more I was able to follow long and meandering conversations between fans from Hyde, Rochdale, Oldham and Stockport. Before long I became brave enough to join in some of these exchanges. I liked to give my opinion on a player or on a goal I'd thought was fantastic. I'm lucky I don't have a heavy accent: when I spoke, it was difficult for people to pick up that I was French. A friend from college had advised me to avoid the 'Queen Elizabeth accent' we'd been taught to use during our English lessons in France.

The first thing I always looked to buy were fanzines, the often quite home-made magazines that expressed the voices of supporters. I used to appreciate the quirky, humorous tone of *Red Issue* (launched March 1989) and *United We Stand* (October 1989). I happily read the articles and loved the cartoons. The content frequently fascinated me and enabled me to understand the various aspects of what defines a Manchester United fan.

When I got close to the footballing cathedral of Old Trafford, I took a different path from the majority of supporters. I headed for gate 4B, the place where every Man United player dropped off tickets reserved for family and friends. An envelope would be waiting for me on which Eric had written 'Claude Boli'. There was always a little cartoon too: a face without a nose, a man without arms, a face with a big smile. Inside, I'd find my match-day ticket for the Family Stand and a small card of varying colour that enabled me to access the players' lounge before the start of the match, at half-time and after the game had finished.

For matches kicking off at three o'clock, I liked to be inside the stadium forty-five minutes beforehand so I could take some time to flip through *United Review*, the club's official match programme. On the opening two pages, it listed the club's list of honours along with words from Alex Ferguson.

In the middle, there would be some striking photos from the last game and, on the last page, the line-up of both teams, including what then seemed to be sometimes bizarre player numbers – Terry Cooke at number 27 or Viv Anderson at number 28. The names of the referee and his assistants would also be listed in a small column, along with the stadium evacuation procedures, this being one of the measures implemented following the Taylor Report in the aftermath of the Hillsborough disaster in 1989.

I would watch closely as the players come on to the pitch. Head held high and chest puffed out, Eric would be one of the first to emerge from the tunnel and enter the 'Theatre of Dreams', as Old Trafford was nicknamed. He rarely glanced at the Family Stand. More often than not he warmed up meticulously, paying special attention to stretching exercises. 'The warm-up is an important moment that influences both your game and the pace of the games in England,' Eric told me when we were discussing player injuries. 'Touch wood, I've had very few muscle injuries and strains during my career. I pay attention to what I eat, of course, but I also make sure I warm up well before a match.'

The other thing I liked to do in the stadium was watch the almost empty stands steadily fill up and become full just seconds before the game started. Not far away from where I used to sit, I could see the supporters filling the Stretford End, known for being the most fervent and vocal section of the stadium. Often standing, despite the ban imposed by the Football Association, the fans there sang, clapped, applauded, shouted with joy. The Stretford End clearly wanted to remain a bastion of traditional support. For these fans, football was still the people's game.

From the start of the 1994/95 season, I noticed hundreds of blue, white and red flags bearing Eric's portrait, the result no doubt of the remarkable season he'd had the year before culminating in the league and FA Cup double. I was also happy to hear some different songs dedicated to him in addition to the 'Oooh, aaah Cantona' chant that had emerged during his spell with Leeds United. One stood as the most iconic song of the 1990s. It had been written by Peter Boyle, one of the fans who led the chanting and who, by chance, Eric and I ran into in a pub close to the Hacienda nightclub. We were playing table football when Peter appeared, surprised and happy to see us in this quite ordinary pub, and a friendship developed as we often went back there. At every match, the fans would sing 'Eric the King' to the tune of the Scaffold's 1960s hit 'Lily the Pink', and its chorus became their anthem:

> We'll ... drink, a drink, a drink
> to Eric the king, the king, the king.
> He's the leader of our football team.
> He's the greatest French footballer
> that the world has ever seen.

Obviously, every game had a slightly different flavour, and there were some with particular teams that stood out. The games where I felt the tension most extreme weren't those between Man United and its historical rivals, such as Man City, Liverpool, Aston Villa or Arsenal. It was the meetings between Manchester United and Leeds United, I quickly realised, that were much tenser than any of them. These were the only games when I made a point of avoiding being outside

50

the stadium an hour before kick-off, after a bad experience before the first match I'd attended between these two rivals.

On 1 January 1994, as I stood in front of the megastore outside the stadium, I found myself rooted to the spot as I witnessed virulent exchanges between mounted policemen and a group of particularly aggressive Leeds fans who were hurling insults at Man United supporters. For the first time in England, I could see the police becoming exasperated by the actions of a group of fans. The nervousness of the horses, with their beautiful manes, was very apparent too. The crush of fans, galloping horses and the strong-arm tactics of the police resulted in confusion and fear on Sir Matt Busby Way.

Eric had warned me what it would be like when we came up against the team with which he had won his first English championship title two years earlier. 'Leeds was a great love story that ended badly.' During that New Year's Day match, some of the Leeds players had set out to provoke Eric, and succeeded, leading to a memorable photo that Manchester United fans loved of Eric putting his finger up the Leeds midfielder Steve Hodge's nose.

Laughter could also punctuate certain matches. I remember a phenomenon that was then quite common in England: streakers. In France, I'd never seen fans strip off and run onto the pitch. During one league game, a streaker who supported the opposing team managed to elude the stewards and walk over to Eric. On his back was the number 7, with an arrow below it pointing towards his backside. Eric turned to the stand and our eyes met. After the game, we laughed at the audacity of the fan, who'd managed to escape several stewards, surprising them by his turn of speed. We couldn't stop laughing about it.

As far as my research into the club was concerned, match

days were always an ideal opportunity to assess the economic power of Manchester United. In the megastore, there
would be several queues snaking towards the checkout. Fans
from all over the world filled the place, buying all manner
of Manchester United-branded products. Shirts bearing the
name Cantona were among the biggest sellers.

Once inside the stadium, I would look over at the private boxes and luxury seats. Whenever I had a ticket that
gave me access, my curiosity led me to ask these privileged
fans where they came from. Many of them, I noticed, were
from Scandinavia – a phenomenon that owed much to the
success and popularity of United's Danish goalkeeper Peter
Schmeichel and Norwegian forward Ole Gunnar Solskjaer.
During the 1996/97 season, I wrote in my notebook:

> *Private boxes and executive seats*: as you look around the
> stadium, you will see two rows of private boxes. There
> are 181 private boxes including thirty-two Sky Boxes in
> the new North Stand, sixteen that seat six spectators and
> sixteen that seat eight. The other boxes form a ring around
> the stadium and they vary in size from five to eight seats.
> All of the private boxes are equipped with closed-circuit
> television showing replays of the goals and action. A waiter
> service is also provided. In addition, there are a number
> of Executive Seats. These are sold on a season ticket basis
> and entitle the holder to use luxurious bar and restaurant
> facilities which are available for pre-match, half-time and
> post-match enjoyment.

Games were also an opportunity to point out what was
then one of the principal differences between the life of a

football player in England and his counterpart in France. Eric put it well.

Match day is a time when you notice the English mentality. In England, on the day of the match, we approach the game in a normal way. There's no bunker mentality. No hotel where we are 'locked up'. For a match kicking off at 3 p.m., we're told to arrive at midday for lunch. This means that until a few hours before the match, you're at home with your family and you're not focused totally on the match. You're at home, quiet. You approach the game with a degree of serenity. In France, at Auxerre, you'll remember that when we had a match at eight o'clock on a Saturday evening, we would be told to meet at around six on Friday evening before it. The wait at the hotel was too long. Here, though, I only think about the match when I get to the ground. I prefer this way of approaching games.

For away matches, the routine was also quite ritualised. We'd usually meet up in the bar at the Four Seasons Hotel near the airport – a pint of Guinness for me and a pint of lager for Eric. We really liked this place, as a lot of Premier League footballers used to hang out there. We regularly saw the former Man United star Bryan Robson, who had become a coach at Middlesbrough. We liked the family atmosphere and the conviviality of the place, and also appreciated the hospitality and the attention of the staff, in particular the kindness of three ladies, two of whom had crimped and lacquered hair in styles reminiscent of Barbara Knox and Pat Phoenix, two of the leading ladies in *Coronation Street*, the famous soap opera set in Manchester that has been running since 1960.

CHAPTER 5

In the Family Stand

On Sunday, 28 April 1996, I attended the last home game of the season at Old Trafford. Manchester United were playing Nottingham Forest. Seeing their players run out onto the pitch, their shirts bearing the famous club badge of a tree next to a river, reminded me of two things in particular: first, a television series that evoked the good deeds of Robin Hood and his band of merry men, and secondly, and above all, Forest's domination of the European football scene under their controversial manager Brian Clough, whose team was a wonderful blend of English, Scottish and Irish players, including the likes of Trevor Francis, Archie Gemmill, Viv Anderson, Martin O'Neill, Peter Shilton and Tony Woodcock.

I was part of a crowd of 53,926, setting a record attendance for the Premier League, and we were treated to a fantastic spectacle. I felt exhausted after what had been a very eventful year, which had seen Eric's 'return' to the United team after being suspended for several months. This sometimes painful and often emotional period had taken something of a toll on me, which I'd summed up in a single sentence in my notebook: 'The fans suffer for a season, while those who are close to the players suffer for the duration of their sporting career.' The words made it abundantly clear that emotional attachment had overridden the historian's stance of detached objectivity. Heart had triumphed over head. It had been impossible for me to ignore the hours, days and months of uncertainty surrounding Eric's future at Man United.

As usual, I took my seat in the Family Stand. In the 1996 tour guide brochure for the stadium, it's described as follows:

The Family Stand is situated at the far side of the South Stand in the corner adjoining the Stretford End. Only parents and children are allowed to sit here, and they must be either Manchester United Members or on an organised tour from a visiting club. This is the only section of the ground where United and visiting supporters are not segregated. This is done purposely to teach the younger generation of fans to mix in a friendly way with the fans of other clubs. The capacity of the Family Stand, which is set aside for players' families and VIPs, is approximately 4,200. Special entertainment is provided for children prior to kick-off, including clowns, magicians, face painters and various give-aways. The Family Stand is the only part of the ground where smoking is not allowed. Above the seating in the Family Stand sits the TV studio where television presenters provide match coverage. When the matches are not televised this facility is available for hire to supporters. The view from here, as you would expect, is unsurpassed.

Family spirit, fraternity, entertainment for young fans and civic-mindedness were the principal characteristics of this 'friendly place' that was created in the early 1990s. There was something else, though, that made the Family Stand special. It was here that one of the least-known and least-discussed aspects of top-level football was most apparent: the high anxiety felt by the players' families and friends during a match. Depending on the mood in the stadium and what was happening on the pitch, it would be a tableau of faces depicting happiness, sadness, pride or even desolation.

Those lucky enough to be a member of a player's family or one of their friends were, from the outside, a homogenous group, usually described as the 'players' families'. Yet, from the inside, this group was actually a constellation of 'individual families' whose first consideration was to their relative or friend on the pitch, and only then to the team. For each family, the performance of their son, brother, husband or friend was far more important than that of the team. It has been said that football is the most individual of team sports. The same could be said of loyalties in the Family Stand: we always focused on the player we knew or loved before worrying about any another player or indeed Manchester United itself.

Throughout those years in that area shaped like an unfinished U, I shared the same sorrow, joy, disappointment and delight as every other member of the players' families. We were united in the way we showed our love and support for 'our player'. We were singular in our focus, but similar in attitude. We rarely showed our anguish, for instance – we didn't want to reveal any degree of fragility, of vulnerability, that could be interpreted as a 'family' characteristic. The family of a player who was regularly among the substitutes never displayed any public sadness or distress at seeing their relative sitting on the bench along with the others who hadn't been picked. When 'our' player spoke to us about a falling-out with or dislike of a teammate, we never revealed any hint of it beyond our little clique. Our duty (unstated, naturally) was to represent our player in the best way we possibly could. They were the focus of our attention.

When Eric was the victim of a hard tackle, I'd feel I'd been hit too. I watched everything he did forensically: his body language, his hand gestures, whichever part of his body might be troubling him at that time, how he looked when he was left prone on the pitch. I cursed the player who'd been guilty of the 'unforgivable' foul. I had no objectivity whatsoever. We all lack objectivity when it comes to someone who is close to us. Love makes you blind, and so does friendship.

When Eric received a yellow card for a foul, I would instantly be able to say how many times the player he had fouled could have been penalised in the same way. We were judge, defender, prosecutor and victim all at the same time. Reason had no place in our hearts. Emotion prevailed over everything and anything. We would explode with joy. Our heads would sink into our hands when our loved one missed an opportunity that 'couldn't be missed'. When Man United wavered our faces would darken. The Family Stand was *Coronation Street*, *Brookside* and *EastEnders* all rolled into one ninety-minute episode. We were actors in and spectators of extraordinary moments that were collectively shared. Football and Manchester United provided the setting for funny, tragic and unforgettable stories.

When Eric shone, I received a share of the admiration, in

congratulations, knowing smiles and a few words from the other families. In people's eyes, the 'Cantona family' had (I still don't know why) played a part in every moment of lobbing, juggling and back-heeling genius Eric served up. I can remember numerous examples of this. Sunday, 19 December 1993, for instance, when Man United played Aston Villa: the Red Devils won 3-1, Eric scoring a goal in the twenty-first minute and again in the eighty-ninth. After each of these marvellous moments, I received thumbs-ups, winks and hugs from the other families. At the end of the match, some of them came over to congratulate *me* on King Eric's performance with an enthusiastic 'Well done!'

I remember something similar at another match in March 1996, this one where the stakes were very high, as the opposition were one of the teams challenging Man United for the Premier League title: Arsenal. The Gunners had a very talented team, which included goalkeeper David Seaman, arguably the best player in that position in the Premier League and one of the best in Europe. He kept out attack after attack from Andy Cole, Ryan Giggs and Eric. It looked as though the game was heading for a draw until Eric produced a moment of real class. After the ball had been headed out of Arsenal's box, Eric cushioned it on his chest and hit a precise, dipping shot from about 30 yards out over Seaman and into the net to open the scoring in the sixty-sixth minute. You could see the look of indescribable happiness mixed with relief on everyone's faces. Eric had once again played the role of saviour. At the end of the match, people kept coming up to me to express their joy thanks to the Reds' number 7.

As I took my place in the Family Stand for each game, a familiar scenario would unfold, just as it might if you went into the same pub year after year. I'd get a friendly pat on the back from Nicky Butt's brother, say hello to David Beckham's parents, receive a lovely smile from Ryan Giggs's mother, kiss Ole Gunnar Solskjaer's wife on each cheek, exchange a few words in Spanish with Jordi Cruyff's girlfriend. When the players came out of the tunnel and onto the pitch, each of them had their own ritual. Ole always looked our way and smiled at his wife. Eric, with his head held high, had his gaze fixed on the centre of the pitch. Denis Irwin would take a furtive glance at his loved ones. Peter Schmeichel, white towel in hand, would greet the crowd on both sides of the stadium, Andrei Kanchelskis would pray before stepping onto the field. We all stood up to applaud the players as they came out, each of us with our particular connection to the player who was our reason for being there.

Every player had their own little entourage in the Family Stand. There were usually three of us in the Cantona group: Isabelle, his wife, Gary King, a former Leeds United fan who had decided to follow Eric when he transferred to Man United and become a good friend, and me. I used to sit next to Isabelle because we knew each other so well. Although the three of us were together, we experienced the game in our own individual ways. Gary would talk and joke with members of the other players' families, and got on really well with everyone. When he came to games he only had eyes for Eric: Manchester United weren't the club he'd grown up loving, but he had been to enough of Eric's games at Old Trafford and other grounds to be accepted by everyone as a 'Red'.

Isabelle didn't attend many of the first few games I went to, but gradually, as the stakes increased, she missed very few. I knew Isabelle and her brother, Bernard 'Nino' Ferrer, who was also a professional footballer, from Auxerre. Eric had spoken to me at length about his 'marvel', a student at the University of Aix-en-Provence before she became his wife. He also told her a lot about me, praising my 'extraordinary' qualities as a cook. Isabelle was also friends with Geneviève, my brother Basile's wife. They had got to know each other in Auxerre, Marseille and when their husbands had been called up to play for the French national team. Their friendship deepened when the players' wives got together, notably in Sweden during the final phase of the European Championship in 1992.

Isabelle also had a good relationship with Anne. Isabelle and I became very close in Manchester, seeing each other not only at games but often also on other occasions. Each time we met, we had the opportunity to joke, to laugh, to discuss the latest mischief their son Raphaël had got up to, and to reminisce about our time in Auxerre – the town, the team's coach, Guy Roux, our friends at the training centre, the surrounding countryside, the matches ... We would talk about Manchester, its beautiful buildings, the pace of life, and her fond memories of working as a French teacher at the University of Leeds. We were both very happy in Manchester, a burst of laughter never far away whenever we met.

Even though I was concentrating on Eric, I would still keep an eye on what was going on around me, and I noticed one feature that was very interesting from a sociological point of view. I became very aware of the level of anxiety among the players' wives. For some wives, match day was an oppressive time, when they had to play the 'role' of a wife, containing their emotions so that they wouldn't be judged, as well as ensuring that their children, with Raphaël sometimes among them, didn't get over-excited amid the immense clamour within the stadium.

The game was the focal point of every family's week. Their lives revolved around their husbands' sporting activities. Several of the players' wives had had to put their own professional careers on hold to support their husband's footballing commitments. Sacrifice might not be the right word to describe this undertaking, but in certain situations the women had to devote themselves completely to maximising their husband's chances of footballing success.

To provide their husbands with the best possible framework to focus solely on his profession, these women often became the guarantor of family stability, taking on the heavy responsibility of organising all 'non-footballing' responsibilities, the whole emotional labour of the family. They had to make sure their husband did the minimum amount of household chores, that he had enough sleep and recovery time from the almost incessant flow of matches (England remains the only league in Europe that doesn't have a mid-season break), that he only needed to devote a 'limited' amount of time, say, to monitoring their children's education or organising moves between different cities at short notice, and even be a sole parent for spells if a player decided not to move his family. Everyday life has improved considerably for footballers' wives, however, mirroring the change in circumstances and earning power for the players. In the hundred or so books I read about the lives of footballers in the 1950s and 1960s (including those on Sir Stanley Matthews, Sir Tom Finney, Francis Lee, Ian St John, Jimmy Greaves and Sir Alex Ferguson), in the 1970s and 1980s (Trevor Brooking, Bryan

Robson, Peter Beardsley, Paul McGrath and others) and in more recent decades (Paul Gascoigne, Kevin Phillips, Andy Cole, Roy Keane, Wayne Rooney and Steven Gerrard, for instance), the importance of the family and especially of the footballer's wife is fundamental. Reading them, it was very clear that football could change the destinies of players and families.

In Isabelle Cantona's case, I saw how the games literally transformed her. The numerous demands made by fans, team-mates and the media on Eric resulted, quite unconsciously, in a gradual build-up of stress that became increasingly difficult to hide as one season morphed into the next. Sitting next to Isabelle during matches, we were racked by uncertainty, often devoid of joy. Victory, which might usually be a cause for celebration, sometimes simply sparked relief.

At times I suspected that 'Isa' felt more tense about what was at stake than the King out on the field. Sometimes, although I didn't say anything, I could see Isabelle's thoughts had drifted to an agonising place. Like me, she wasn't very expressive, but I'd known her long enough to realise that the game had taken an over-arching place in her life as a wife. Her passion for football became very apparent after Eric had scored an extraordinary goal against Newcastle United at St James' Park in March 1996, a goal that enabled Manchester United to close the gap on Newcastle at the top of the table. Following it, Isabelle decided to get a Red Devil tattoo on her arm. It was more than just a symbol.

The families' time in the Family Stand divided into three distinct parts. Before the match, we went to the Players' Lounge for a hot drink and a sandwich or a pork pie. Then we would sit in the stand to watch the game. Finally, once the game had finished, we would go back to the Players' Lounge to meet our loved one.

Having access to the Players' Lounge was undoubtedly a source of envy for many fans. This is how it's presented in the club's brochure for the thousands of visitors who flock to Old Trafford every year:

> Opposite the dressing room is the Players' Lounge. Here, players can relax after their pre-match meal before the game starts and invite guests and away players to enjoy the free bar afterwards. There are also crèche facilities for players' children. Around the room are photographs of nearly every player to be club captain since the war and an honours board which lists every United player to win an international cap whilst playing for the club. Another exhibit is a plaque made by an inmate of Dartmoor Prison to commemorate United winning the European Cup in 1968. It was presented to Bobby Charlton and has hung in the lounge ever since.

Why was this place so fascinating? For a start, it was where you could see and meet Manchester United's celebrity fans. Among those I was able to see close up and sometimes chat with were the actor Ian McShane, whose father Harry had played for Manchester United, the Salford-born actor Albert Finney, musician Bernard Sumner from the band New Order, the actor Christopher Eccleston, one of the stars of the 1998 movie *Elizabeth* in which Eric also appeared, Danny Boyle, director of the cult movie *Trainspotting*, world champion snooker player Dennis Taylor, TV presenter Eamonn Holmes, the novelist and winner of the 2010 Man Booker

Prize, Howard Jacobson, and the writer and star of the hugely popular TV comedy *Absolutely Fabulous*, Jennifer Saunders – we met again just after United's victory in the 1996 FA Cup Final.

There we learned about the seriousness of the relationship between David Beckham and 'Posh' Spice Victoria Adams, who regularly came to games. It was where we watched the players' sons grow up. I remember Kasper Schmeichel, who's now Leicester City's goalkeeper, and Raphaël Cantona being there from a young age.

It was also the place where players from the opposition team would come for a beer. The full meaning of that very British sense of fair play could be found here: there was mutual respect and courtesy and everybody behaved impeccably. I especially liked to see opposing players with whom I had a good relationship, among them Chris Waddle, who was one of my brother Basile's best friends. Basile had told me to see or call 'his English brother Chris' without hesitation if anything happened to me while I was in England. I did go to see 'Magic Chris' in Sheffield to interview him about his experience at Olympique de Marseille, and he gave me a very warm welcome. So when Sheffield Wednesday came to Old Trafford, I watched the game with some degree of impatience, keen for it to end so I could see Chris once again.

Being there also gave you the chance to get a close look at the players themselves. I had noticed, for instance, that the average height of the defenders was around 1.85m (6 foot 1). Unlike in France, it was very rare to see a goalkeeper standing less than 1.83m (6 foot) tall. We rarely saw United manager Alex Ferguson and the club's directors in the Players' Lounge;

as the name implies, it was a place 'reserved' for the players and their families. Eric didn't stay long there, however. We preferred to go to restaurants in the city centre and then enjoy Manchester's nightlife.

I couldn't mention the Players' Lounge without mentioning one other thing I loved about it, and that was hearing the names of the Scottish teams on Sky TV, which broadcast highlights from the previous day's matches in both the English and Scottish leagues. Sitting on the velvet-covered bench, I relished the sound of the names, which seemed from a bygone era, of Scotland's league teams: Airdrieonians, Albion Rovers, Inverness Caledonian Thistle, Cowdenbeath, Forfar Athletic, Hamilton Academical, Heart of Midlothian, Livingston, Montrose, Queen of the South, Raith Rovers, Stirling Albion ... Hearing them now transports me back there in an instant.

CHAPTER 6

Inside the Dressing Room

We were in Pizza Express in the centre of Manchester in early January of 1995. I'd arrived stunned, after hearing about Manchester United's intention to sell a player I really liked: 'Hughesie', Mark Hughes, the team's Welsh striker. Even before ordering my usual Regina pizza I was telling Eric how disappointed I was. 'I don't understand it! Why's the gaffer decided to buy Andy Cole? You and Hughesie are one of the best attacking combinations in Europe – the way he plays just in front of you and you in the false nine role. I thought you complemented each other perfectly!

'This'll make you laugh,' I went on, 'but I also think you've got a lot in common. Neither of you is one for talking. You're both winners and never overawed by any of the defenders you come up against. You're both very focused and ebullient out on the pitch, but very calm away from it. And,' I added, tongue in my cheek, 'you've both hit defenders. And you know Hughesie was a good musician too – he played violin in his school orchestra.'

On and on I went, not letting Eric get a word in. He sipped his tomato juice; I was a man racked by disappointment and needing to get it off my chest. I ended my monologue by pointing out the media's scepticism about this unlikely Cantona and Hughes double act and the stats that underlined what a success their partnership had actually been. 'When you and "Sparky" played alongside each other during the double season [1993/94], you scored eighteen Premier League goals and Sparky got twelve. Lots of United's goals came from the understanding between you. The media said you coming in would make Hughes less important in United's attack, but it turned out exactly the opposite: he's never been more effective and selfless! I think he'd be a great loss for United—'

'Claudio, you're right,' interrupted Eric, 'but Andy is the future of United. You saw what he did in Newcastle. He's a great striker – he's scored nearly seventy goals at Newcastle in two seasons, and he's a great passer. I think the club was right to buy him [for a record fee of £7 million]. He's been named the Premier League's best prospect,' he said calmly.

Then Eric reflected on playing with Hughes. 'I was sure we were going to get along on the pitch. What I like about him was that he always looked to go forwards, and he's both powerful and very technical – he doesn't lose the ball very often. Sometimes he can break down a defence when he's up front on his own. He's always on the move, and he's a fearless attacker. Sometimes he might give the impression of being individualistic, but he's very much a team player. He's often trying to play one–twos with me, Giggs or Kanchelskis. We make a good attacking partnership. He rarely misses a match, always gives a hundred per cent.'

I listened to what Eric had to say, and his argument

convinced me. I didn't want to know about any other reasons for Hughes's departure other than those to do with football. I could have asked about the relationship between Hughes and Ferguson, or what the other players thought about his impending transfer, but instead I resolved to move on, as if this were no more than another run-of-the-mill episode in the life of a modern-day club and the professional footballers playing for it. But then a thought came into my mind: that of the conditions footballers had faced until the 1960s and, specifically, the abolition of the 'maximum wage' by the Football Association in 1961. Up to that point, professional footballers didn't enjoy economic security: they were prisoners of arbitrary decisions made by club directors. They could be transferred without having any say in the matter.

I still felt bad for the Welsh striker, though. I couldn't help dwelling on it: the man who had reopened the door to success for Man United in that historic season when they took the league title and FA Cup, by equalising forty seconds from the end of the Cup semi-final against Oldham Athletic, was on the verge of leaving the Red Devils ... I wouldn't hear the fans at Old Trafford chanting 'Hughe-sie! Hughe-sie! Hughe-sie!' any more. I was sad, if a little less so after hearing Eric's eloquent and sincere words about his colleague. And though he hadn't necessarily meant to, what he said also gave me a glimpse into the United dressing room.

Every professional footballer naturally has a distinct relationship with each of their teammates. Friendships are based on a number of things: age, social origin, how near you live to one another, musical tastes, friends in common, a common purpose on the pitch, shared personality traits, and so on. Even though Eric never said anything unpleasant about a team-mate, I could tell from his words and body language what he thought of them. During my years in Manchester, a number of players particularly caught my attention, including Ryan Giggs, Roy Keane, the 'Ferguson Babes' – David Beckham, Paul Scholes, Gary and Phil Neville and Nicky Butt – Ole Gunnar Solskjaer and Andy Cole.

The first player I noticed Eric showing great interest in was Ryan Giggs. I'd never heard of the Welsh wizard before I got to Manchester. During one of my first visits to the Cliff, our paths crossed, and straight away I sensed an ocean of kindness in his brown eyes. I also noticed how young players like Giggs used to scrutinise Eric's gestures and behaviour: they looked at the boots he wore (which never had steel studs), the way he tucked his shirt into his shorts, his stretching sessions, the casual dress he went in for, what he listened to, what he read, what he said . . . Beckham, Scholes and Butt were mesmerised by Eric's sense of calm and strength. For the club's young-sters, Eric was a role model, and the aura he radiated was to them spellbinding. He was perceived as the footballer from elsewhere, the 'enigmatic Frenchman'. He may have been the star, but he never put any distance between himself and the younger players. He was an accessible star.

As far as Giggs was concerned, I was sure every kind ges-ture of his towards me was a way of indirectly expressing his admiration for Eric. This made me thrilled and happy. When he was at Old Trafford with his mother, Giggs would always give me a smile. When our paths crossed in Manchester, he would stop and chat. One day Eric told me that Giggs's grandfather was Black and had come from Sierra Leone, a country in West Africa close to my home country of Ivory

Coast. I was delighted to hear this, and felt it was one reason we got on so well. Of all the people at the club he was definitely one of those I liked the most.

When it came to Giggs's performances on the pitch, Eric was full of praise for the brilliant left-winger. I was always pleased to see the understanding between Eric and 'Giggsy' when I saw them play at Old Trafford. There was absolutely no doubt that they complemented each other extremely well. Eric told me he had been impressed by Giggs in a match in 1993 against Oldham Athletic at their tumbledown Boundary Park ground. The young winger had been at his elusive best. United won the match 5–2, with Giggs scoring two goals. Having heard Eric talk so much about him, I was keen to see him repeat those exploits at Old Trafford.

On 22 January 1994, United met Everton in a game that paid tribute to Sir Matt Busby, who had died a few days earlier. Giggs served up an outstanding display, capped with the only goal of the afternoon. Less than a month later, he provided a repeat performance. In front of 43,294 spectators, Manchester United struggled to beat a Sheffield Wednesday team that featured Chris Waddle. Once again, Giggs scored the only goal of the match.

Like any 'big brother', Eric could be tough on Ryan, especially when he told him how he could improve and become the best left-winger in the world. The Welsh prodigy's inexperience became apparent during matches against continental teams, as Eric was quick to point out. 'In the European Cup we lack experience,' he told me again after one of United's sorties abroad. 'You can see that in certain phases of the game, we tend to rush things. But just you wait: when Giggsy is more mature, he'll bring even more to the team. At the moment, he tends to depend on his speed down the wing, but I'm sure that in a few years' time he'll venture into the centre of the pitch more and direct the game. With his technique and touch, which is second to none, he'll have much more influence on the game. I really like Ryan a lot, and I can see that you like him a lot too.'

During one of my research trips around the charity shops of Manchester, I came across a copy of *Ryan Giggs, Genius at Work* (published in 1996 by Manchester United Books). In it, Giggsy expressed his admiration for my friend.

Eric's got more outgoing the longer he's stayed at the club. We all respect him because he's one of the best players in the world, and the club's fortunes have changed since he's come. He's a dream to play with: I've never come across such perfectly weighted passes. He knows exactly the place we can meet it. He's such a cool customer (he can wear anything and get away with it). And look at the way he takes penalties. He hasn't missed one for the club yet, and I don't think he ever will. He's not at all arrogant, though, as some people who don't know him make out. If you go out for a drink Eric's always there, and he's quite witty. He likes a joke. His English is better than he lets on. In fact, his English is perfect if he wants it to be. Sometimes he just doesn't want it to be.

Another player Eric had a special understanding with was his 'blood brother'. When Eric talked about Roy Keane, his eyes lit up. Every time he talked about the Irishman, it was like listening to someone talking about Eric. They were two sides of the same coin. In all the accounts that have been written about Manchester United, hardly anyone has looked at this extraordinary relationship, where Mediterranean blood met Irish, and a beautiful alchemy was created.

When contemplating what Roy did, Eric very often saw his alter ego. The relationship between the two of them was an unwritten and inviolable pact of sincerity, based on a deep and unconditional mutual respect. Except perhaps when he talked about Steve Bruce or Paul Ince, I don't think I ever heard Eric utter as much praise of a Manchester United player as he did of Roy. He loved Roy, and the feeling was reciprocated. It was an adoration expressed in public only modestly, as both of them were well known for their reluctance to wear their hearts on their sleeves during their playing days.

As players they were similar. Like Eric, the Irishman offered total commitment on the pitch, and he was an instinctive performer. As with Eric, Roy's attachment to the club and his hatred of defeat often resulted in him getting into trouble on the pitch that more than once led to him being sent off.

I sometimes wondered whether the bond between the kid from Marseille and the kid from Cork could stem from the adoration Irish fans felt for the Frenchman. 'We often go to Ireland to play pre-season friendlies,' Eric once told me, 'and I'm always surprised by the fervour of the fans. They're crazy about United! I really like how much they love us – it's weird, but I always feel like I'm in a place I've known for a long time. I feel good when I'm there. Maybe I have some Irish blood.'

One day we were walking down Whitworth Street and decided to go into an Irish pub. We both asked for a Guinness and, as you'd expect, the barman served it with a clover 'drawn' in its creamy head. The historian in me kicked in, and I was soon explaining for Eric the strong historical links between the city of Manchester, Manchester United and the Irish community. Manchester United's long-standing ability to unearth and nurture players from both the Republic of Ireland and Northern

Ireland, I told him, was one of the great strengths of the club's recruitment policy. Of those who had crossed the Irish Sea to join United, the most famous was certainly the Belfast prodigy George Best. But the club's first Irish star had emerged three full decades before him; Johnny Carey was an elegant midfielder-turned-defender in the 1930s, recruited from the Home Farm club for £200 – a paltry sum even at that time.

Naturally the conversation eventually got on to 'Keano', as Roy Keane was nicknamed. 'He's become one of the best midfielders in the world,' enthused Eric. 'He has all the qualities of a modern midfielder: tough, powerful, combative, a goal-scorer, generous with his effort, selfless, a leader ...' I didn't dare interrupt. It was quite incredible to hear Eric so fulsome in his praise and superlatives about a player. I was already starting to think that perhaps Keane would be the next king, and history would prove me right.

The mid-1990s also saw the emergence of the generation known as 'Fergie's Babes'. The best known were David Beckham, Paul Scholes, Nicky Butt and Gary and Phil Neville. They all came through the club's youth system, and were quickly promoted by Alex Ferguson to the first-team squad, where they were 'guided' by Eric. For him, this generation was 'exceptional'. Once or twice we tried to draw a comparison with the young players we'd known at the AJ Auxerre training centre, but Eric pointed out a key difference: 'At Auxerre, most of the players that featured in the teams that won youth titles never played in the First Division. On the other hand, here at United, Ferguson didn't hesitate when it came to throwing them into the "big time", never mind how young they were.'

They first began to make a real impression at the start of the 1995/96 season. Gary Neville, Nicky Butt, David Beckham and Paul Scholes all started regularly in the team, and produced some excellent performances. I remember two moments in particular. The first was the match between Chelsea and Manchester United at Stamford Bridge on 21 October 1995. The young redhead Scholes made a huge impression, scoring two of the four goals as United won 4-1. When the players got back from London, Eric and me inevitably discussed the game.

'It was one of our best away performances since I've been at United,' he told me. 'You've seen Scholes. I love him. He can do anything: he can play midfield, centre-forward, defensive midfielder . . . He has such great vision. You saw his two goals – great class.'

'You've found your successor,' I suggested. 'Scholes is definitely the most gifted youngster you've got at the club.'

'You know, he reminds me of [former Sochaux player] Philippe Anziani – just as versatile. Being so good in so many positions can be a drawback, but today he really impressed me.'

The second occasion was also an away game, this one a derby match against Bolton Wanderers at Burnden Park on 25 February 1996. The stars that day were Beckham, Scholes and Butt. Of the fourteen players on the team sheet, six were home-grown, and between them they produced a performance close to perfection. The youngsters were breathtaking: the precision of Beckham's passes was a delight, as he showed himself a true midfield master; Gary Neville demonstrated his strength of character in defence; Butt won all of his midfield duels. As soon as Scholes came into the game as a second-half substitute, he confirmed his eye for goal. The match ended as an incredible 6-0 rout for United. Beckham, Scholes (with two) and Butt were among the scorers.

That season was a landmark in Alex Ferguson's career, as it proved he was right in his decision to integrate the young players into the team. Right at the start of that 1995/96 season Alan Hansen, a former Liverpool player who had become one of the pundits on BBC's *Match of the Day*, had predicted that Manchester United's youngsters were not yet good enough to win trophies. At United there were claims of conspiracy and jealousy, that they were 'standing up for Liverpool'. Consequently, what a pleasure for United fans at the end of the season when their youngsters enabled the club to achieve its historic second double! Perhaps the happiest of all was Alex Ferguson. 'Some pundits suggested we couldn't win the title with kids,' he pointed out on television with great irony and pride, 'but they reckoned without the force of a rejuvenated Eric Cantona and the respect and admiration our "kids" have for him as a footballer.'

Another young player was emerging. From the very first matches he played alongside Eric, I knew he was going to thrive. There are players who are ready to play from their very first training session. When you have played football and watched great players in action, there are signs – details like their positioning on the pitch – that immediately reveal them as having the potential to become world-class. When I watched how he positioned himself when he was playing in tandem with Eric, kept his cool as he approached the goal, observed and listened to Eric on the pitch, I could tell Ole Gunnar Solskjaer was going to be a great teammate for Eric and a formidable striker for Man United. What's more, as with Ryan Giggs, Ole and I hit it off from the start. Although we didn't know each other, there was something between us that made it seem like we did, almost as if we'd been friends in another life.

The first time I saw him in person was at the club museum. I was there researching how the club presented its history, jotting down things in a notebook, when this player with a very youthful countenance appeared. I watched carefully as he related the history of both the club and, above all, its legendary players. That we were both foreigners may have brought us closer. Even during those first exchanges, I felt we were going to get along very well.

Eric and Ole only played together for one full season, but their understanding on the pitch made a big impression on me. They complemented each other so well you would have thought they'd known each other for a very long time. In fact, Ole's rapid acclimatisation to Eric and Manchester United's direct style of play accelerated his success. During games I would sometimes focus my attention on Ole's runs in relation to Eric's positioning, and it was just phenomenal to see how well he understood Eric's game, and also how well Eric responded to the former Molde centre-forward's instinct for goal. When Eric had the ball, it was not uncommon to see the Norwegian make a run without even glancing to see what the Frenchman was intending to do with the ball. Ole instinctively knew what Eric was planning, and he was rarely wrong.

This filled me with elation, because the two players epitomised the kind of football I love: based on improvisation, joy and the movement of players who don't need to utter a word to know the other's intentions. As amazing as it may sound, the symbiosis between Eric and Ole came to seem to me one of the most beautiful attacking combinations I ever saw on a football pitch. Naturally, the phases of the game I enjoyed best were those where their magnificent understanding climaxed in a superb goal, and there was no shortage of such moments of grace.

On 14 September 1996, playing in front of 54,984 spectators at Old Trafford, Manchester United crushed Nottingham Forest 4-1 in what was a sumptuous spectacle. United's attack was on fire. The combination play between Eric and Giggs, and Eric and Ole, had the crowd in ecstasy. The goal Ole scored was the product of a beautiful collective move.

On 9 December 1996, the Monday after Man United had played against West Ham in East London, Eric and I had lunch together at Pizza Express. As we chatted, I recalled the biggest moments of the previous day's match. Although the 2-2 draw was a disappointment for many fans and even for Eric, for me one moment stood out. I'd barely started talking when Eric interrupted me. 'I know what you are going to say. Funny, I'd just thought of it. You're going to talk about the first goal, Ole's goal, aren't you?'

The passage of play that had resulted in Ole scoring, I told him, encapsulated their on-field relationship. 'When you received the ball, he knew exactly what you were going to do. His run provided you with the best option, and when you made that pass with the outside of your foot, I was already thinking, *If he scores now this will be a magical move.* That kind of thing should be shown to kids learning the game. Ole really is a world-class forward.'

'Did you see him shout and make his run to get into the best position to score?' responded Eric. 'It was really impressive.

He's a very intelligent player, a great centre-forward.' His words were, as usual, reflective rather than impassioned.

Out of all the players who lined up alongside Eric, there's one relationship that leaves me with a sense of regret, of things left unfinished. And that's Eric and Andy Cole. Given Andy's performances during his two seasons at Newcastle United and my knowledge of Eric, I thought these two would form quite a pairing in Manchester United's attack. Yet somehow it didn't quite work out that way, which left a lot of people surprised, myself very much among them.

From their very first moments playing together, as was Eric's custom with young players, he tried to put everything in place for his new striking partner to be successful. Eric saw Cole as the centre-forward who would enable the club to dominate national competitions and shine on the European stage simultaneously, and he was really looking forward to playing with him. 'He's bringing something new, something different,' said Eric. This was my friend all over: always resolutely optimistic and ready to help a new player integrate into the team. Cole had impressed the football world with his speed and scoring ability; that he would quickly develop an understanding with Eric seemed a foregone conclusion.

The first time I met Andy Cole it seemed to me he exuded inner strength and confidence. With Paul Ince, Ryan Giggs, Nicky Butt, Ole Gunnar Solskjaer and Jordi Cruyff, I became friends, but with Andy Cole things never got beyond cordial. We would say hello, and that was it. I didn't dare approach him; perhaps I was intimidated by his London accent – in fact, I've always found it really difficult to understand Londoners, because they speak so quickly. He came across as quite reserved, and that made me in turn a little distant.

Several months after his arrival, however, it turned out that we had two mutual friends. One was Saltz Anderson, a Mancunian musician and actor, and someone of unparalleled generosity who knew the 'people of Manchester' as very few do, and was appreciated by everyone for his kindness. He was a fixture of Manchester life. The other was the Liverpool player Michael Thomas, whom I'd met through Saltz at J. W. Johnson's on Deansgate. Michael had known Andy Cole for a very long time, as they had both played in the Arsenal youth team. When Michael asked me if I ever saw Andy away from Old Trafford, I didn't dare tell him that I didn't really know him. However, even these mutual friends weren't able to turn a polite acquaintance into a warm relationship. In fact, I proved to be remarkably shy around Cole.

Something else that certainly influenced my behaviour was the fact that I hardly saw Eric playing alongside Andy, or at least to the extent that I had with the 'old guard' of Steve Bruce, Denis Irwin, Gary Pallister and Peter Schmeichel and the 'young guns'. Perhaps subconsciously I felt closer to the 'Fergie Babes'. Andy Cole was an enigma to me, a puzzle I didn't dare try and piece together in the hope of a better understanding of him. All the same, a kind of Black solidarity prevailed. Andy's distant attitude, which from afar could be perceived as arrogance, was more the result of wanting to protect himself.

I understood this completely. Andy had great self-esteem and self-confidence, just like Eric. One thing that marked out the new generation of Black people in England, sociological studies of Black populations showed, was their willingness to show real ambition and confidence in their abilities. Andy Cole personified the proud Black man, and I could relate to that.

Above all, however, I was looking forward to a felicitous association developing between Eric and Andy at the head of United's attack. In the first matches they played together, I saw some nice combination play between them. On 30 December 1995, Manchester United met Queens Park Rangers at Old Trafford. That my friend William Prunier, a former Auxerre player who was on trial at United, was playing in defence that day didn't stop me watching Andy Cole's performance closely. Wearing the number 17 shirt, he was very industrious alongside Eric, and in the games that followed the Cole–Cantona partnership improved.

A month later, one particular incident strengthened that bond. On 22 January, United were playing West Ham at Upton Park. Andy found himself on the end of a horrendous tackle from the West Ham defender Julian Dicks, and nearly got himself sent off – only for Eric, who'd been appointed club captain just the previous month, to step in as peacemaker and smooth things over. From this game on, the relationship between Eric and Andy continued to deepen, but I still never felt there was quite the same synergy between them on the pitch that I'd witnessed in the Cantona–Hughes, Cantona–Giggs or Cantona–Ole partnerships. It's a shame they didn't have more time to get to know each other and, above all, score more goals. For my part, I got a little closer to Andy by being one of the fans who used to encourage him by chanting this song:

Andy Cole, Andy Cole,
Andy, Andy Cole,
He gets the ball and scores a goal,
Andy, Andy Cole ...

CHAPTER 7

The Man from Govan

It was some time now that I'd been engrossed in working my way through the archives researching Manchester United's early history. I'd been studying the extent to which the roles of director, secretary/manager turned full-time coach, and professional player had evolved or stayed the same as English society and sport had changed. One important theme emerging from my reading was the power struggles within the club. The position of the manager within this power play was particularly interesting.

As Eric and I sat in a Peter Street bar that was within sight of the Free Trade Hall, the headquarters of the free trade movement in the 1840s, I told him I wanted to interview Alex Ferguson. Hitherto, shyness had prevented me from asking his assistance in setting up an interview with someone from the club's management. Maybe this reluctance also stemmed from my childhood self-sufficiency, when I prided myself on getting what I wanted by my own efforts, and also the conviction that all academic research is an individual ascent to a summit of knowledge and self-sacrifice. What all this added up to was only asking for help if I had no other option.

Eric wasn't in the least bit surprised by my request, because I kept him updated on how my research was progressing, indeed often to the extent of monopolising the conversation. Out of politeness and also genuine interest, he was always keen to listen, especially when I turned up facts that illustrated the passion the managers, players and supporters had for the club.

One day, for instance, I was delighted to be able to inform him that in 1909 the club's donations to charitable causes had been higher than its spending on medical care for the players. Another time, I told him about the essential role played by Charlie Roberts, the club captain when United won their first league title in 1907, in the creation of the Players' Union, which represented all professional footballers. An excellent defensive midfielder and a key figure in the Reds' early glory years, Roberts, I explained, had pulled off a media stunt designed to attract the attention of journalists by showing them a photo of 'rebel players' captioned 'The Outcast Football Club'. It was a masterstroke.

'I like the sound of this Charlie Roberts,' said Eric.

These little nuggets of history about the club made a real impact on him. Suddenly, I'd realise, I had his full attention, and he'd smile as if to say, 'Go on, I'm interested in hearing about the past.' I found it important to be able to discuss my work with someone who would not examine it from an historiographical perspective, and consequently, instead of lapsing into complicated academic jargon that might bewilder the average person in the street, I became more of a storyteller.

Of course, I was also hoping to find a sympathetic ear, to confirm I was on the right track with my work, and shouldn't be prioritising something else. Often I found that the answers to such quandaries came to me during our conversations. I needed Eric's reaction too to tell me whether what I was doing really was of interest to the general public. In some ways he was my first audience, my first critic, my audience in the present who would interrogate the past. Gradually, our individual perspectives became intertwined and shared.

Among the episodes I recounted to Eric was the story of the first trip the Busby Babes made to the continent. In the Swiss city of Zurich some of the players owned up to feeling embarrassed at their table manners: sitting down to lunch in a decent restaurant was a surreal experience for these kids from poor backgrounds. How did you eat a salad? Which fork should you use for this dish, which spoon for that one? Another thing I'd discovered was the incredible bond between Matt Busby and George Best's family – so close that Best's parents decided to christen his little brother 'Busby'! There was plenty to laugh about too: I shared some funny and even quite raunchy stories with Eric, like the affair between the United manager Tommy Docherty and the wife of the club's physio!

But by now I'd come to feel it was both relevant and important to interview Alex Ferguson in order to get a full picture of how the club was run. No sooner had I asked than Eric told me he would ask the gaffer. I was pretty sure the manager would respond positively, as he and Eric got on famously.

I prepared by watching and reading every documentary, article and every biography on Alex Ferguson's life, day and night, and in the posh Didsbury district of Manchester I stumbled on a treasure trove: a bookshop with a very low ceiling and a pervasive smell of dust. Its shelves harboured innumerable useful publications. I was overwhelmed, spent more than four hours in this 'grotto' and, for less than £20, walked away with all kinds of treasures. Elsewhere, I happened upon endless VHS tapes and sports books, most of them on British football. Within a tottering stack of VHS cases I spotted a documentary on Scottish football and Aberdeen's impressive European campaign of 1983 when, with Ferguson as their manager, they won the European Cup Winners' Cup. I immersed myself in the autobiographies of players who had worked with him – Gordon Strachan, Steve Archibald, Lou Macari, Paul McGrath.

At Manchester Central Library I discovered microfilm, and took up residence at its viewing machines to go through articles from the Scottish press, including the *Herald* and the *Scotsman*, and the English press, notably the *Manchester Evening News*, the *Guardian*, the *Independent*, the *Daily Telegraph* and *The Times*. I was particularly pleased to find articles on Ferguson written by the Scottish journalist Hugh McIlvanney, one of the star writers at the *Sunday Times*.

I also studied the manager's comments in the club's various official publications, including the *Manchester United Official Yearbook*, *Just Champion!*, *A Year in the Life: The Manager's Diary*, and *Ten Glorious Years: 1986-1996*. I wanted to get acquainted with every facet of Alex Ferguson's personality and sporting career before interviewing him. I wanted it to become evident to the manager how much research I'd done on his life and career. Also in the back of my mind was that I wanted him to tell Eric how serious I was about my work. Eric had told him I was a student who was interested in looking at British society through the prism of football, and had told me that Ferguson was reassured to hear his star striker was hanging out with a student, an intellectual, rather than someone who lived for nights out. I was also fortunate to have my brother Basile in my corner, as he'd played for two seasons with Glasgow Rangers, where Alex Ferguson had spent three years as a player.

I'd first met the United boss at the Cliff. I was standing near the dressing room, and he approached me in a blue Umbro sweatshirt with the initials AF on it. His warm smile reassured me, and immediately I felt charmed by him. He offered me a '*Bonjour*' with an impeccable French accent and said he would tell Eric I was waiting for him.

On 17 October 1996, I found myself back at the Cliff to interview Ferguson. Smiling once again, he led me into his office, from which you could see the players running and training on the pitches below. Did I want anything – a tea or a coffee? I declined, wanting to take in everything I possibly could: the signet ring on his left hand, the photos on the walls, the layout of the office, the notices . . . It was part of a strategy I'd developed in similar situations: drawing on the environment around me to yield three or four improvised questions to provide additional insight into the interviewee.

And there, pinned to his wall, I spotted what on first sight was an incomprehensible word. 'What does that word mean?' I asked: '"Ahcumfigovin"'? What is that?'

'"I come from Govan,"' the United manager replied. 'That's my home. I come from Govan, a district of Glasgow. That's where I spent the big moments of my life.'

Then I picked out a phrase in Latin. 'And these words in Latin: "*Nihil sine labor*" – Nothing can be done without work?'

I could see he was a little surprised by my beady eyes. 'That comes from my social background, you know,' Ferguson replied: 'you always have to try to do the best you can.' He went on to explain that he liked to surround himself with all these echoes of Govan. I could really relate to what he was saying, and the reminders of his background that he had in his workplace.

Ferguson represented the ideal of the working-class hero, and I was absolutely aware of that. Later, I would venture further down this path that had led Ferguson to adorn his office with all kinds of reminders of his working-class roots. Yet his office was not the only place where the Scot proudly affirmed his origins. His house, in the affluent Cheshire town of Wilmslow, was called Fairfields, after the shipyard where his mother and father had worked. The first racehorse he acquired was named Queensland Star, in reference to one of the impressive ships his father had helped to build.

I was very moved by this insight into Alex Ferguson's life, which gave me a better understanding of the conditions a working-class British family faced in the mid-twentieth century. The Manchester United manager encouraged me not to lose sight of the important role played by the working classes in the world of professional football. Yet one question nagged at me as we talked about his experiences as a player and a manager: what was the secret to his special relationship with Eric?

As a player, I discovered, Alex Ferguson had himself been known for his strong personality. He'd fitted the mould of the rugged centre-forward and never let himself be intimidated by his opponents. During three seasons with Rangers (1967–69), the press repeatedly mentioned the left-footed striker's 'volcanic' temperament. One of Ferguson's idols had been Scotland's Denis Law, the brilliant and sometimes temperamental Manchester United striker in the 1960s. 'A bit like Eric, I was a player who never backed down when confronted by my opponents,' Ferguson reflected. 'I used my elbows to gain respect. A real centre-forward at that time was rough, hard . . . less technical than Eric, I must confess. I also scored great goals,' he added with a smile.

This 'volcanic' temperament was something the United boss and Eric had in common. He seemed to understand Eric's outbursts of anger on the pitch, even though he didn't always accept them. Whenever Eric was penalised by a referee, Ferguson was always his principal advocate. In public, in front of the cameras, he always protected Eric, often acting as a shield against attacks from the press. Even though he acknowledged the Frenchman lost his composure at times, Ferguson repeatedly highlighted the unjust decisions referees had made, on occasion pointing to a referee's lack of courage or competence. It was partly a way of diverting attention from the regularity with which Eric got sent off.

On 19 March 1994, United travelled to Swindon Town for a Sunday game in the Carling Premiership, as it was then known. For the first time ever, United were playing at the small County Ground. The Reds were at the top of the table, one point above Alan Shearer's Blackburn Rovers. The game started well for them, Roy Keane scoring in the thirteenth minute following a superb move that underlined the accord between United's strike force of Cantona and Hughes.

Twenty minutes later, Swindon equalised. Ten minutes into the second half, Paul 'the Guvnor' Ince put United back in the lead again. However, seven minutes from the final whistle, the home team equalised once more and the game ended a 2-2 draw.

All the headlines, however, concentrated on Eric's latest sending-off, trumpeting the game as an example of the two sides of his personality. 'Beauty and the Beast' wrote Trevor Haylett in my newspaper of choice, the *Independent*. I kept replaying in my head the incident that had resulted in Eric's dismissal. I thought the referee had been over-hasty. Alex Ferguson had been furious about it: as he saw it, the culprit was Mr Brian Hill of Market Harborough, the referee, and when he had appeared in front of the television cameras he had been extremely angry and railed against the injustice done to Eric. The year before, indeed, the United boss had already declared that Hill 'shouldn't be allowed to referee another Manchester United game'.

Sometimes I wondered why Ferguson defended Eric quite so much. But to a large extent it stemmed, I came to realise, from the way he'd come to view Eric. 'Eric's not the enigma people often suppose,' he had been quoted as saying in *Just Champion!*,

> but he is very different from all the other players. Different in his nature, his temperament, his cultural background, almost everything in fact. Little wonder he's not on the same wavelength as the rest of us. This *vive la différence* all wrapped up in the legend of an idiosyncratic football-poet is what makes us all very wary of how long our mutual relationship can last. It could be a lengthy honeymoon,

who can say? ... I have had to change my whole attitude, maybe do a bit of a U-turn on my usual policy, and accept that we have a different type of player around the house.

The right to be different, and a certain fascination with an extraordinary player, could explain Ferguson's attachment to *le Frenchie*. During my interview with him, he talked about his love of France, its wine (Bordeaux being his favourite), its landscapes and the French way of life. Did Eric embody this ideal of the Frenchman in the eye of his manager?

'Eric was the catalyst for our title win in 1993,' Ferguson was telling me. 'Simply with his presence, he brought something that very few players possess: confidence and serenity.' Another thought now struck me: that the deep admiration Ferguson clearly felt for Eric was also demonstrated by the special attention he gave him, and by extension me. I was never prevented from accessing the club's changing rooms, and Ferguson's staff – Brian Kidd, Eric Harrison, Norman Davies, Albert Morgan – showed me a great deal of kindness. One day, as I was waiting for Eric at the Cliff, Ferguson called me 'son'.

Touched by this, I told Eric later how much I liked his manager.

'Ferguson is one of the reasons I'm happy at United,' he explained. 'Thanks to him, everything is in place for me to be happy as a footballer and as a man. I've known many coaches during my career, but Ferguson is really something special. We don't speak very much, you know. But we understand each other in all kinds of ways ... And when I don't understand his Scottish accent I just say "All right". He always finds the right words to use with me, even in a tense situation. Ferguson is an exceptional man, Claudio. Of all of the coaches I've worked with, he's the best I've had and the one I respect the most.

'From the first moment I arrived and we spoke to each other, I knew he was a good and sincere person. He's always supported me, even in the most difficult moments. I know he's often ended up on his own when standing up for me against other people. I owe him a lot. Ferguson is a great guy.'

'Can you imagine what your career would have been like if you had met him sooner?' I joked. 'We might not have known the cold of Auxerre and the Morvan region, or Duarig football boots.'

When it comes to people he loves deeply Eric has always preferred to keep his own counsel, and on this occasion he didn't go down the path of what might have been. However, when I interviewed him on 6 September 1995 as part of my research, he confided to me: 'I have a special relationship with Alex Ferguson, a complicity that's underpinned by mutual respect. He brought me to United without worrying about everything that had been said about me, whether in France or here in Sheffield and Leeds. He showed a lot of courage, and also the flair to make me a success.'

One act would further cement what was already a close relationship between them: Eric's promotion to captain. As the games went by, I could see how Eric's influence and importance on the team were growing. He quickly became one of its essential elements. Ferguson regularly pointed out the number of games they lost when Eric wasn't in the line-up. On the pitch, I could see him talking more and more to the other players, pleading a teammate's case to the referee, complaining about decisions that went against the Reds, encouraging United's players, telling the younger ones what to do, approaching the bench to listen to Alex Ferguson's instructions. He became an intermediary between the manager and the players, gradually taking on the role of leader.

I'd studied the club's previous captains – Steve Bruce, Paul Ince, Peter Schmeichel – but Eric was markedly different. He was a captain with real charisma. Compared to Schmeichel, for example, he had a less exuberant attitude, his behaviour was more restrained, and he was an almost silent presence in the dressing room and on the pitch. Like Zinedine Zidane, Eric Cantona wasn't very talkative as a captain, but led by example. He had an almost mystical presence on the pitch, one fan told me: his physique and bearing left you speechless. He was appreciated for his qualities as a player and, above all, as a person. He never showed an individualistic streak – in fact, sometimes he was reproached for his altruism. In life and on the field, Eric always put the interests of others before his own. In the dressing room, he was a quiet leader, his presence alone enough to fill his teammates with a winning spirit. 'When he's there', Ole once told me, 'the air is different, the team is different, the opposition look at us differently.' Awarding the Manchester United captain's armband to the number 7 seemed just the right thing to do.

On 27 December 1995, a cold evening with the temperature barely above freezing, Manchester United met Newcastle United at Old Trafford. Kevin Keegan's team were leading the Premier League with 45 points, with Manchester United second in the table with 38. The media had been hyping the match as a key moment in the championship race, and so it would prove.

The Magpies' attack featured one of the best players of the era, the flamboyant Frenchman David Ginola. Meanwhile, the Reds' defence had been seriously weakened by the absence of three key members: Steve Bruce, Gary Pallister and Paul Parker. Alex Ferguson showed his faith in the young Neville brothers by selecting both of them to help fill the gaps. What's more, he chose this game to 'promote' Eric. In the presence of 42,024 spectators, I watched my friend walk out onto the pitch with his jersey collar pulled up, as usual, and wearing a black armband bearing the word 'Captain' in white. It was his first time wearing it in an official match, and I felt very happy, although not entirely surprised that he'd been handed the honour.

A new chapter in the club's history was unfolding before my eyes. Eric became, after Peter Schmeichel, United's second foreign player to wear the armband, and the first Frenchman ever to captain an English club. It also sealed his place among Manchester United's legendary players: Billy Meredith, Charlie Mitten, Duncan Edwards, Denis Law, George Best, Bobby Charlton, Bryan Robson. The evening ended well as, thanks to goals from Andy Cole and Roy Keane, United ran out 2-0 winners, trimming Newcastle's lead to just four points after it had recently been as high as ten.

Eric excelled wearing the armband. His run of form reached a peak in March 1996. In that month's opening game, the return fixture at Newcastle's St James' Park, he scored the only goal, which lifted the Reds to just a point behind Newcastle at the top of the league. He then scored in the ninetieth minute to secure a draw away at Queens Park Rangers. Four days later, he got the only goal of the game against Arsenal at Old Trafford, a result that put United level on points with Newcastle, who now led the table only on goal difference.

Four days on from that, United played Tottenham Hotspur at Old Trafford, and Captain Eric scored his sixth goal in six consecutive matches. This one had a special flavour as it allowed United to move to the top of the league for the first time since September. At the end of the match, Alex Ferguson's face was a picture of happiness. The Newcastle team, so long the league leaders, now seemed to be running out of energy, and it was down to the pressure United had been applying. I had seldom seen the Players' Lounge in such high spirits.

In the car on the way to the city centre, I told Eric how much this victory meant to the fans. 'I've rarely heard Old Trafford so happy and in such perfect harmony with the players. There are times when football takes you so far away from all the worries in life that you wish it would never end. It wasn't a great match but the tension was unbearable! When you scored, I looked towards the fans in the Stretford End and exchanged looks with people I'd never noticed before, but their expressions will stick with me forever. There was such happiness.'

'We had to win today to put more pressure on Newcastle,' Eric replied. 'From here on, they're going to have to win every game to catch us. We always finish very strongly at the end of the season. I'm sure they'll crack. I remember that in December some people were saying the championship was over because Newcastle were ten points ahead of us. We've pulled them back point by point, and today we're in front. That's what a great team does.'

*

The relationship between Alex Ferguson and Eric also involved the gaffer putting a protective arm around the Cantona family. When Eric decided to move permanently to Manchester at the beginning of the 1993/94 season, the family lived in Worsley, on the outskirts of Salford, close to Old Trafford and the Cliff training centre. Unlike the majority of players, who lived in Cheshire, Eric had decided to live in a relatively modest and popular residential area. It wasn't uncommon for people to come to the house seeking an autograph. They were sometimes surprised to look through the window and see Eric sitting in his kitchen. When fans knocked on the door, they were gobsmacked when Eric opened it.

During the day, when Eric was training, Isabelle would have numerous people calling at the door, hoping for a photo or to get the King's autograph. It happened all the time and it could get embarrassing. With journalists often appearing outside the house as well, Alex Ferguson advised Eric and Isabelle to move, to somewhere quieter and more exclusive. Indeed, the United manager took personal charge of finding Eric, Isabelle, Raphaël and new arrival Joséphine a new abode. This turned out to be a two-storey house with four bedrooms in Prestbury, a small village in East Cheshire, near Macclesfield. Former residents included Mark Hughes and his family, and among the neighbours were a number of local celebrities, including the Manchester City captain Keith Curle. Ferguson also found them a nanny to look after the children, while his secretary became a trusted helper and friend to the Cantona family, and especially to Isabelle. Ferguson's wife Cathy also got to know them well.

Ferguson and Eric's relationship was further reinforced by the Frenchman's ability to meet the manager's ambitious demands on his team. As captain, Eric was the player who most clearly understood and channelled the manager's unstated ambition.

From the moment he joined the club in 1986, Ferguson's overriding aim was to end Liverpool's supremacy in English football and for his United team to dominate the games between the two clubs. Liverpool had been the best English and European club of the 1980s, but in the early 1990s the tide began to turn, and in Eric the United manager found the player who would enable him to fulfil this mission of knocking Liverpool off their perch and installing United in their place. In all his autobiographies, Alex Ferguson talks about the importance of United's title win in 1993, their first for twenty-six years. According to him, this success was the trigger for United's emergence as the new dominant force, and the player who embodied the club's resurgence was Eric Cantona.

Subsequently, every confrontation between Manchester United and Liverpool effectively became a battle for national supremacy. Looking at this rivalry from an historian's perspective, and seeing how the media built up this fixture, I soon realised the special flavour these games against Liverpool had. On *Match of the Day* it was the most eagerly awaited contest of the season. The papers would devote several pages to the duel between the two neighbouring cities for the title of England's football capital. Consequently, when it came to the action on the pitch, the tension was palpable. I remember a match at Anfield in January 1994 when the rugged Liverpool defender Neil Ruddock used all kinds of provocations to try and unsettle Eric in what was his fiftieth game for United. The game ended a 3-3 draw.

*

Three years later, in April 1997, Eric's brothers Jean-Marie and Joël came with me to Anfield for the United game. A few days before, Eric and I had met the Liverpool playmaker John Barnes at La Gitane, a bar in downtown Manchester. When the two players greeted each other, there was no tension whatsoever between them: the respect and appreciation were mutual. I considered going across to speak to Barnes; he was a player I'd always liked. I asked Eric if he remembered the great English team from the 1986 World Cup, which had featured several players who didn't fit the stereotype of the typical English footballer: Chris Waddle, Glenn Hoddle, John Barnes, Ray Wilkins, Peter Beardsley. 'It was quite a team,' Eric agreed. 'It took all the talent of Diego [Maradona] to beat them.'

That same week I met a friend, the Liverpool midfielder Michael Thomas, who predicted that United would taste defeat at Anfield. In the end, though, the Red Devils won 3-1 thanks two goals from defender Gary Pallister and another from Andy Cole. When we got back from Liverpool, Eric's joy was irrepressible. 'Matches against Liverpool are undoubtedly the most important of the championship season. In fact, there are times when I wonder if they're not more important than the European Cup games. For the manager, Liverpool is special,' he told us.

Games between Manchester United and Manchester City were special too, but in a different way. They mattered to the managers and the players, but also to the entire city of Manchester, which looked forward to them with real relish. Pubs and bars favour one team or the other, and heaven help anyone who finds themselves in the wrong place at the wrong time. Yet, whether United were playing Liverpool or Manchester City, Eric was often the decisive player, much to the delight of his manager.

CHAPTER 8

How the Euro Stars
Changed the Premier League

I often bought the papers at the Manchester University Students' Union. The mid–1990s 'price war' between the broadsheets was a godsend for a passionate newspaper reader like me. To attract the widest possible readership, on week-days dailies like *The Times*, the *Independent* and the *Guardian* were sold at 'student prices'. I could buy all three for less than £2. At weekends, though, in the absence of those student offers I tended to choose my paper more carefully.

However, on the morning of Saturday, 16 December 1995, I splashed out on all three, eager to see what they had to say about the likely effects on English football of the Bosman ruling, the decision made the previous day by the European Court of Justice that meant that players from within the European Community could no longer be considered as foreigners within other EC countries. Britain, which had long resisted unrestricted recruitment of players from the continent, was being forced to open up. Would this signal the end of English football's splendid isolation? Would the recruitment of German, Italian and French players influence the game's identity? And how would fans react to their arrival?

That morning, therefore, I rushed to one of the Pakistani-run newsagents in Rusholme to pick up everything that had been written about the Bosman case. Even though the Saturday papers cost twice as much as on a weekday, I wasn't the slightest bit concerned about the expense. Not only did I buy my usual three, but I also added the *Daily Telegraph* and the *Financial Times*. I was also interested to see what the tabloids had to say, so the *Sun*, the *Daily Mirror* and the local daily, the *Manchester Evening News*, also went into my shopping basket.

The sheer abundance of newsprint didn't put me off. On the contrary, I was eager to find out what journalists' views were on this issue that, for Britain, marked another step in its rapprochement with the continent following the opening of the Channel Tunnel in 1994. After the arrival of Eric Cantona at Leeds in February 1992 and David Ginola at Newcastle in July 1995, were we going to see the invasion of *Frenchies* at English clubs? What would be the ramifications for leagues across Europe? I was desperate to find out what might happen next.

I shoved the papers into a plastic bag and rushed back to my flat, where I laid them out on a large table that was already home to my voluminous Robert/Collins French–English dictionary. I started reading, writing occasionally in a notebook with my four-coloured Bic pen. I wanted to digest both pro and anti-European analyses, and took particular pleasure in reading a captivating article in the Sport section of *The Times* by David Maddock and John Goodbody, which laid out nothing less than a new reality that would completely change the landscape of British football.

The revolution had begun with 'my' team, Manchester City. I lingered on these lines from the paper's 23 December edition:

> The deadlock after the European Court's ruling on the case of Jean-Marc Bosman was broken yesterday when Manchester City named four foreign players in their squad to meet Chelsea in an FA Carling Premiership football match at Maine Road today. In a pioneering move, City decided to follow European laws, rather than the regulations of UEFA, European football's governing body, and forced the FA Premier League reluctantly to lift the restrictions that a maximum of three foreigners and two 'assimilated' players could appear in a match. There was an air of celebration at Maine Road last night, which was not linked with the staff Christmas party taking place at the club. Francis Lee, the chairman, and his board of directors were claiming a breakthrough, which will allow Premiership clubs to field as many European Union (EU) nationals as they want.

In short, England no longer had a choice. The Premier League and the divisions below it were set to receive the most talented, and sometimes not so talented, European players.

Between the launch of the Premier League in the 1992/93 season and the Bosman ruling at the end of 1995, the number of foreign players had risen from eleven to sixty-six. In 1997, the year Eric Cantona's adventure in England came to an end, 218 foreign players were playing in the country's top four divisions. This revolution on the pitch was mirrored in managerial appointments, where the French were also well represented. Arsène Wenger and Gérard Houllier had taken up management positions at Arsenal (in 1996) and Liverpool (in 1998) respectively. Chelsea, meanwhile, opted for Italian know-how in the shape of Dutch and AC Milan legend Ruud Gullit, signed in 1996, and former Juventus centre-forward Gianluca Vialli, who joined two years later.

The Premier League had changed slowly but steadily, but those changes were extremely significant when viewed through the eyes of an historian. From the 1996/97 season, the 27th edition of the *Rothmans Football Yearbook*, the statistical bible on British football that runs to close to 1,000 pages, marked the growing influence of the contingent of foreign players in the Premier League and Endsleigh League with a section entitled 'The Foreign (International) Legion'. At the same time, match reporters had to learn how to pronounce often unfamiliar names of players from equally unfamiliar backgrounds. Clubs themselves rushed to find interpreters, who were not always very proficient when it came to the language of football. The London-based French consular service suddenly had to devote a lot of its time to dealing with the influx of French players arriving in England who needed assistance with all the red tape. Fans too had to familiarise themselves with these players who'd come from other parts of the world. At Old Trafford, their presence was marked by an increasing number of national flags flying atop the North Stand. Manchester United was becoming a truly international club.

A few days before the announcement of the Bosman

ruling, Eric and I were talking about it, which led to him asking me a question. 'Tell me, Claudio, who was the first foreign player at United?'

I wasn't too surprised to hear him ask this. As usual, I answered by giving as many details as possible about the player's arrival, the historical context of his signing, the attitude of the manager at the time and the standing of the player within United's broader history. 'It was in the late 1970s – 1977, to be precise – and after sacking Tommy Docherty Manchester United had taken on one of the best coaches of that era, Dave Sexton. Sexton had come from Queens Park Rangers after the West London club had enjoyed the most successful period in its history, finishing just a point behind a great Liverpool team in the championship in the 1975/76 season, which enabled QPR to compete in the UEFA Cup for the first time the following season.

'In July 1977, Sexton accepted a lucrative offer [£20,000 a year for four years] to become Manchester United's manager. Sexton was a coach with innovative ideas who would leave his mark on the club in three ways: first, the introduction of new coaching aids, such as video cameras; secondly, by reorganising the roles of assistant coaches, including the hiring of a coach to work specifically with the goalkeepers; and, thirdly, by scouting out foreign players.

'It's this last point that's the key one. Sexton had a very open mind when it came to football and travelled abroad a lot to watch games, particularly in Germany, Italy and Spain. He was also a cultured person: he liked to read books on training methods, on other sports, on sport psychology, on football culture around the world. In December 1978, having been impressed by the performance of some of the Argentinian players that had been part of the team that had just won the World Cup, he informed United's directors that they had the opportunity to sign the team's defender and captain Daniel Passarella and goalkeeper Ubaldo Fillol.

'Two other Argentinian players arrived in England at that time. Osvaldo Ardiles and Ricardo Villa had joined Tottenham, making them the first South Americans to play in the English Football League. Foreign players were very rare in England, partly because of the restrictions put in place by the Home Office and the football authorities. Between 1931 and 1976, the English FA imposed a residential qualification that required professional players to have lived in the UK for two years.' I pointed out to Eric with undisguised satisfaction that one player had made his mark on his era: the German Bert Trautmann, the Manchester City goalkeeper, who in 1956 had been the first foreigner voted by journalists as Footballer of the Year. As for Manchester United, however, they failed to complete the signings of Passarella and Fillol for financial reasons.

'Sexton, though, wasn't discouraged. He switched his attention to a Yugoslav player, Nikola Jovanovic, a defender who was part of the Red Star Belgrade team that appeared in the 1979 UEFA Cup Final. Consequently, Jovanovic became United's first foreign player. Unfortunately, he didn't adapt to English football or to the club. He played twenty matches for United, several of them for the reserves. In December, he returned to Yugoslavia, and his departure was a bitter setback for Sexton and also for the image of foreign players at United.'

This led to us reminiscing happily about the game in the early 1980s. Spontaneously, a face and a name appeared: a young, short-haired blond boy with a shy smile and a purple

Umbro jersey – Gary Shaw, the nippy striker in the Aston Villa team that won the European Cup in 1982. We remembered his brilliance, the great technical ability that allowed him to score some incredible goals. His idiosyncrasy was rarely going over the top with his goal celebrations: simply raising his left arm – enough to express his joy. Eric and I both had a soft spot for him.

The English league seemed far away to us back then – fascinating and wonderful. There were few opportunities in France to watch and admire Division One games: we were essentially limited to two options. One was on Sunday afternoons, the *Stade 2* programme, on France's second channel, which offered us the chance to admire the talent of players from Liverpool (Kenny Dalglish, Graeme Souness and John Barnes), from Nottingham Forest (Peter Shilton, Trevor Francis, Viv Anderson), Tottenham (Glenn Hoddle, Paul Gascoigne, Chris Waddle), and Manchester United (Frank Stapleton, Bryan Robson, Norman Whiteside and Arnold Muhren).

The other time English football entered French homes was the FA Cup Final. We used to be glued to the match at Wembley, with all its traditions and timeless spectacle, the game usually taking place in bright afternoon sun, its dazzling effect sometimes softened by light rain. Close to 100,000 fans packed into the mythical stadium, all desperate to see their club lift the trophy. The teams would come out of the tunnel side by side, the two managers suited up and leading the way, their ties matching their club's colours. It was always an enthralling occasion.

Strangely, of the three finals we could remember, two of

them were won by Manchester United teams featuring two fabulous players, Bryan Robson and Norman Whiteside. The first was against Brighton and Hove Albion in 1982, the second versus Everton in 1985. The third final we could recall pitted Paul Gascoigne's Tottenham Hotspur against Brian Clough's Nottingham Forest in 1991. The London team won the Cup, but the incident we remembered most clearly was Gascoigne being carried off the pitch with an injury.

English football had already been in our minds when we were still in France, but that one day we would find ourselves in the country where modern football was born was unthinkable. The thought of a Frenchman playing in England was not a dream so much as madness. English football shone so brightly on the European stage that it had no need for foreign players. For one to succeed in England would require a considerable mental and physical adaptation.

In his interview with me, Eric highlighted the difficulties continental players had in adapting to English football: 'Here, everything is completely different. The training sessions are sometimes like matches where everyone's completely committed. There are matches scheduled on Boxing Day – sometimes at midday! The training conditions are different, and there's a big difference between the coach and the manager. At United, Brian Kidd is in charge of the training sessions as the coach.

'There are also differences from what I experienced in France when it comes to preparation for matches, the number of professional footballers, the physical commitment during the matches, the fixture list – no winter break – the press, charity activities. Here in England it's very important for the players to be involved in social projects and other initiatives designed to boost the morale of fans, like visiting young children in hospital. The food is different, and you just have to get used to that. The managers aren't all that interested in your life beyond the club: what's important is what you give in a match, and this mentality is completely different from what I've experienced in France, where there's a tendency to infantilise players. Here, the players are given a sense of responsibility. I prefer this way of doing things. Here, if you give a hundred per cent on the pitch, everything else is of little importance in the eyes of the directors or the fans.'

The attitudes within English football were radically different from what we had known in France. Alcohol is a good example. When Eric and I went out, it was rare for us to drink more than three bottles of lager, to the astonishment of some players. It was quite normal for players to drink a lot of beer, I discovered, which to some extent reflected a 'lads' culture' where the qualities of a 'real man' could up to a point be measured by how much beer they drank and how quickly. We *Frenchies* took our time getting through a beer. There was never any rush. We also rarely drank without having something to eat, like chips or peanuts, and we rarely drank standing up at the bar. We preferred to be comfortably seated. As a result, our habits and behaviour were very different to English players'.

I also studied carefully Eric's attitude towards English players and the other foreigners he came up against. His relationship with Vinnie Jones was a case in point when it came to the former. Jones, it could be argued, was the archetypal 'English player', a genuine 'lad', and it was interesting to see how he performed when up against Eric, the best foreign player in the league at the time. The first encounter between the pair was rugged but courteous. However, a subsequent game took a more violent turn. On Sunday, 20 February 1994, Wimbledon hosted Manchester United in an FA Cup fifth round match at Selhurst Park. I decided to watch it in a pub that broadcast games on a giant screen, one of many huge establishments that had sprung up after the pay-TV channel BSkyB had bought up the right to show the majority of Premier League matches following its launch in 1992 – paying, it's worth noting, what now seems the modest sum of £191.5 million.

From the start the match had a heated atmosphere, beautifully described by one of my favourite commentating duos, Martin Tyler and Andy Gray, a grammar school boy from Guildford with a measured and calm tone and a former Aston Villa and Scotland centre-forward whose insights were incisive and often quite passionate. United were wearing a retro 1890s jersey of yellow and green with a lace-up collar, a nod to the colours of Newton Heath and Yorkshire Railway (founded in 1878), the club that preceded Manchester United (formed in 1902). With almost twenty minutes played, Jones revealed what had become the defining aspect of his game. During an innocuous United move a few yards from the centre circle, he made an abominable tackle on Eric. To the great surprise of many, the Frenchman didn't react, having no doubt been warned about the Wimbledon player's tendency towards intimidation. Not only did he not confront Jones, he also didn't even look at him. He just got up and watched as the referee, David Elleray, known for his severity, showed a yellow card and not red to the most emblematic player of Wimbledon's 'Crazy Gang', as they were nicknamed.

In the end, United won the match 3-0, Eric opening the

scoring with a magnificent volley, a goal Andy Gray described as 'sensational, magical, a perfection' and, added Martin Tyler, the best response to Vinnie Jones's awful tackle. Just after he'd scored, the Reds' fans could be heard singing their love for the French footballer, 'Ooh, aah, Cantona! Ooh, aah, Cantona...'

A few days later I spoke to Eric about the game and that Vinnie Jones foul that could have done him serious harm. He smiled, at pains to play down his rival's aggression: 'Wimbledon are a team that can play well on the ball, but they've chosen antagonism as a way to intimidate the opposition. We didn't fall into the trap. We knew exactly what we had to do to foil their plan. We were far superior, and as for Vinnie, I like him – he's funny, he's not mean! I know in his heart he's not mean. He's a good actor, a good comedian, and he plays that bad boy role very well on the pitch. You notice that quite quickly, as he's laughing and joking with the opposition players. He plays the tough guy, Vinnie, but he's not really a tough guy. He's a good guy, very funny. We had some good nights out in Leeds with Gary McAllister. We never stopped laughing.'

Three years later, I went to Old Trafford to watch United play Wimbledon in a Premier League game. I don't know why, but I had to wait for the players to come out onto the pitch before I could take my place in the Family Stand. This turned out to be a stroke of luck. I watched the players closely in the tunnel just before they came out onto the pitch, the two teams lined up next to each other, their faces a picture of concentration. Vinnie Jones, who had become Wimbledon's captain, said something to Eric, by then the United captain, which was obviously very funny. Eric smiled for a few moments, and it struck me that I'd rarely seen him so relaxed with an opponent.

Before they went out onto the pitch, Vinnie went up to Eric to shake his hand. The two captains swapped greetings and exchanged a smile. On the field, I didn't notice any rough treatment towards Eric. Respect and some form of gentleman's agreement had been established between these two strong but quite different personalities. At the end of the match, as they were standing in the corridor to the Players' Lounge, I saw Vinnie give Eric a friendly wink before heading to his team bus. It was a small but quite touching moment, and significant because it confirmed how the players in the Premier League had not only accepted the Frenchman, but also had great respect for him as a result of his exploits on the pitch.

The opinion of local journalists was a good way of measuring the impact of European players, and especially Eric, on the Premier League. Through seeing him regularly at the Cliff and in the corridors of Old Trafford and, above all, reading his reports and stories in the *Manchester Evening News*, I ended up meeting David Meek, a journalist who had witnessed forty years of Manchester United's history. Among the press and radio journalists who followed Manchester United closely (and which included Tom Tyrrell, Peter Smith, Stuart Mathieson and Roger Johnson), David was the best known, and the one I chatted to most often about Manchester United matches, how my studies were progressing and about the city itself. I always listened carefully to what he told me, and appreciated his unique knowledge of the Busby Babes, George Best, the City–United rivalry, and the changes that had taken place at Manchester United since the 1950s.

In Manchester, David was a well-known figure – 'a journalist institution', Guy Hodgson put it in an article in the *Independent* on 20 May 1995 to mark the journalist's last match: 'For thirty-seven years he has reported on the goings-on at Old Trafford for the *Manchester Evening News* and probably knows more about that other institution, Manchester United, than any other man alive. Today, after some 2,000 match reports, he retires.'

I asked if I could interview him for my research, and on a spring day in 1996 I went to meet him in a pub near the *Manchester Evening News* offices on Deansgate. David spoke passionately about the evolution of Manchester United, English football and the city. I was deeply moved by his words on Duncan Edwards, a player of immense and largely untapped talent who died in the Munich air disaster. I could see his eyes shining as he spoke about the magical trio of Bobby Charlton, Denis Law and George Best, and also when he recalled Sir Matt Busby, defender Bill Foulkes and midfielder Bryan Robson.

Then I got to the question he'd certainly have been expecting: where did Eric Cantona stand in United's history? David answered at length, his words reminding me a little of my university lecturers, full of detail and analysis. 'When he arrived', Meek confessed, 'we were honestly sceptical about his ability to make a mark at such a big club. But Eric pleasantly surprised us with the speed with which he adapted. With every match I could see that he was integrating more and more, and it didn't really look like he'd just arrived at a new club. He was really different to the other players I saw during all of my years here. I remember his early games well, especially his first derby against Manchester City. He produced a great performance. Gradually he became the team's leader after Bryan Robson left. Eric transformed the club with his exceptional talent, just as George Best did.

'When analysing Eric's success at United, we mustn't forget one person: Alex Ferguson. He was instrumental in Eric's dazzling adjustment to the club and to English football. As regards the impact of foreign players and Eric in particular on the English league, it's undeniable that our vision of football has changed. The continental players – Schmeichel, Ginola, Vialli, Gullit, Klinsmann – have instilled a different mentality thanks to their qualities, but also their faults. By far, and no journalist and football enthusiast could contradict me, the best of them all is Eric Cantona. His success changed everything. His class on the pitch and his passions off it – as a painter and poet – gave football here a new breath of life. Eric paved the way for clubs to hunt for that "rare pearl" from the continent.

'At United, no other player since 'Robbo' [Bryan Robson] has had such an influence on the club's results. I think the successes speak for themselves, but what impressed me about him was his desire to help the younger generation – Giggs, Beckham, Scholes – develop a perpetual thirst for victory. It's often said that he's arrogant, and you know him better than I do, but I think that what characterises him, as it does Alex Ferguson, is the determination to perform well and maintain that level of performance for as long as possible. We owe Eric Cantona a great deal for the way in which he enabled our football to be perceived differently abroad. Since Eric's been here, I've never had so much contact with foreign journalists, especially French ones.'

Eric's popularity in England had an undeniable impact in France, especially with Canal Plus, the channel that generally broadcast Premier League matches. French football lovers discovered a new passion thanks to matches between the likes of Manchester United and Liverpool or Arsenal. Games that pitted David Ginola's Newcastle against the 'King of Old Trafford' provided an opportunity to talk about the success of the *Frenchies Outre-Manche*, the Frenchmen making strides on the other side of the Channel. I became aware of an increasing number of French journalists coming to Old Trafford to witness Eric's extraordinary celebrity in England. I often saw the Canal Plus cameras approaching him just before the whistle in big games to get his impressions.

During the unforgettable duel between Newcastle and Manchester United in the 1995/96 season, British and French newspapers tried to pit Cantona against Ginola, but Eric paid little attention. I don't ever remember him talking about Ginola's performances. They played together in the French team but the former Paris Saint-Germain striker, who became an idol at St James' Park, was never in Eric's circle of French friends, which included the likes of William Prunier, Laurent Blanc, Fabien Barthez, Éric Di Meco, Pascal Olmeta and my brother Basile. Despite their origins in the south of France, Cantona and Ginola never became close.

Eric's attitude towards the French players and managers was more politeness than extreme warmth. At Old Trafford, I saw him go out of his way to greet Frank Leboeuf when United played Chelsea, and Lionel Perez, his former teammate from Nîmes Olympique, who played for Sunderland and Newcastle, but he didn't spend long chatting with either of them. That he kept people he didn't know well at a distance and had a certain shyness about him might have suggested a degree of arrogance, but it wasn't so.

It's also been said that he had a degree of ambivalence towards Arsenal, who became Manchester United's principal rivals during the late 1990s. But I always noted how Eric would nod respectfully to Arsène Wenger and admired their players. One in particular caught Eric's attention. When the clubs met at Old Trafford in November 1996, the London team featured a young midfielder with the number 4 on his back. Patrick Vieira really stood out that day, although United won 1-0 thanks to an own goal. Later, I asked Eric if he'd noticed Vieira's performance.

'He's young but talented. I can see him going far. In any case, when you've been captain of your team at the age of eighteen, as he was at AS Cannes, and you are signed by the great AC Milan in order to become the new Rijkaard, you must be very good. He'll make a lot of progress here, especially if he can measure up to midfielders capable of defending, attacking and scoring like Roy Keane.'

The presence of foreign players was a subject that went beyond the framework of football to take on wider cultural significance, to be a subject worthy of analysis in university and museum circles. Historians and sociologists from different universities were conducting extensive and stimulating research. In April 1996, I was on the cover of the newsletter for a social history museum in Manchester, the National Museum of Labour History.

As part of the cultural events running in conjunction with the Euro 96 Championship in England, during which several matches took place at Old Trafford, I was approached by the curator, Catharine Rew, about becoming part of the team producing an exhibition entitled *The Beautiful Game*. The impact of foreign players in the Premier League was one of the exhibition's major themes. I had responsibility for pulling this part together, and managed to source some notable items from some iconic players. I talked to Eric about the project: he liked the sound of it and asked what he could do. Without hesitating, I said the PFA Player of the Year trophy he'd won in 1994, and a red Manchester United jersey with Cantona on the back.

CHAPTER 9

New Manchester United,
New Manchester

Between the autumn of 1993, when I got to know the area around Old Trafford, and my departure from Manchester in the summer of 2004, that part of the city changed dramatically. During Eric's time in Manchester the buildings that surrounded it, like the stadium itself, underwent a total makeover. A whole new world appeared, impossible to miss, because what emerged was stunning.

From my point of view, as a keen observer, as a foreigner, as a historian and, above all, as a regular visitor to Old Trafford, everything became bigger, wider, higher, more impressive and more international. Following the upheavals at Manchester United and within the city of Manchester year by year was like watching a child's transformation from adolescence to adulthood. I witnessed profound social, economic and architectural change, and was affected in very different ways by it. Bound up in my fascination with this transformation was the feeling that a particular idea of England was gradually disappearing.

For a historian, it was strange to see an area marked by the scars of a very immediate past being revitalised; to see a new world in the making. Manchester embodied this new England, and Manchester United this new vision of British football, which was set to reconquer Planet Football by employing a very particular kind of know-how: the capitalisation of sporting success.

That era was undoubtedly one of change, as was most obviously demonstrated in 1997 by the arrival of the new prime minister, Labour's Tony Blair. His party's slogan, 'New Labour, New Britain', perfectly captured the zeitgeist. By that time, I'd been going to Old Trafford regularly for four seasons, and was meeting and chatting with more people outside the stadium each week. I'd always been aware of Irish voices, but now there were a growing number of them, and I was also picking up accents from countries much further away – from Malaysia, South Africa, the USA, Argentina and China. I also spotted more and more coaches parked in front of the club shop with Scandinavian and Eastern European registration plates.

Starting the day before United's home games, the city was transformed, not only by these new fans but also by the commercial opportunities they presented. From the airport all the way to the stadium, taxi drivers, shopkeepers, hoteliers and restaurateurs began to thrive, thanks to this internationalisation of United's Red Army of supporters, as did the image and economy of the city, which benefited hugely from the club's immense popularity across the world.

I regularly remarked to Eric about the links between Manchester United's performance and the city's development.

Often he would interrupt me in the car and point to a building, a street, a frontage that had changed dramatically since he'd joined the club. 'When I arrived here, none of the new buildings you can see as you head towards Salford along Sir Matt Busby Way were there. Back then, this area was a reminder of a period of intense industrial activity that had disappeared. It was affected by economic decline. You'd see factories that had closed down, buildings in disrepair and scarred by wild grass. It was sad to see. I was told this area was going to change in the years ahead, that there were plans for hotels, cultural venues, big businesses in Trafford Park . . .'

As part of my research, I was particularly interested in Trafford Park, the huge industrial area that bordered the Old Trafford stadium and which from its creation in 1896 right through to the 1960s had been a source of local pride, and a barometer of the city's economic prosperity. I decided to study the area's regeneration, noting the projects that were being developed. Thanks to the annual report of the Trafford Park Development Corporation, which was established in 1987, I was able to track the transformation that was taking place.

I was interested in the sums invested, the urbanisation plan, the new developments. To get an idea of the latter, I called on the staff at Sale Library (Trafford Metropolitan Borough Council), who supplied me with maps and other details of these projects. Over several weeks, I spent hours studying the changing topography of the area around the 'Theatre of Dreams'. I noticed passers-by giving me strange looks when they saw me laying out plans and making notes as I worked my way around the many streets and avenues using my Manchester *A–Z*. My curiosity was insatiable.

I supplemented this survey by reading leaflets and

documents about Trafford Park obtained from Trafford Town Hall and several libraries in the area. Between February 1987 and March 1998, £274.2 million was spent by the TPDC (Trafford Park Development Corporation), of which the largest amount, £85.76 million, related to expenditure on what was described as 'Physical Infrastructure'. I could see where the funds had come from, and it included a significant amount from the European Community (£6.07 million). The money from Europe was a key part of the regeneration process of an England which, without ostensibly displaying the fact, was becoming Europeanised.

One foggy morning in April 1998, I decided to go there to see the changes for myself. With the aid of my *A–Z*, I walked along Sir Matt Busby Way, across Wharfside Way and then Trafford Wharf Road, drawn into the area around Salford Quays. I passed the Copthorne Hotel, its frontage illuminated by the bright Manchester United signs across the road. I admired the Lowry Centre, named in tribute to the local artist who painted the famous work *Going to the Match* (1953). I looked at the planned extension to the Metrolink, the city's tram system, the HMS *Bronington* factories, Colgate Palmolive . . . The whole area was undergoing a morphological evolution in every way.

At the same time, Old Trafford was fast becoming a vast commercial district itself. I was familiar with the three separate club shops where fans could buy all manner of products that showed their affiliation to the Red Devils. As the ground's capacity increased, the range of these products diversified ever more. In the shop next to the station exit, where fans would arrive on the chartered shuttles from Manchester Piccadilly station, the young United fan could dream of a room completely decorated with Red Devils merchandise: curtains, 66 inches wide with a 54-inch drop, £24.99; 66 inches wide with a 72-inch drop, £29.99; autographed wallpaper, £6.99 per roll; border, £5.99 per roll; striped wallpaper, £6.99 per roll; Ryan Giggs quilt cover and pillowcase set, £29.99.

The second shop, covering almost 10,000 square metres, was located on the east side of the stadium (the Stretford End) as part of the renovation and expansion of Old Trafford started in 1992. Distinctive portraits of George Best, Denis Law and Bryan Robson invited you in to an immense space where fans, and even some rather more unexpected customers, would gather. During Euro 96, for instance, several members of the French team who were set to feature in the semi-final clash against the Czech Republic spent time in the shop. I once saw Zinedine Zidane at the till with several souvenirs.

In 2000, the monumental 17,500-square-metre mega-store opened on Sir Matt Busby Way. In the same year, two more United megastores opened in Singapore (17,000m²) and Dublin (15,000m²). From a commercial point of view, Manchester United had gone to a new level. The club had established the economic model for everyone else to follow, and the development of commercial activities had transformed the club's image. Between 1992 and 1997, the directors showed they had the vision to make United much more than a football club, which was highlighted by several successful projects:

- In 1992: the launch of the monthly *Manchester United Magazine*
- In 1993: the launch of a monthly video magazine, *Manchester United on Video*, the start of wholesale distribution of associated products

- In 1994: the formation of Manchester United Merchandising Ltd; the launch of Manchester United Radio
- In 1995: the announcement of a plan to extend the stadium's capacity from 44,000 to 55,300 spectators
- In 1996: the creation of a website
- In 1997: the agreement of a contract with the HSBC Midland Bank, which had a strong presence in South-East Asia; the opening of the Red Café restaurant in the North Stand.

The year 1995 was a turning point. For the first time in the economic history of a European club, match receipts (£19.648 million) were outstripped by another commercial activity: merchandising (£23.488 million).

The Old Trafford stadium I had got to know was also changing. When I went to my first match on 21 October 1993, I marvelled at the 39,396 people who packed the stadium for the European Cup clash between Manchester United and Galatasaray. Almost a year later, on 15 October 1994 to be precise, I was thrilled when Eric scored the only goal of the game in a championship match against West Ham United in front of 43,795 spectators. On 23 April 1997, less than a month before the end of Eric's career at United, I left the stadium immensely sad after United's defeat by Borussia Dortmund in the semi-final of the European Champions League, which was witnessed by 53,606 fans.

Even though they were still establishing themselves as a major force in Europe, Manchester United dominated English football. The club had dethroned Liverpool. The capital of British football was now in what was once Cottonopolis. The reasons for the Red Devils' supremacy were obvious and impressive, and Eric had played a huge part in it. It's worth remembering that the club had been waiting twenty-six years to win the league title. United then went on to win two doubles (league championship and FA Cup) in less than five years. It was universally agreed that Eric had been the crucial factor.

Eric's impact also resulted in him winning some significant awards at local level. He became a permanent fixture on Manchester's list of legendary heroes, and to some extent part of the city's collective memory. Although he gave little attention to the fact and may not even have realised, he became a historic figure. From day to day he led a normal life, but on the pitch he achieved extraordinary things.

In 1994, in a ceremony at the Midland Hotel, near Manchester Central Library, I watched with pride as Eric was awarded the Sports Personality of the Year prize by the famous Manchester beer company Boddingtons Breweries and the *Manchester Evening News*, the powerful local daily paper. He won it thanks to the votes of the paper's readers, a real achievement for a foreigner and a footballer. In 1994 and 1996, the Sir Matt Busby Player of the Year trophy, which serves as the voice of fans across the UK and around the world, was awarded to the *Frenchie* without any debate.

At the national level, his achievements were also remarkable, and included the PFA Player of the Year title awarded by his fellow professionals in 1994, and in 1996 the Footballer of the Year awarded by sports writers.

The image of the new Manchester merged with the revival of Manchester United, the best club in England. Confirmation of their joint renaissance was especially notable on match days. The city that had been formed by its industrial strength had been transformed into a service industry centre. With this sector booming, Manchester stood out as a city of dynamic economic growth.

Thanks to a French friend, David Lachimy, who was the manager of the Radisson Hotel Manchester Airport, I had an excellent vantage point on the day before home games for observing the evolution of the Manchester United fan. They flew in from many different places – Dublin, Oslo, Aberdeen, the Isle of Man, London, Limassol, Belfast, Zurich ... Most of them were among the 115,000 members of the Manchester United fan branches (1995/96 season) around the world. These supporters, many of quite modest means, delighted in telling me about their attachment to Manchester United 'no matter what the cost'. I remember a Glasgow City Council employee telling me that he would rather watch United than go on holiday. A woman from Germany confessed to me that Manchester United was her 'most beautiful lover'. A Danish estate agent outlined to me in great detail the budget (hotel expenses, taxi fares, beer consumption, purchase of match programmes, souvenir gifts) he devoted to the Reds. A young, elegant London broker told me quite simply that his life had changed since Cantona's arrival.

In my investigation of the city's metamorphosis I also interviewed black cab drivers from the Mantax company in the run-up to United's home games – about fifty in all. One taxi driver of Pakistani origin, a Manchester City fan, told me his takings reached their peak when 'the city's other team' was playing. A divorced father confessed that he needed to work on United game days to be able to afford his child support payments. An Indian from the Sikh community who had been in Manchester since 1977 revealed to me that he used to prepare himself mentally for the long hours he worked on match days, because of the intensity of the workload ferrying around hundreds of supporters. A Manchester United fan confessed that he was always really happy talking to fans coming in from the airport.

I honed in too on other indicators of Manchester's shift to the service sector. In the university district in the city centre, I noticed new office facilities for banks and insurance companies, as well as hotels and restaurants springing up. At the start of the 1995 academic year, on Oxford Road, the main thoroughfare for students of Manchester University and Manchester Metropolitan University, there were nine banks: Barclays, Co-Op, Lloyds, Midland, NatWest, Royal Bank of Scotland, TSB, Abbey National, Halifax. BSkyB's dissemination of Manchester United's success internationally, and Manchester's burgeoning reputation as a party city, attracted scores of students, some of them from Malaysia, one of the countries where United's support grew fastest.

Thanks to its international student population and a growing middle class who travelled a lot, the city was starting to look and seem very different. A European influence was becoming increasingly apparent. 'Manchester's city centre has been undergoing a seismic cultural shift recently,' noted the *City Life Guide to Manchester* in 1996, 'bringing a whole new European ethos to its eating and drinking scene.'

The mid-1990s was when the virtues of healthy eating were becoming more apparent in England. New culinary flavours were emerging, including those of the Mediterranean. The flagship product was olive oil, which was supposed to reduce cholesterol levels and other harmful effects of junk food. It first reached the Withington suburb of Manchester not far from where we lived with the opening of one of the area's first Sainsbury's – it might even have been the first in Manchester. Sainsbury's was presented as the trendy place to find products from Italy, France, Greece and Spain. Some days I would rush there and buy a 'French stick' (pre-baked) to get some of the flavour of the hot baguette you'd find in French bakeries.

Where Sainsbury's led, other supermarkets followed, selling food imported from France. We found other sources for French cuisine too. Every Thursday, Isabelle Cantona used to go to the delicatessen at House of Fraser to source familiar titbits, and we relished finding products imported from France. One Saturday evening I surprised myself by enjoying some low-quality pâté I'd bought at the new Tesco on Market Street – the kind of thing it would never have occurred to me to buy in France, but I savoured it just the same. Another day I found myself craving French cheese, and was delighted to find some at Tesco, the taste of it carrying me straight back to France in an instant. Every weekend after that I maintained my cheese obsession, gorging on a different one each time: Camembert Président one weekend, Bresse bleu the next, then Comté, always accompanied with the inevitable baguette.

This quest for continental flavour encouraged the establishment of many new restaurants, French, Italian and Spanish among them. Since 1969, the Beaujolais on Portland Street had been the only place in the centre where you could eat French food. Yet 1994 saw the opening of Café Bonjour, then Pierre Victoire on Peter Street, Café Rouge on Deansgate, and Malmaison, a superb hotel-restaurant facing Piccadilly Station. Italian gastronomy was represented by, inevitably, Pizza Express in South King Street. Its reputation was well-deserved, said *City Life*: 'The biggest, busiest and best Pizza Express in the country (recently it expanded up onto the first floor), a cut above its London brothers in decor, ambience and quality of cooking. An instant favourite with Manchester's trendiest diners (a place to see and be seen), it has taken the pizzeria into the twenty-first century.'

Cocotoo's on Whitworth Street was the other popular Italian restaurant, partly because the illustrious tenor Luciano Pavarotti had dined there, but also owing to the interior redesign by Michael Browne, who a few years later produced *The Art of the Game*, which featured Eric in a divine posture, the work inspired by Piero della Francesca's *The Resurrection*. The flavours of Spain could be found in La Tasca, a restaurant Eric and I often used to visit, at 76 Deansgate, two doors from J. W. Johnson's.

Strolling through the city centre, we also noticed that Manchester was undergoing something of a fashion revolution. Alongside the so-called alternative fashion boutiques in Affleck's Palace and the Corn Exchange, where young urban fashion talents were blossoming, were a growing number of internationally renowned brands.

One day, leaving the Atheneum bar to walk towards King Street, I pointed out to Eric that this area was becoming a serious presence in the fashion industry, symbolising 'flamboyant Manchester'. From the mid-1840s, King Street had been the heart of the banking and insurance district but, more than a century on, it was being made over into one of the most important fashion streets in England, featuring illustrious *haute couture* shops: Emporio Armani, Vivienne Westwood, Karen Millen, Ralph Lauren, Whistles, Pink, Ted Baker, Jigsaw, Liberty, Moschino.

The architectural heritage of the industrial era was giving way to new buildings and innovative configurations. The number of café-bars cropping up on former industrial sites was staggering. We'd go and have the renowned ciabatta at the Atlas on the end of Deansgate, and some afternoons would head to Alaska, in the Arches at Whitworth Street West, putting the world to rights to the rumble of trains overhead.

In the Castlefield district we frequented Dimitri's, Dukes 92 and, most often, Barça, named in tribute to FC Barcelona and located in Catalan Square. It was owned by Mick Hucknall, the lead singer of Simply Red, a huge Manchester United fan and a friend of Eric's. It too was built under the railway tracks, the architecture mixing old (red bricks, metal arches, exposed beams) and modern (flower-filled spaces, large windows, outdoors eating). In the spring of 1996, we were invited to the opening, along with many musicians, actors and artists who were local celebrities. A table was specially reserved for Manchester United players to savour the flavours of Catalonia, with the food produced by master chefs. The warm decor of the interior contrasted with the dampness outside. We were served sun-dried tomatoes, wonderfully juicy melons, thinly sliced Serrano ham, olive oil-seasoned bread, seafood, fruit salad, sangria . . .

The 1990s also saw the city attempting to establish itself in the community of renascent metropolises, through projects designed to boost both its national and international visibility, with sport very much at the forefront. Manchester put itself forward as a candidate to host the 1996 and 2000 Olympic

Games and, although it lost out to Atlanta in the first instance and Sydney in the second, it was nevertheless important to feature as a city capable of organising the world's premier sporting event. 'I'm convinced that Manchester must continue to "think big",' said Bob Scott, president of the city's Olympic Bid Committee.

There was, of course, a successful bid too. In 1995, the city was awarded the 2002 Commonwealth Games, and as a consequence a number of new sporting venues emerged. The eastern zone of the city (Ancoats, Beswick, Openshaw, Miles Platting, Ardwick, West Gorton), which had been severely affected by the economic recession of the 1980s, received £2 billion in public and private investment for a radical facelift. The area became the heart of Sportcity, which included the new City of Manchester Stadium, a multi-sport arena with 38,000 seats which, in the wake of the Games, became Manchester City's new home, with the capacity raised to 48,000. Designed and built by John Laing, it cost close to £110 million. Near by was the National Cycling Centre, opened in 1994 and home of British Cycling, which included Britain's first permanent indoor velodrome. In 1997, an Olympic swimming pool was built on Oxford Road, the student quarter. 'Manchester's failed bid for the Olympics, and its successful bid for the Commonwealth Games in 2002, plus the revival of Manchester United as one of the world's leading football clubs, put the city on the world map,' stated *City Life 1996*, a sentiment with which Eric and I fully agreed.

CHAPTER 10

'We Are the Nineties'

It was Saturday night in Manchester. As was often the case, United had won and Eric had put on a sublime performance. We came out of La Tasca, the Spanish restaurant on Deansgate, and headed towards to Yesterdays in Alderley Edge, one of the region's most popular nightclubs. Our mood was very upbeat.

Gradually the lights of Manchester faded away and we were in the countryside. As we drove, listening to *Now, That's What I Call Music! 32*, we sang along to some of the current hits: 'Big River' by Jimmy Nail, 'Hold Me, Thrill Me, Kiss Me, Kill Me' by U2, 'Broken Stones' by Paul Weller, 'Fairground' by Simply Red, 'Roll with It' by Oasis, 'Inner City Life' by Goldie, 'Missing' by Everything But the Girl . . .

We arrived at our destination without Eric putting his foot down too much. Eric likes racing cars and motorbikes, but he's not a speed freak. We offered polite hellos to the imposing doormen, who nodded their heads and smiled, wishing us a good evening. Once we were inside the huge building, we soon realised that plenty of other Man United players were there too: I saw Ryan Giggs chatting with someone, and when we made our way over we realised he was talking to Liam Gallagher. Eric and Liam hit it off immediately, chatting in a calm and friendly way as though they'd known each other for ages.

To some, such an encounter might seem abnormal, improbable. How could the king of Manchester United and one of the kings of Britpop, a life-long and unconditional fan of Manchester City to boot, hit it off so well? But for Eric, there was no dividing Liam the musician from Liam the City fan: football and music were fundamental to the uniqueness and pride of the city. Oasis belonged to all Mancunians, whether they were Reds or Blues. There was no ambiguity: music and football were harmonious.

Eric was a big fan of Oasis, in fact, and liked Liam a lot. 'I like everything about them,' he told me: 'their love of football, their attachment to Manchester City, their music, which both resembles and is very different to the Beatles. I also like them because they're from Manchester, they're guys from working-class backgrounds. The way those Gallagher brothers complement each other is fantastic: Liam is the performer and Noel the composer. I think that's great, and it also shows how different they are – opposites, even. They are exceptional.'

There was something else that seemed to bind Eric and Liam together: they both embodied the 1990s. There had never been a period when the links between football and popular music had been so close: it was as if football had found its way into pop music and vice versa. A number of songs had become hymns that highlighted the passion and fervour of football. Although football was not necessarily mentioned, these songs were heard in stadiums at half-time, inside pubs, supermarkets, taxis, inside buses, in the halls of university campuses.

Football and pop music reflected the hallmarks of British culture in a particular way, emphasising its vibrancy. No one, for instance, who lived through this period in the UK could possibly forget the cult song 'Three Lions' by Baddiel, Skinner and the Lightning Seeds, which became indelibly associated with the Euro 96 Championship in England. Among the other songs that had similar collective resonance were Oasis's 'Supersonic', 'The Riverboat Song' by Ocean Colour Scene and 'The Changingman' by Paul Weller. The fusion between Britpop and football became even more obvious when Paul Weller featured a portrait of George Best on the cover of his *Stanley Road* album. The allusion to the beautiful game had been even more pronounced when the jazz-funk band Incognito used a photo of the 1970 World Cup-winning Brazilian team on the cover of their song 'Piece of a Dream', that came out on the famous London label Talkin' Loud.

In the stands, the influence of pop music was omnipresent. Most of the songs that fans chanted used melodies that were very familiar from the radio and TV. Among the best was the adaptation by Manchester City fans of Oasis's 'Wonderwall' – written of course by Blues fan Noel Gallagher – that celebrated the fabulous Georgian dribbler Georgi 'Kinki' Kinkladze, German goalkeeper Eike Immel and team manager Alan Ball, one of the heroes of England's World Cup-winning team in 1966. The refrain has always stayed with me:

And all the runs that Kinki makes are winding
And all the goals that City score are blinding
There are many things that I would like to
    say to you
But I don't know how
I said maybe
Eike's gonna be the one who saves me
And after all
You're my Alan Ball.

The appeal of football broke down class boundaries. The passion for it was becoming ever more apparent among the well-to-do and even classical music artists. The violinist Nigel Kennedy never hid his deep attachment to Aston Villa. The pianist and film soundtrack composer Michael Nyman, a product of the Royal Academy of Music and King's College London, proudly declared his passion for London club Queens Park Rangers. In 1994 the playwright Howard Brenton and composer Benedict Mason, a former student at King's College, Cambridge, joined forces to produce *Playing Away*, a powerful opera that evoked a fictional European Cup Final, whose dominant theme was football.

The sport was having an impact and influence on almost every part of the culture. Eric and I were particularly alive to football's place in literature. I often enthused about the books I felt had revolutionised sports writing in Britain in the 1990s. We both enjoyed and discussed *Fever Pitch*, Nick Hornby's account of the fanatical love he had had for Arsenal since the age of eleven, and marvelled at the photo of the kid on the cover of the edition I had bought at Sportpages near Barton Arcade, a heavenly place for lovers of sports literature. A year later, Hornby edited a terrific book called *My Favourite Year*, an anthology of football writing featuring excellent writers from literary, journalistic and sporting backgrounds, including Roddy Doyle, Harry Pearson, D. J. Taylor, Olly Wicken and Jorge Valdano. The 'soccerati' had been born.

I shared my discoveries with Eric. I told him about John King, an author I found rather disturbing, an 'outsider' in my library at the time, and his 1996 book *Football Factory*. The characters in it, hooligans mainly, were representative, perhaps excessively so, of the voices of a white working class decrying its bitterness, its pain, its inevitable demise, its disenchantment with the world. The writing was deliberately unfiltered; the tone was fierce, brutal, virile, politically incorrect. I wrote down the opening paragraph:

> Coventry are fuck all. They've got a shit team and shit support. The only good thing to come out of Coventry was the Specials and that was years ago. Now there's sweet FA and we've never had a decent row with Coventry. The best time was two years ago in Hammersmith with a bunch of Midland prototypes looking for a drink down the High Street. About fifteen of them. Short cunts with noddy haircuts and tashes. Stumpy little legs and beer guts. Looked like they should be on Emmerdale Farm shafting goats for a living. They clocked us coming the other way and took off.

I read it out to Eric.

'Whaou!!!' he said. 'You're right. It's amazing!'

I showed him the magazines with a new, offbeat tone that were changing the way the world of football was being written about: *Four Four Two*, with its 164 pages concentrated on English football, was launched in 1994; *Total Football* came into being a year later, concentrating on the international game. We started to move away from literature focusing purely on football and discovered a wider range of books and writers, including a new generation of brilliant authors evoking very different perspectives on England. During my Sunday reading of the *Observer* and the *Sunday Times*, I would select the must-read books, then go out and buy them and afterwards talk to Eric about them.

The Nineties saw the emergence of many major authors who helped us understand new sides to Britain and British life. I was enthralled by the squeaky satire of Thatcherism in Jonathan Coe's *What a Carve Up!* and *The Winshaw Legacy*. I became infatuated with the Scottish humour in Irvine Welsh's *Trainspotting*. I was intrigued by David Lodge's writing in *Therapy*. I was captivated by Hanif Kureishi's *The Black Album*, which dealt with the difficulties of feeling both English and Pakistani.

We were also in thrall to the cinema, and particularly films by directors who depicted people from the grassroots, the marginalised, the underprivileged, the forgotten, the anti-heroes. Often there would be some connection with football. We would talk for hours about what we'd seen, never short of things to say when it came to the genius of filmmakers who captured the solitude of the big city, the struggle of the working class, the complexity of social mixing, social inequality, the 'self-derision of the poor'.

I would go to Manchester Central Library, where I was allowed to borrow up to five films on VHS cassette. I was drawn to committed filmmakers who were socially engaged, the Emile Zolas and Charles Dickenses of the camera. I was keen to discover another angle on English social reality via cinema and relished watching, sometimes again and again, the films of Mike Leigh (a Manchester native, it's worth noting): *High Hopes* and *Life is Sweet*. I moved on to Ken Loach's films and documentaries: *Riff Raff*, *Raining Stones* and *Carla's Song*. Like many, I was captivated by Danny Boyle's *Trainspotting*, Maria Giese's *Jimmy* and Steve Abbott and Mark Herman's *Brassed Off*. And when Eric and I discussed them, we noted so many familiar places and features: the north of England, the red bricks of the terrace houses, the football stadium.

One phenomenon often identified with football players and becoming much more apparent to millions of fans, was alcoholism. It was not new: in 1979, the former Tottenham, Chelsea and England centre-forward Jimmy Greaves had released a book with the shoutline: 'My name is Jimmy Greaves . . . I am a professional footballer. And I am an alcoholic.' The career of George Best, one of the legends of world football, the man nicknamed 'the fifth Beatle', was tarnished by alcohol abuse, which eventually led to his death at fifty-nine. In one of his many autobiographies, *The Good, the Bad and the Bubbly*, published in 1990, Best described the evil of alcohol in a chapter entitled 'The Demon Drink':

> Booze. Mention my name and the word comes staggering into the conversation a moment later. Which, when all things are considered, is understandable enough. I have drunk my way through an ocean of the stuff, drunk myself through days without memory or recall, point or purpose, except to blot everything out in a swirl of alcohol.

During the 1990s, footballers' alcohol problems received unprecedented media coverage. Generally the issue was tackled in an extremely sensitive and moving way, highlighting the wider social problems that resulted from addiction to alcohol. The football authorities, including the Football Association and the clubs, showed they now had more awareness of the vulnerability of footballers. While it was hardly news that this scourge was affecting a large part of the footballing population, hearing Premier League stars like Paul Merson and Tony Adams talk about their difficulty in coping with alcoholism was poignant. In 1995, Merson, the 26-year-old Arsenal midfielder and England international, opened up to the *Daily Mirror* about his addiction to cocaine, alcohol and gambling. He was later seen in tears at a press conference, a shocking sight. He received help from the Football Association, the Professional Football Association (PFA) and his club, and went into a rehabilitation clinic.

A year later, Tony Adams, Arsenal's captain and stalwart at the heart of the team's defence, also confessed to a serious alcohol problem. In 1990 he became one of the first footballers to be jailed for drinking and driving. Following his case, the FA accelerated the introduction of random alcohol testing within clubs.

The image of footballers being rich, invulnerable and carefree was revealed as flawed: they might be perceived as living the dream, but it became apparent that footballers could be vulnerable too. Merson, Adams and, later on, other players, most notably Paul Gascoigne, movingly exposed an issue that was well known within the football world, but had been largely hidden from the general public.

Eric and I talked about the alcohol problem in English

football, but perhaps we were too French to understand. What was evident to us was that there was a culture of drinking at English clubs; that among British players at all levels a heavy consumption of alcohol, and especially beer, was almost the norm. It had become a shared tradition. This tendency was alien to us.

During these years, despite being wrapped up in a resolutely macho world, we were aware too of women's voices becoming increasingly loud and expressing a visceral attachment to football. Women football writers were starting to emerge. Numerous initiatives, some backed by the Football Association, enabled the gradual entry of women into the world of football, and revealing how many women had long had a passion for football but hitherto few opportunities to express it.

I got to know one undying fan. She used to tell me she had two loves, 'animals and Manchester United'. I met her in one of the charity shops in town. She worked at PDSA, the animal welfare organisation, and was at the till when we first got chatting. I had in my arms a pile of books on contemporary English history – David Cannadine, Jan Morris, Arthur Marwick, the *Cambridge Illustrated History* edited by P. J. Marshall – as well as volumes of *Wisden*, the cricketing almanack, and biographies of former Manchester United and Manchester City players including Lou Macari, Paul McGrath, George Best, Alan Ball and Francis Lee. She asked me if I collected memorabilia, and I told her I was a student interested in the history of England, and football in particular.

'If you're interested in football, then you should drop all those books on City players,' she replied in a flash. 'The real team here is United. The only team worth studying hard is Manchester United.'

I listened to her as intently as I always had during my university seminars. I was amused by her response, which I'd heard countless times from the Manchester United fans I met all over England. I liked the way she talked about football. She told me she'd been married twice and each time been unlucky enough to fall for a man who couldn't name the players in the United team that had won the European Cup at Wembley in 1968. 'I'm a mixture of Keane and Cantona,' she often used to remind me, alluding to her Irish origins and a name that suggested French ancestry. She was 'crazy' about football – wouldn't miss a Manchester United game for anything. With a season ticket beyond her means her settee was her private box, she used to tell me, and *Match of the Day* her home cinema. She'd been introduced to football by her brother, a Manchester United fanatic who had unfortunately got mixed up with the wrong company and led a difficult life that had ended tragically.

I used to like dropping in to the PDSA shop to listen to the radio commentary on the BBC when Manchester United were playing away from home. She knew football inside out, and especially the players from the 1980s, but she wasn't nostalgic. She was also never unkind when she talked about players – except of course those from Manchester City – but that's something I've always found funny about football. She loved to talk to me about Cantona: his upraised collar, his impetuous outbursts, his dashing looks, his goals against City . . .

She knew all the players in the Manchester United squad, plus all the youngsters in the reserve team. She didn't talk much about the national team: her whole conversation was Manchester United. 'I'm a fan who doesn't necessarily need to watch every game at home and away,' she said. 'My blood is the red of United.' I was quite happy to spend time talking about Manchester United rather than football in general. 'Football was my life,' she told me, 'and United was my heaven and hell.' I promised to surprise her by bringing a United player into her shop. 'That's nice,' she told me, 'but you shouldn't bring a player in here. My shop is in danger of being labelled pro-United, and that could result in me losing customers. And I prefer to see them on television.'

This woman's passion for football was hardly unusual. The 1990s was a time when the flame was unleashed without restraint, without fear. In David Bull's book *We'll Support You Ever More: Keeping Faith in Football*, a diverse spectrum of supporters (academics, former prime minister John Major, priests, journalists) offered their take on the game. 'The "true supporter"', wrote the sociologist Tessa Davies in her article entitled 'Why can't a woman be more like a fan?',

as defined by the footballing establishment − and also, sadly, by some of the alternative, fanzine culture − is by and large a man. The devoted lad who is rooted to the terraces, season after season; who may well cancel his wedding day, should it coincide with a Cup tie; who could name a first-born after first-team players; and who is capable of struggling with relegation over lager and curry. After years of struggle against institutionalised sexism, we women fans have learned that, as long as we adopt these norms of fan culture, we may make the grade. Those unable or unwilling to be initiated into the rituals are pooh-poohed as phoneys, members of the armchair brigade – never a true fan. For us who are unwilling to become 'ladesses' – or, indeed, for us at home looking after the lads' children and cooking the lads' sausages – the only way we can participate in the game we love is to watch it on the telly. And make no mistake: we do love the game.

Two aspects of life in England struck me particularly as unimaginable in France: seeing groups of gleeful women making their way to the pubs on Friday evenings, and the fervour and true faith of these female Manchester United and City fans around the stadiums when it came to talking about their clubs. At Old Trafford I'd see lots of women get excited about a Peter Schmeichel save, or a typically rugged tackle by 'the Guvnor' Paul Ince, or one of Giggsy's mazy dribbles, or leap up in rage when the referee didn't give a penalty. Seeing female fans regularly in the stadiums, I didn't pay them any more attention than anyone else. It just showed how many women now loved the sport.

Academics were observing this trend closely. Sociologists such as John Williams at the Sir Norman Chester Centre for Football Research at the University of Leicester were conducting surveys to investigate it. The institute was also assessing (via the FA Premier League National Fan Survey) the profile of fans, as the growth in numbers of female fans was a significant factor in the explosion of football's popularity in the mid-1990s. According to the study, in 1996 and 1997 they represented 11.9 per cent and 12.3 per cent of the attendees at Premier League games, respectively. The change was noticeable in the press too. I particularly liked Alyson Rudd's sharply-worded columns in *The Times* every Saturday under the tagline 'The Astroturf Blonde'. In literature books like Pete Davies' *I Lost My Heart to The Belles*, and *One of the Lads: Women Who Follow Football* by Anne Coddington were big sellers.

The federation also played a key role. In 1990, the FA decided to lift the ruling preventing girls aged under eleven from participating in mixed football. Other important initiatives followed. A brand-new national championship, the National Women's League, started in 1991. Two years later, Julie Hemsley became the first woman to serve on the all-male FA Council. Change was taking place within the management of clubs too. In 1993, Karren Brady, then just twenty-three, was appointed managing director of Birmingham City, a pioneering move. Three years later, the TV cookery star Delia Smith joined the board at Norwich City.

Discrimination was decreasing, but it wasn't disappearing. This was particularly evident in the racist actions carried out against the Black community both on and off the pitch. April 1993 saw the appalling death of Stephen Lawrence, the 18-year-old Black Londoner brutally murdered by white youths while waiting for a bus. The story shocked me, but led to the issue of racism being debated in the press, on television, at university, in the streets.

Meanwhile, I immersed myself in the subject of racism in football. I discovered the work of the historian James Walvin, a specialist in both slavery and football and author of *The People's Game*, published in 1975 and republished in 1994. I studied the history of the Black British community through the works of Paul Gilroy, Stuart Hall, Peter Fryer and Dave

Hill, and the family story of the Phillips brothers, Mike and Trevor. I also built up an extensive bibliography comprising press cuttings and players' biographies (including those of Viv Anderson, John Barnes and Paul McGrath), and consulted the stories celebrating the centenaries of great clubs such as Aston Villa, Arsenal, Liverpool, Tottenham, West Brom and Manchester City.

In the course of my research I noted the numerical evolution of Black players in the elite league. During the 1972/73 season there were just three in the First Division; by 1993/94 in the Premier League there were 244. England was taking on new colours, with football becoming a remarkable showcase for Black talent. I closely followed the career of John Barnes, whom I saw quite often in Manchester with Eric. During his first games for Liverpool, he was the target of obnoxious heckling from individuals sympathetic to the National Front. One encounter transfixed me: the Merseyside derby, Everton vs. Liverpool. Everton fans had been singing: 'Niggerpool' and 'Everton are White'. I came across the front page of the *Daily Mirror* from 31 October 1987: 'Stay away, you scum' was the headline, the courageous words of Everton chairman Philip Carter, who wanted to dissociate himself from the racist attacks of his club's supporters on the talented striker.

In his autobiography John Barnes wrote that he had experienced racism throughout his life:

Racist abuse stained my life even before I moved to Merseyside. Walking home from school, in one of the better areas of London, kids shouted 'black bastard' at me. The situation in the East End was far worse. At Watford, opposing fans from countless clubs, but particularly

140

Millwall, West Ham and Chelsea, showered me with spit and abuse. Banana after banana came flying from the terrace throngs towards me. Hundreds of them.

The problem was profound. Even players were using racist insults against other players. On 20 December 1994, at the request of Gordon Taylor, then chief executive of the Professional Footballers' Association, the Nottingham Forest defender and England international Stuart Pearce apologised after making racist remarks to the Manchester United midfielder Paul Ince. On 6 January 1995, the Arsenal centre-forward Ian Wright complained about racist chanting by Millwall fans during a Cup match. There were other incidents too, underlining that society was gangrenous with racism. In due course the Macpherson Report of 1999, following the Stephen Lawrence case, highlighted 'institutional racism' in the police force.

In the face of this scourge, there were signs of change, of social mutation, of a legislative response. Racist chanting became punishable by heavy sentences under the 1991 Football Offences' Act, and in 1993 the Kick It Out organisation was created with the aim of fighting racism, and supported by the football authorities, the Football Association, the Professional Footballers' Association and, later, by the Commission for Racial Equality. Its slogan was straightforward: *Let's Kick Racism Out of Football.*

The players were also mobilising. In 1995, discreetly but effectively, Eric became involved in an anti-racism campaign led by the sports equipment manufacturer Nike, appearing with my brother Basile Boli, at the time a Glasgow Rangers player. The recognition of Black players was growing within

clubs and the England team. The stereotypes about noncha-
lance, weak character, their 'innate' qualities, were gradually
diminishing. In 1988, John Barnes became the first Black
player to win the Players' Player of the Year award, a prize
awarded by professional footballers themselves. The following season he again distinguished himself by winning the
Player of the Season trophy awarded by the football writers.
On 9 June 1993, Paul Ince went down in England history
as the first Black player to wear the captain's armband. At
Manchester United he was a fundamental part of those glorious years – winning the championship title and the FA
Cup. He was one of the players Eric appreciated most for
his winning temperament and kindness. On the pitch, Paul
was always one of those who always defended Eric in heated
situations. For this reason, I liked him a lot too.

CHAPTER 11

Kiss and Tell

Every time we were in a bar or pub in the city centre, some-one would offer to buy us a beer. It was often a Man United supporter or a local who loved France. We always refused, although I can't put my finger on why. There was an element of shyness in it, a desire to protect ourselves from any misunderstanding, as well as simply wanting to have a quiet conversation without being interrupted.

One evening after a match, we had one of these encounters with a stranger that particularly disturbed me. I quickly picked up on the elegance of the mysterious character who had offered us a drink. He looked athletic, was tall and was about forty. When he spoke, I couldn't detect a northern accent. He spoke calmly and eloquently, giving the impression that he'd been well schooled and was from an affluent background. He was decked out finely in luxury brands, wearing an anthracite grey suit, a white shirt with an Italian collar and gold cufflinks, a Rolex Daytona watch on his right wrist, and wearing a very nice red pair of Church's Shanghai shoes. His aftershave had a subtly sweet scent. In short, he was a true gentleman, who reminded me a little of the Brett Sinclair character played by Roger Moore in the TV series *Amicalement Vôtre* (*The Persuaders!*) that I'd enjoyed so much during my childhood in Ivory Coast.

The man was sitting in one of the armchairs used by the regulars at the Four Seasons Hotel bar. That evening, we were there with Eric's two brothers, Jean-Marie and Joël, and some friends, including Jean-Jacques Bertrand, Eric's lawyer. The stranger beckoned me over and politely asked me to sit down with him for a few seconds. I was used to situations like this, which tended to follow a certain routine. Often they were very funny, and usually they ended amicably with a good deal of laughter. I was frequently asked if I was Eric's bodyguard.

'He doesn't need a bodyguard,' I would answer without missing a beat. 'And look at me next to him: do I look like someone who could be intimidating or scary?'

Sometimes the question would be: 'Am I allowed to ask him for an autograph?' I would jokingly say that my answer depended on how much they were willing to pay, before quickly adding, 'Of course you can ask him for it,' and enquiring whether they had a pen handy. Often, to their delight, I'd offer them one of my own, which I'd usually never get back.

At other times I'd be asked if I was Andy Cole! One evening someone even came up and said, 'Excuse me, are you Basile Boli who plays for the Glasgow Rangers?' A student asked me, 'Are you a player with the Manchester United reserve team?' A woman's query was simpler still: 'Are you a famous footballer?' Generally, the requests were very politely made and my responses usually well received, although one day someone who didn't have a pen was brazen enough to tell me that 'With what he earns he could afford to carry a pen with him at all times for the fans!' I was lost for words. Eric, meanwhile, gave him a cold look.

That evening at the Four Seasons, however, the stranger started asking me all sorts of questions: what I did for a living, what differences I noticed between France and England, my opinion on the weather in Manchester, the Mancunian accent, concert venues, English theatre, rugby league ... I told him I'd come to Manchester to study English history since the nineteenth century.

'Then you must be interested in the press,' he said.

'I like reading the papers,' I told him.

'Then you must be aware of the importance and influence of the tabloids – the *Sun*, the *Daily Mirror*, the *News of the World*. Do you know these newspapers recruit beautiful girls to entrap footballers? If a player succumbs to the charms of these "temptresses",' he went on, 'they often end up being on the end of compromising stories in the press, sometimes with a photo that reveals these trysts.'

I was a little surprised by how swiftly he had shifted to revealing this aspect of the tabloids' behaviour. I listened attentively, without interrupting. This encouraged him, and he was soon explaining that 'this practice is known as "kiss and tell".'

At first I didn't say anything. Then something rang in the back of my mind and a memory suddenly came back to me. I recalled exactly where I'd heard this term before. It was the title of a song I liked on Bryan Ferry's *Bête Noire* album. When I'd first heard it, I'd no idea what it meant, but I could still remember a few lines.

The stranger was now providing a quasi-scientific and almost police-like description of these girls. He was apparently an expert on the subject, and I was curious to hear what else he had to say. 'There are several different profiles, but I'll outline the three most common,' he told me. 'Let's start with "the student". She'll approach quite shyly, say a few words in French and, if you answer, she'll tell you that she's a student and that her dream is to continue her studies at a French university, with a preference for Paris. She loves French culture and the mentality of the French people. These "students" are mostly young – let's say around twenty. She'll be very well turned out, will speak without any noticeable accent. She won't be vulgar in any way, in what she says or what she wears, and her make-up will be discreet. She wants to be seen as a model student. She's interested in football, but nothing more. She has relatives who love football. She's not a fan of any particular club. She enjoys the passion and fervour at football matches. She'll tell you that she's never had any kind of relationship with a footballer. She'll say that she's wary of football players as they come across in the press as fickle and very misogynistic.'

With barely a pause, he carried on: 'The second type you might come across is an independent, financially well-off woman, "the modern woman". She's more self-assured than "the student". She's in her late thirties. She'll never let you pay the bill when you invite her out. She'll tell you that she works in business, probably in finance or for a law firm. She'll look impressive, with clothes from chic shops like Karen Millen, Joseph, Aquascutum. She'll have lots of self-confidence. She'll tell you that she's very busy at work and has very little time for leisure activities. She loves to take holidays abroad, often in glamorous resorts. She'll claim to know Monte Carlo, Milan, Paris. She studied at the best English and American business schools. She doesn't know much about the world of football, except what she's picked up from the kind of clients who talk about their private boxes at the biggest clubs. She'll have been invited to attend cricket matches at Lord's or rugby union internationals at Twickenham.'

Then he outlined the third type of woman looking for a kiss-and-tell encounter. 'She's a football fan. She'll tell you that she loves football and comes from a family where football is very important. Her favourite team will be one of Manchester United's main rivals – Liverpool or Arsenal. She'll give you the impression that she is committing a "sin" by talking to you because you're considered the enemy. She'll be smiley, extremely friendly and very good company. She'll say she studied at university but had to drop out for financial reasons. She follows football on radio and television and enjoys fanzines. She also enjoys music, especially R&B and Britpop. She's sporty and goes to the gym regularly.'

I was dumbstruck, a little frightened, but also impressed by what he was saying. I was fascinated by the details he provided, in a tone both serious and clinical, yet with a touch of humour that made his words pleasingly hypnotic and engaging. In the end, I simply thanked him for his advice and rejoined the group. From time to time that evening our gazes met, then we lost each other again in the noise and cigarette smoke of the cheerful throng that had gathered in the bar.

I was rather puzzled by what this stranger had said. I'd heard about the tabloids ravaging the personal lives of some players. At the same time, I'd never known a player that I socialised with falling victim to this kind of trap. Yet, although they didn't admit it publicly, every Premier League player had heard about these charming creatures with silver tongues. When you did hear that a player had been caught out in this way, it would be a source of amusement among other players for a day or two. Usually the 'willing victim' would be from one of the many London clubs – the capital was regarded as something of a honeytrap, filled with elegant women primed by the tabloids' editors to be on the look-out for footballers who might get caught out straying.

Traditionally, club managers had encouraged players to settle down to a peaceful family life as quickly as possible. The coaches' thinking was clear: *The sooner the player 'gets his head straight', the better he can concentrate on his profession.* Being single was seen as detrimental to a serious career. Marriage and fatherhood were among the virtues of the model footballer in both France and England. At Auxerre, when a young player joined the professional team, the coach, Guy Roux, would try to get to know his girlfriend. I remember him pestering his players about this. He didn't hide the fact that he was keen for players to get married and start a family so they wouldn't be distracted by talk about going nightclubbing. So he was delighted when, for instance, both Eric and my brother Basile got married when they were barely twenty, and even more when each of them became a father shortly afterwards.

In Manchester, many of the players fitted this model and were married with children, so when we went out with Eric we rarely encountered them. I've no recollection, for example, of spending an evening with Peter Schmeichel, Steve Bruce, Mark Hughes or Brian McClair. Yet very often we'd meet the younger players who were then unattached, the likes of Ryan Giggs, Nicky Butt (and his brother) and David Beckham and one of his best friends, David Gardner. When we went out, all eyes would be on the players, who always got envious glances because they attracted so much female attention. 'Giggsy' and 'Becks' in particular always received lots of beautiful smiles. Young, handsome and rich were the three words I heard most often when women were talking about these two United players.

Were they afraid of a dalliance with a stranger? Undoubtedly. All the players were aware of the kiss-and-tell rumours or of the danger that might arise as the result of an encounter with one of the *Sun's* Page Three girls. One of the first things I noticed when I began to rub shoulders with players was how much they favoured the tabloids. I'd often notice copies of the *Sun* or the *News of the World* on car seats at the training ground, inside the team's dressing room, on the table in the players' dining room, or in his hands in a hairdressing salon. The tabloids might have been hated and decried, but they were omnipresent. Many players bought or at least read them to see the match reports or to find out the latest gossip – after all, essentially newspapers derive their success from this fascination people have with the happiness and misfortune of others.

'I'll never spend my money on these rags, or even look at them,' Eric told me. Although the tabloids made frequent requests, he never agreed to an interview with a single one of them. I shared his opinion, but I was always interested to find out a little more about how they had gained such popularity and especially how they were able to influence such a vast readership. I'd quickly noticed that the tabloids clearly understood they could boost their sales by devoting considerable space to football news and scandals. Sex, money and football were three components that always sold well. In November 1994, for instance, the *Sun* revealed a grim story of corruption involving the former Liverpool goalkeeper Bruce Grobbelaar, who had allegedly been caught up in a match-fixing ring. The 'Grobbelaar scandal' hogged the headlines for several days, while the story shook the integrity of the English Football League and highlighted the irresponsibility of some players. It even led to an investigation into corruption within the game. The taboids, inevitably, lapped up every salacious detail.

Eric and I scrupulously avoided becoming a target for the tabloid press. Maybe we were lucky to have lived in the spotlight at a time when the smartphone didn't exist. What freedom! I say that because we did have some unusual experiences. On one occasion, we were at the Band on the Wall, which was located in the northern part of the centre on the road that ran out towards Oldham. Built in the 1860s, the building is one of the remnants of Manchester's industrial revolution, and these days it was a popular venue for music lovers, particularly for world music and jazz concerts. We really liked going there and hearing rhythms from Asia, Africa and Scandinavia. During one concert, while the musicians were on a break, we decided to leave the crowded hall to get some fresh air. A doorman was kind enough to point out somewhere where we could talk in privacy, but Eric declined the offer and told him we'd be fine just a few steps from the entrance.

No sooner had we started chatting to each other than a young woman in her twenties, who'd clearly been waiting for the end of our exchange with the doorman, approached us. Straight away she started to tell Eric about the passion for Manchester United she'd had since she was a child. 'I'm a United fan!' she exclaimed. 'You're the best! You're beautiful! I adore you. Eric, I love you! Are you married? Do you have children? Whatever – it doesn't matter: I love you. You're beautiful. I never imagined I'd see you in a place like this. They used to say that all footballers stayed in their luxurious mansions in Cheshire. You're really different. I adore you. You're a painter and a musician, aren't you?'

The doorman, who must have seen the woman approach us, came over and asked if we wanted any help. 'That's kind,' Eric replied, 'but we're okay.'

Happy to be talking with Eric, the woman carried on telling him that she loved him and that she found him intelligent, classy and really charming. She disappeared for a few moments, then came back with a big black felt pen in her hand and asked for an autograph. We noticed that she didn't have a piece of paper for him to sign. With a mischievous smile, she turned around and pulled down her trousers. We stepped back and asked her to stop what she was doing. We were totally stunned, but quickly found a piece of paper for the autograph. We hurried back inside, laughing with the doorman. 'Eric, sorry about what just happened, but you are the King,' he said. 'People love you here and are ready to show that. Come back any time – we're always happy to see you here.'

On another occasion, we were in a bar a few miles from Old Trafford when we were suddenly interrupted by a tall, elegant woman. Could she join us at our table? she asked. We said yes. She began by saying that she wasn't a Manchester United fan, but that she liked Eric's personality. She talked non-stop, not allowing us to get a word in, her sentences coming out in rapid-fire bursts: 'I'm a businesswoman, president of a company with a turnover of several million. I have companies in several countries. You'll understand, then, that I'm very rich. I travel a lot on the continent, in the United States, in Africa, in Latin America, in South-East Asia, in Dubai. I frequent the best hotels in the world. I like to eat in the best restaurants in the whole world. I don't deprive myself of anything. Whenever I want something, I've got enough money to be able to afford it without giving it a second thought. I enjoy life. I had a marriage that didn't last because my work took over my life and made me lonely and too dependent on my business. I have a son. He's crazy about you, and I'm sure he'll be upset and maybe won't even believe me when I tell him I've had the opportunity to talk to Eric Cantona. It would be his dream to be in my shoes right now. He's twenty. His birth was a youthful mistake but I love him. I've never been maternal, but I think about him every day. I'll do everything I can to make him succeed in his professional and personal life. You're certainly married to a beautiful model, and your children, are they beautiful like you?

'And you,' she said, suddenly turning her attention to me: 'You're obviously a footballer too, certainly as famous as Eric, but unfortunately I don't know much about Premier League players. I'm sorry, but I don't know who you are. You're not famous enough for me to know you. Maybe I'm wrong? Let me guess . . . With your leather cap, you work in the cinema, certainly in the art world? Are you famous? Are you French too? France. The city of love. The city of cafés, beautiful women, *haute couture*: Dior, Chanel, Yves Saint-Laurent? I would have liked to marry a Frenchman. I hear that you are great lovers, you are romantic, you cook for your wives. I love France, French men and women. I'm sorry to bother you but I wanted to meet you and Mr Cantona. I wanted to talk. Thank you for listening to me. It's time for me to leave you in peace. I won't ask you for an autograph because I suppose it must be annoying and boring for you to be constantly approached to sign a piece of paper. What I wanted was to get to know you and talk to you.'

She stood up, apologised again for taking up our time, said she was delighted to have met us and left without looking back. We felt overwhelmed by her torrent of words and rather confused, and mulled over what she'd said at the start and at the beginning of her monologue. 'You see, she has everything she wants in life: professional success, money, beauty,' Eric pointed out. 'But she feels terribly lonely. Her work is her passion. If her passion was football, she would certainly have moments of sharing, moments of collective happiness when she went to the game.'

'We're all alone,' I added. 'But the stadium can be one of those places where you meet a group that you get on with, a kind of family.'

It's fair to say that the presence of footballers tended to provide a useful measure of a nightclub's notoriety. It was in these places, it was said, that one could find the most beautiful women and the most renowned celebrities. In cities like Glasgow, Birmingham and Liverpool, nightclub owners displayed pictures of famous footballers very prominently precisely to highlight their reputation as the place to be. In Manchester, the regular patronage of footballers from across

England made J. W. Johnson's bar 'the place to be and to be seen', as I used to describe it. Footballers were the attraction, the reason for so much fascination. Celebrities, wealthy young men on the look-out for conquests, clubbers and indeed anyone looking for a memorable night out naturally gravitated to these places, and by doing so became part of a relatively homogenous scene.

I spent one happy afternoon wandering between the city centre clubs where we used to hang out, just to get an idea of what they were like during daylight hours, and how different they seemed. They sat within four cardinal points that delineated what I ended up calling 'the Night Quarter'. The joyous soul of the north could be found within this district, characterised by dancing, flirting and clandestine love. Friday or Saturday nights here were blissful.

The real heart of Manchester's nightlife could be found at the southern end. There was a string of bars that ran alongside the GMEX tram station. Whitworth Street was home to the famous Hacienda, the Ritz was known as a place to 'grab a granny', while trip hop fans flocked to the Venue. It was said at the time that the craziest parties, the prettiest girls and the most charming men could be found in this part of town every weekend.

Thanks to a friend, Saltz Anderson, we got to know all the nightclubs in Manchester. This Manchester native was the singer in the group the Jazz Defektors and an actor who had appeared in Julian Temple's 1986 film *Absolute Beginners* that featured David Bowie and Sade among its stars. Saltz was a well-known and popular character among the city's doormen, and with him as our guide we explored every happening corner of Manchester. United's young players, and particularly Giggs, Butt and Beckham, also advised us on the coolest places. We were open to any kind of music: hip hop, drum & bass, Britpop, trip hop, indie . . .

Thanks to the city having some of Britain's trendiest nightclubs, a night out in Manchester was full of surprises and unexpected encounters. One night at the Manchester Reform I saw two faces that looked familiar, which was no surprise as so many people frequented the same clubs. They were two women in their twenties, and as we passed we exchanged polite hellos. We were in good spirits because we were celebrating the birthday of a United player.

Later, as I was talking to one of the bartenders, one of the girls asked me if I could come to their table quickly. I glanced across at Eric to let him know where I was. Once I'd made my way over, one of the girls asked me if I could help her make a wish come true. 'Are you a footballer too? Do you play at United? My friend is on her hen night – she's getting married in a few weeks,' she explained. 'We'd like to play a joke on our other friends. Could you ask Eric to kiss her on the mouth and allow us to take a picture? There's nothing in it, really! It'll just take a few seconds and we won't bother you any more. It's for a bit of a laugh and you seem very nice. I'm sure you'll manage to convince him. It's just a joke. Eric's a gentleman and I'm sure he'll trust you when you tell him that it's just for fun.'

Caught up in the club's buoyant atmosphere, I didn't imagine for a second that she might be lying. She seemed sincere, and I thought her request was quite daring and funny. I got up and went over to tell Eric. As I told him I became more and more aware of where this seemingly innocuous story could be leading.

'Claudio', said Eric: 'I can just picture your face if you were to see me on the front page of the *Sun* or *News of the World* tomorrow morning kissing this girl!' Instantly my lucidity was restored, and we spent the rest of the evening laughing about a set-up that thanks to my naivety would have resulted in one of the tabloids selling millions of copies.

CHAPTER 12

Allez les Bleus!

Eric's history with *Les Bleus*, as the French football team is nicknamed, can essentially be summed up in the famous Serge Gainsbourg song, '*Je t'aime moi non plus*'. It was a love-hate relationship. Eric and *Les Bleus* is a story of real passion, featuring moments of pride, tragedy, happiness and extreme disappointment. It was a saga that had many happy twists and turns, but which, unfortunately, ended sadly.

Outside his immediate family circle, few people were able to understand just how important France's blue shirt was to Eric. He loved *Les Bleus*, in exactly the same way that he loved to immerse himself in his art, committing himself to it with total absorption and fervour, finessing it until he felt it was complete – the same rigour, torment and passion always apparent. During the time he played for the national team, and even after his competitive career was over, when he talked about *Les Bleus* his comments were rarely dispassionate or bland. His perspective was always based on a real love for the game, while both his personality and his standing as a former player meant he could hardly remain insensitive to France's performances. *Les Bleus* have always mattered and will always matter to him. For my part, *Les Bleus* were a part of my life that I saw from two perspectives: Eric's, of course, and also my brother Basile's.

Although many articles and books have been written about Eric, not one has managed to calibrate the importance he attached to the national team. Every time he was called up, it was to what he described as the joy he drew from being with certain 'colleagues', the change of scenery, the clash of cultures, the stimulation that came with playing in a very different atmosphere, the diversity of playing styles, playing with and against the best players on the planet. Being part of the French national team fulfilled his desire for innovation. Being selected wasn't just satisfying his professional passion but also enriching his way of playing, his friendships, his inspiration for painting, his desire to discover other cultures. Eric was utterly dedicated to the national team while playing at all his clubs, ready to make any sacrifice to ensure success. With the other players, the coaches and the backroom staff his behaviour was always exemplary.

For every footballer representing your country is the pinnacle. It brings with it the opportunity to take on the best players in every nation. For both Eric and Basile, wearing the blue jersey adorned with the French cockerel was a moment of pride and happiness. For several years I followed their international careers very closely, initially when they were part of the under-23 set-up and then when they had graduated to the national team. They both knew how closely I would be watching them when they lined up for France. Their successes and disappointments affected me deeply:

when they were happy I was proud of them, and when they weren't I silently and to a more modest degree felt the same sorrow. Footballers' relatives tend to be quick to show their joy, but often conceal their sadness.

By an odd coincidence, Eric and Basile earned the same number of caps for *Les Bleus* – forty-five. Both also played their first match with the national team away from home and in the month of August. Both experienced the bitter taste of defeat on their international debut. Basile's came earlier. He won his first cap in 1986 in Lausanne against Switzerland. Eric's debut came a year later when he scored the only goal for *Les Bleus* in a 2-1 loss to West Germany in West Berlin.

They would both tell me about incidents that had taken place during international matches – a decisive bit of action, funny moments – but what I liked most were their stories about the new environment they'd experienced, the country they'd just visited, the things that happened away from the games. I recall Eric transporting me to Gabon in 1985 during his short spell with the French military team. 'It was the first time I'd experienced Black Africa, and all kinds of things made a mark on me. It was completely new, exciting and bewitching. It made a real impact on all my senses. I was particularly affected by the vividness of the colours: the sky, the ground, the vegetation. I was fascinated by the strength and difference of the smells, the way people dressed, the music in the street, the passion for football. The change was dramatic and fantastic.

'Libreville was a city of profound paradoxes. We were staying in a luxury hotel but poverty wasn't far away. We visited the market and there I was captivated by the dark alleys that led to the stalls selling fetishes and, especially, masks. These masks piqued my curiosity. I had read about the influence of African art on the paintings of European artists, Picasso in particular, and his famous *Demoiselles d'Avignon*, a major work in the very early days of Cubism at the beginning of the twentieth century. I'd read that he'd been inspired by the masks of ethnic groups [Mahongwé or Ngaré] in the Congo. I went up to, studied and touched the masks. The vendor, happy to see white tourists, played up the authenticity of "ancestral pieces" like this, often with a lot of exaggeration. I half-listened to him. I was enthralled by the "spiritual force" of the masks – they seemed to project a soul that attracted me, that delighted me. I was so pleased to discover the unique nature of these Gabonese masks. Each had a particular name and a distinctive use. I learned about the Vuvi, with their faces painted white, which came from the centre of the country. They appeared in night-time rituals that were accompanied by beating drums. Another mask also caught my eye. Its face was white too. It was the Punu or Lumbo, which are widespread in the west and centre of Gabon.'

Eric's stay in Gabon furthered his interest in mysticism, in a part of Africa that was both mysterious and beguiling. The spirit of Black Africa had entered his mind. He not only welcomed it with huge eagerness, but would also never abandon it. 'What's the Ivory Coast like? What are the most fascinating aspects of its art? Is football as important on the streets there as it is in Brazil or Argentina? When's the best time to go? I want to discover the magical places!' These were Eric's questions when we talked about Africa and in particular my home country. We promised each other that one day we would go.

Eric and Basile told me about their adventures in the Eastern Bloc – East Germany, the USSR, Czechoslovakia, Hungary,

Poland – before the fall of the Berlin Wall in 1989, about the Nordic countries of Norway and Iceland, about Israel, about Kuwait. They enabled me to travel free of charge and without leaving home. I was handed a map of European football without paying a penny for it. I loved to hear them talk about the stadiums whose names both delighted me and made me shiver. The stories of their trips were almost like lessons in a foreign language. They played at Leipzig's Zentralstadion in the German Democratic Republic, the Népstadion in Budapest, the Villamarín in Seville, the Ramat Gan in Tel Aviv, the Kazma in Kuwait City, the Laugardalsvöllur in Reykjavik.

I stored away their tales of *Les Bleus* that I heard over the years in a corner of my memory. In many cases, their accounts of their experiences have endured longer than the facts about the matches they played there. For instance, Basile told me about an unusual adventure during a trip to Kuwait in January 1990: 'A frightening thing happened to me. I got lost on my camel in the desert. There were three of us: my teammate Pascal Vahirua, the guide and me. I don't know why, but I headed off in one direction and kept going. When I turned round, I couldn't see anyone behind me. I looked left, right, everywhere: I couldn't see anyone. I kept calm, kept telling myself that someone would definitely come to my rescue. I trusted the guide but I was still very apprehensive. I was completely on my own for an hour, maybe even an hour and a half. It was scary. Finally, I was found. I was so grateful I offered the guide whatever he wanted: my jersey, an invitation to France, a French team bag, a nice jacket ...'

I recall another one of Basile's anecdotes. Every time the French team went to an Eastern European country, a delegation of African students of Beninese, Congolese, Guinean,

Senegalese, Ethiopian or Nigerian origin would be waiting for him at the stadium exit or near the hotel where the
French team was staying. These students would ask him for
help – very often they wanted currency or new and even
second-hand clothes. With huge generosity, Basile always
tried to fulfil their requests. 'Every time I went to one of
the Eastern Bloc countries, I took clothes and some French
francs. I thought a lot about those students, who were leading an extremely difficult life a long way from their own
country. I loved their courage and adventurous spirit. Most
of them were studying subjects that impressed me: aeronaut-
ics, biochemistry, computer science, mathematics, industrial
engineering, nuclear physics.

'We only spent a small amount of time together, but I
really appreciated meeting these "brothers" who were living
in these cold and distant countries. By witnessing what they
had to deal with on a daily basis, I knew what they wanted.
Obviously financial help, but also "things from the West", as
they put it. When it came to clothing, they wanted French
and especially American brands – they were crazy about Levi
501s. Those items weren't available in Moscow, Warsaw or
Sofia, for example. I knew that selling these clothes on the
black market brought them some money and, as a result, brief
moments of happiness. Many of them had been sent under
agreements between their country, which had become so-
called 'socialist republics', and the communist states. Each
student relied heavily on a state scholarship, but the money
didn't reach them on a regular basis and often didn't amount
to much. My arrival brought some joy to people who perhaps
went on to become the brains of their country.'

*

Michel Platini had made a major impact on a whole generation of young players. We followed his exploits at Euro 84 and his great performances at the 1982 and 1986 World Cups. Basile admired him so much that during his first matches with *Les Bleus* he decided to sit next to the famous number 10 to hear him talk about the Juventus players (Bettega, Cabrini, Scirea, Zoff, Rossi, Gentile), the coach Trapattoni and the president Gianni Agnelli, known as 'the Lawyer'. 'Sitting next to Platini was a childhood dream,' Basile told me. 'Being with *Les Bleus* allowed me to be on the same team as one of the gods of football. It was wonderful.'

In March 1990, Eric played brilliantly in a friendly match in Hungary. 'While we were in Budapest, I was amazed by the city's beauty. I never imagined I would see such architectural wealth. When I was a child, my father told me about the famous team of the 1950s with Puskás, Kocsis, Bozsik, one of the best teams in the world. The Hungarians won the 1952 Olympic tournament and lost to Germany in a controversial final at the 1954 World Cup, and a year earlier had humiliated England [unbeaten at home against continental teams] at Wembley, winning 6-3. Hungary, for me, were a monument of football. Oddly, I thought of my father in that country and in that stadium. It's strange, but I felt good being there. It's hard to say why, but there are places like that where you feel something positive, something transcends you. We won 3-1 and I scored twice. I felt so good on the pitch that day.'

On 12 August 1987, Eric got his first cap. The match was a big one: West Germany–France. The last time the French had won on German soil was on 16 November 1954 in Hannover. The match had a special flavour. In the summer of 1986, France had been defeated by their perennial rivals in the World Cup semi-final. Four months before the Hannover friendly, Michel Platini had played his last match in blue. A page was turning. A new generation now had to take up the baton passed down by their glorious elders. At twenty-one, Eric was called up and formed an attacking partnership with Jean-Pierre Papin. Basile was on the substitutes' bench. I was happy for my friend, but unhappy for my brother.

Les Bleus lost the match 2-1, Eric scoring the French goal. The day after the match, the press praised him for his performance. 'Matches against Germany are always tense,' Eric told me afterwards. 'Even if it's a friendly, we know all too well that when you're playing certain teams such as England, Germany or Italy, the term "friendly" doesn't really apply. These are always high-stakes games, whatever the setting. The journalists were surprised by my confidence. But I approach all matches like that, with great confidence.'

I'd been looking forward to this match for a long time for two reasons. First, to see how Eric would get on in his first match with the 'big boys'. I was reassured to see that he kept to his normal habits as he prepared for the game to kick off. He looked focused, but relaxed. He did a few stretches at the end of a group training session, and was wearing his Adidas 'Copa Mundial' boots that didn't have metal studs. Secondly, I was hoping this match would be the first of many that would see Eric and Basile playing together in France's colours. As it was, I had to wait another few weeks for that ambition to be fulfilled.

On 14 October 1987, at the Parc des Princes, France met Norway in a qualifying match for the 1988 European Cup of Nations. For the first time, Eric and Basile lined up together in the French team. I was very moved seeing them both representing *Les Bleus*. Back in Auxerre, before they'd set off for Paris, I'd felt butterflies in my stomach, triggered by the prospect of seeing them wearing this 'sacred jersey', of watching them stoically listening to the Marseillaise, hoping they would return with smiles on their faces after a victory well won with a goal or two from Eric.

The match was so agonising to watch that it erased any joy I'd felt. The French team was nervy against a very average Norwegian team. The match was played in an oddly disjointed fashion, with no clear rhythm imposed by either team. The French team was struggling. Basile and Eric didn't have much of an influence, although the same could be said of the rest of their teammates. I was anxious, worried how the match would go. Eric, playing as the principal striker alongside his AJ Auxerre teammate Philippe Fargeon, wasn't making an impact. *Les Bleus* finally managed to score in the sixty-third minute, Eric passing to Fargeon, who put them 1-0 up. But a quarter of an hour later the Norwegians equalised from a free-kick. I watched the television replays anxiously to see who had scored the goal. Phew! I realised it wasn't the centre-forward Basile was marking, so my brother wasn't at fault.

The match ended in a draw. A big setback. I looked at the disappointed faces of Eric and Basile as they trudged off to the dressing room that cold and rainy October evening. My optimism returned with the thought that they would have plenty of opportunities to shine together in the French national team.

They both kept their places in the French squad. Eric was also called up to the under-21 squad, who were engaged in a very different kind of adventure, and one that ultimately left me feeling conflicted. On Wednesday, 12 October 1988, at the Leo Lagrange Stadium in Besançon, the French U-21 team were crowned European champions. They crushed Greece 3-0 in the second leg of the final, the first having finished 0-0. There was no missing the happiness on the faces of the players in the photos that appeared in the sports daily *L'Équipe* and the weekly magazine *France-Football*. The French football world celebrated the talented youngsters, drawn from the best training centres, from Sochaux, Lille, Nantes, Auxerre. I remember the radiant faces of Franck Sauzée, Stéphane Paille, Jocelyn Angloma, Laurent Blanc, Christophe Galtier, Vincent Guérin, Eric Lada ...

But one face was missing from the photos: Eric's. And yet my friend had been the architect of the under-21s' epic run. He carried this team, but was denied the chance to savour the winning moment. He scored against Hungary in a 4-1 victory, scored the two winning goals in a match against the formidable USSR team. He helped France reach the quarter-finals with a win over Norway. In the semi-final, the French were up against the English. In the first leg, on 13 April 1988 in Besançon, *Les Bleus* won 4-2. Eric was amazing: he scored a goal and delivered a sumptuous back-heel to Stéphane Paille for the fourth goal. In the return match, on 27 April 1988 at Highbury, the English, led by Paul Gascoigne, were keen to get revenge. The match was spectacular and very intense. Eric kept the French in the game by scoring two superb goals. Gascoigne scored a goal. In the end, the teams played out a 2-2 draw.

I was looking forward to the two-legged final against Greece, eager to see Eric light it up. I wanted the football world to see my friend's creative genius. It looked set to provide a great showcase for the exceptional talent of a player who had now been approached by the biggest European clubs – AC Milan, Internazionale, Ajax. Towards the end of May, the two teams played out a scoreless draw in Greece. Then, in the run-up to the second game, which took place five months later, there was a dramatic turn of events. On 20 August, French football was shaken by events at the end of a Ligue 1 match between Eric's new club, Olympique de Marseille, and Racing Club de Strasbourg. He distinguished himself by scoring a magnificent goal, but even more with his post-match comments about France's coach, Henri Michel.

Unhappy at not being selected for the national team, who were due to play a friendly against Czechoslovakia, my friend surprised the media with his softly spoken but explosive words. Dressed in T-shirt and denim jacket, he didn't mince his words when faced with the journalists and television cameras: 'I'll simply say that I've proved that he could pin his hopes on me, and if he thought I was out of form then he shouldn't have made the comments that he did, or he could have warned me, or he could have talked to me, but he didn't do any such thing. I was reading something said by Mickey Rourke, who's a guy I love and who said that whoever was in charge of the Oscars in Hollywood was a sack of shit. I think Henri Michel isn't too far from being that!'

I was watching this 'declaration of war on the coach' on television, and was all too familiar with Eric's cheeky, rebellious posture: I knew this side of him, but it was rarely revealed in public. I could see the bitterness bubbling up inside him – could see it in his expression, his oblique glances at the camera, the time he took to draw breath in order to give his words more impact, the way his chest heaved as he asserted himself, the serious look on his face. These were words of rage, venom, stemming from anger, from a feeling of injustice, that was perhaps unreasonable but needed to be released.

The 'Cantona affair' created a furore. The day after he made his comments, the French Football Federation suspended him from the under-21 team and then, on 9 September, from selection for the French team at any level until 1 July 1989.

Following Eric's transfer to Marseille, Basile became my most faithful messenger. The Henri Michel episode left a bitter taste in my mouth because I had loved him as a player and really liked him as a coach. He'd been an extraordinary footballer with a magical touch, reminiscent in many ways of England's Bobby Moore or West Germany's Franz Beckenbauer. Whether playing for FC Nantes or *Les Bleus*, Michel had been a world-class footballer in both midfield and sweeper roles. It was also Michel who had called up Basile for his debut with the French national team.

Around 2005, I got the chance to meet Henri Michel, who was then coach of the Ivory Coast national team, at Roissy Charles de Gaulle Airport in Paris. He was waiting to fly to Abidjan. When I noticed him in the departure lounge, I approached shyly, introduced myself and asked if he minded if I talked to him. He told me he was happy to meet an 'Ivorian brother' and also a relative of Basile and my nephew Laurent, who had been a member of PSG's academy when Michel had been in charge at Paris Saint-Germain from 1990 to 1991.

During our conversation, I couldn't help but bring up the 'Cantona episode'. I led into it by telling Michel that he'd been one of my favourite players at Nantes, and that I well remembered how he looked in their yellow jersey with the Café de Côte d'Ivoire logo on it. I touched on his performances at the

1978 World Cup, another great memory. Then I took him down the path of my friendship with Eric, told him about our meeting in Auxerre, about Guy Roux, Manchester, Alex Ferguson, and Eric's first games for the national team.

Michel looked at me and said in his beautiful southern accent: 'Well, you've known some great names. As regards Cantona, at the time his statements hurt me, but I'd been a player and, like him, I'm from the south and sometimes we're "hot-blooded". Back then Eric was young, so I forgot about what he said. You know, it proved that he loved the French team. Feeling so upset about a friendly match seemed dispro-portionate to me, but deep down he was someone I liked.

'I'll tell you something else: he was never a problem in the French team. He always seemed to be happy to be back with his mates. I used to see him laughing with Basile, Luis [Fernandez] or Jean-Pierre [Papin]. He was always among the most conscientious and committed players in training and in matches. I had the opportunity to meet him face to face some time after he made his comments, and he didn't get down on his knees and ask for my forgiveness, but he showed me that he was sorry. It was a fit of anger. When I think of the career he had with Manchester United, I'm sure it was because of that personality that he succeeded in England. To do what he did, you have to have a lot of strength of character both on and off the pitch, to overcome the media pressure, and to per-form well in every game. If you see him, say hello from me.'

'You can count on it,' I replied.

The summer of 1990 was eventful. I obtained my baccalaure-ate and continued my studies at the University of Montpellier. Basile left AJ Auxerre for Olympique de Marseille, becoming part of the project being put in place by club president Bernard Tapie to recruit the best French players with the primary aim of ruling European football. With Basile alongside Eric in Marseille, two of the people closest to me were in the team's colours. Every time I went to the Stade Vélodrome in Marseille, I spent some time with Eric, his wife Isabelle and sometimes with the new member of the Cantona family, their son Raphaël. Eric seemed extremely content. He was obviously happy to be with OM, his favourite club.

When he returned to the French team, I felt he showed a real completeness to his game. On 5 September 1990, *Les Bleus* began their qualifying campaign for the 1992 European Cup of Nations that were to be held in Sweden with a game against Iceland in Reykjavik. Following Henri Michel's dismissal on 1 November 1988, Michel Platini had been appointed the new coach, assisted by Gérard Houllier. The pair had been unable to prevent *Les Bleus* missing out rather dismally on qualification for the 1990 World Cup in Italy. That setback meant that qualification for Euro 92 became a major objective for French football. For the Iceland game, Basile was playing in central defence and Eric was the main striker. He shone as *Les Bleus* won the game 2-1, Eric scoring the second goal. Iceland scored near the end of the match and caused some real problems for the defence before the final whistle blew, provoking some minutes of torment for those of us watching the game back home. Yet the victory marked a change of fortune, as 'Platini's gang' enjoyed unprecedented success. They eventually finished the Euro 92 qualifying campaign with a perfect record: eight victories in eight matches.

'There were several OM players in the team,' said Eric.

'Platini understood that all great national teams are built around the country's best club. We all knew each other so well. Each time the squad got together there was a feeling of immense joy, and that came across on the pitch. Baze [Basile], Lolo [Laurent Blanc], Caso [Bernard Casoni], Ber [Bernard Pardo], Luis [Fernandez], Joce [Jocelyn Angloma], Meco [Éric Di Meco] and me were at the heart of it, in training, in the restaurant, in card games. It was the "southerners" team. It was a pleasure to both play and spend time with these guys.'

On the field, the team's enthusiasm was palpable. The Papin-Cantona strike force scored goal after goal, creating what many fans considered to be one of the best partnerships in Europe. The press praised the defensive qualities of the Marseille trio: Boli-Casoni-Angloma. Ahead of a key game against Spain on 20 February 1991, *Onze-mondial* magazine decided to feature Basile on the cover, dressed as a toreador. It proved prophetic, as the Spaniards suffered their first defeat for twenty-eight games in Paris.

Off the pitch, a similar kind of rapport evolved between some of the players' wives. Isabelle Cantona and Geneviève Boli became good friends during this period, which I was particularly pleased to see, given the closeness of the relationship between their husbands. The friendship between Isabelle and Geneviève grew stronger with each game, and especially so in Sweden during the final stages of the tournament.

19 November 1993, Conyngham Road, Manchester. Two days after the World Cup qualifying game between France and Bulgaria. The telephone rang and I hurried to answer it. Eric told me he was going to pick me up from my house after training for a tour of the city and a trip to Owens Park. This undoubtedly meant that first we would go to Pizza Express,

then walk around St Ann's Square and the Royal Exchange and finish up in Café Renoir in Fallowfield, an area in which a lot of students lived.

Sitting by my window, I could hear his car coming into our building's car park. We greeted each other as we always did, in traditional French fashion with a kiss on each cheek, and I slipped into the passenger seat. 'When did you get back from Paris?' I asked him. 'Was it a tough game?'

From his expression I knew he could tell I didn't know the result, that I'd got no idea the unimaginable had happened. He hesitated for a moment, then turned to look at me. 'We won't be going to the World Cup. The USA is all over for us.'

A bit taken aback, I eventually replied: 'How come?'

'We lost the day before last. We lost in the last seconds, even though we only needed a draw and I'd scored to put us 1-0 ahead. The USA's over for us. Perhaps we don't deserve to go there. We weren't professional enough. Everybody was already thinking about America: the staff, the guys at the federation, the journalists, the players, the players' wives. We overestimated ourselves. That's football. It's beautiful and cruel at the same time.'

He stopped abruptly. A long silence filled the car. Strangely for Eric, there wasn't any music playing, not even at low volume. We both just stared straight ahead. I said nothing; neither did Eric. I wasn't bothered about the result or the score. My only concern was how the match had gone. Basile hadn't played because of injury, but I wanted to know how Eric had performed. But I didn't have the bottle to ask how they had lost such an important match. How had they squandered the opportunity to go to the United States, an ambition we'd spent so much time talking about?

We were both fascinated by the USA, and especially New York. The city was an iconic place to us, thanks to Madison Square Garden where mythical boxing fights took place, the famous Blue Note jazz club, and scenes from Sergio Leone's great movie *Once Upon a Time in America* starring Robert De Niro in one of his most masterful performances. As I'd been so certain of the match's outcome, I hadn't even looked up the result in the newspapers on my living room table.

We were totally deflated, each momentarily contemplating this cruel fate. I'd rarely seen Eric so affected by a defeat, and this one was very hard to swallow. Two or maybe three minutes went by. Gradually we returned to the present, our spirits lifting a little.

'Let's go, Claudio. There's nothing that can be done now. There's no turning back, and on Saturday we've got Wimbledon at Old Trafford. We have to win,' he said, his words almost a call to arms. Eric's good humour had started to return and off we went again, towards the city centre. Life in Manchester was our priority once more. Our happiness was back in the hands of the Reds.

18 May 1996. It was the day that France's selection of players for Euro 96 in England was due to be announced. I was in a relaxed mood, mooching around Vinyl Exchange on Oldham Street looking for bargains. I could spend hours and hours looking for albums of all types – jazz, acid jazz, funk, easy-listening, R&B, Britpop, Californian or African music, and of course French music. The place was almost my second home. I always discovered a few CDs that delighted me. That day, I left the shop with about twenty records at unbeatable

prices, the most expensive costing me £3.99, the cheapest £1. In short, a very good fishing trip.

On my way home, I tried to tune my radio in to the France-Inter station. I could hardly hear what was being said. It seemed a bit unreal. I'd got out of the habit of listening to French radio, but nevertheless waited impatiently for the sports news. Finally, it came on, and the main headline was, 'Manchester United striker Eric Cantona has not been included in the list of players who will take part in Euro 96 in England.'

I was heartbroken, knocked sideways. A feeling of injustice and sadness permeated my body. As always in such moments of intense sorrow, and I don't know why this happens, the words that went through my mind were in my mother tongue, Bété, the language spoken in the western part of the Ivory Coast.

At first I wasn't sure what I was hearing. I'd thought the French coach, Aimé Jacquet, would select his players based on their current form. From that perspective, there was no question Eric would be in the squad, despite all the controversies. How could Jacquet make such a decision given Eric's history with *Les Bleus* and the impact Eric could have playing 'at home' in England? I'd heard that the coach was banking on a new generation led by Zinedine Zidane, but I didn't buy that. Eric could play in this team. Since he'd made his debut with *Les Bleus*, he'd always been ready to adapt to the coach's decisions without ever voicing any kind of disagreement.

The question regularly being asked in the French press was whether Eric would be prepared to sacrifice his individuality for the overall good of the national team. I'd followed this debate closely, although with a delay of twenty-four hours as, despite England's proximity, the French papers arrived a day late, and even then weren't available in all newsagents – they cost a lot, too, for someone on a student's budget! I'd found a kiosk run by a Pakistani man near Manchester Central Library that sold *Le Monde*, *Libération*, *L'Équipe* and *France-Football*, so when I wanted to stay abreast of the French news, I could buy the two sports papers and the mainstream press. I'd also get updates and insight on the Cantona and *Les Bleus* debate by phone from friends and relatives in Paris, Auxerre and Montpellier.

Opinions were divided. But those who knew football couldn't understand how anyone could doubt the need for Eric's presence in the national team. Others, more sensitive to the media's opinions, were sceptical about the need to select Eric for *Les Bleus*. 'He's too individualistic,' those in this group complained, like many in the press. 'His personality is too dominant within the group. Will he respect the demands of coach Aimé Jacquet? How can Eric play with Zidane, Djorkaeff? Shouldn't we move on to the new generation of promising players and leave the story of Eric and the French team in the past?'

A few months before the announcement, Eric had said to me with a hint of amusement and also a degree of annoyance: 'I'm hearing things about me and the French team. Apparently my personality could hinder the performances of the young players and I could end up being in conflict with the coach if I don't agree with his tactical choices. Would I really scare the players?

'It's also being said that it would be impossible for me to fit in with Zidane and Djorkaeff! When I hear things like this, it just makes me smile, and I prefer to keep quiet. I don't want to respond to the lies of people who don't know what they're talking about. What's more, they know I won't ever turn to the press to deny what they're saying. The people who know me best are well aware what I'm like when I'm with the club and the French team. Claudio, you know me, you know how I am. In the French team, you won't find a single player who'll say that I try to dominate or that I'm scary. It's all nonsense. Ask Baze [Basile] – he'll tell you I'm the one who talks the least in the dressing room, that I'm always encouraging the youngsters. I may spend a lot of time with Éric [Di Meco] and Lolo [Laurent Blanc], but I'm never stand-offish with the others.

'When young players have come into the French team, I've always gone out of my way to make them feel welcome. People try to set Zidane and me up as rivals. But Zidane is a *Marseillais* like me, shy like me – we like each other. When he arrived in the national team, I made a point of talking to him, just as I did with other players, such as [Emmanuel] Petit and Duga (Dugarry). When he was appointed coach, Aimé Jacquet named me the captain. People seem to forget that. Why would he appoint Cantona as team captain? Why did he decide on me to be the players' representative, as well as the link between him and the players? It certainly wasn't because he thought I was a troublemaker! Selfish, individualistic! Someone with an oversized ego! Jacquet and his staff, especially Henri Émile, knew very well they could count on me to bring the team together, to encourage all the players, and not hide when courage is needed to win key matches.

'Do you think he didn't check beforehand whether or not I was the right person to wear the captain's armband? Did Jacquet know how deeply committed Cantona is to the

French team? Of course he did. The players know me. As a player and team captain, I've always been on their side. When I hear all this crap about me in the French team I'm disgusted, but at the same time I know that the decision about my participation in Euro 96 has already been taken. You know what? I won't be at the Euros. You'll see, Claudio: they'll find all sorts of arguments not to select me. Who really runs the French team? The coach, the press, the federation? I'd have liked people to judge me by my performances on the pitch ahead of all other considerations.'

Eric was right. His career with *Les Bleus* was over, as was Basile's. The only blues left for me now were Manchester City.

CHAPTER 13

Back from Selhurst Park

January 1995 will be remembered as a special moment in time. As an inquisitive observer of the significance football has had for people since the mid-1870s, I was well versed in issues that heralded paradigm shifts, the emergence of a new era. I was also well acquainted with what historians know about the tenacity of beliefs: the perpetual clash between wanting to hold on to the past and the determination to expand towards new horizons. The press provided an excellent means for analysing this.

At that point the media, and especially the tabloids, were abuzz with talk about the suspicious links between money and football. They sought to expose evidence of the Premier League losing its bearings, owing to what was perceived as the growing influence of 'dirty' money. Over the course of several days, Arsenal's Scottish manager, George Graham, became the principal figure in a media drama that held the attention of millions of readers, the suspicion being that he had received illegal payments during the transfer of two

Norwegian players. This led to an outcry against immoral practices within professional football.

Naturally, I was interested in the way the media fabricated, or, rather, constructed, public opinion. I listened to the radio, watched the TV and, as I often did, gathered together newspapers and magazines in order to examine the whole sweep of the debate. It was fascinating to see how some of the comments could have been taken from the 1880s and '90s. I'd found stories from that era in which journalists and other 'moral people' had voiced similar opinions when outlining their ardent opposition to professionalism. For many, 'real football', where the reward stemmed simply from the joy of playing and was bound up in the codes and ethos of amateurism, completely disappeared in 1885 when the right to professional status became official. Echoing a myth that still persists today, professionalism was said to have perverted the true nature of football as it was dreamed up by the game's inventors, namely the bourgeois and aristocratic elites. It was suggested that football's golden age, untainted by any connection with money, had effectively ended forever once people from the working classes chose to make the game their profession. The game's parlous state was the result of the growing influence of the working classes within football and an unhealthy relationship with money.

I talked to Eric about this. As usual, he was fascinated by the historical analysis. 'It's fair to say that football, because it's popular, and perhaps one of the few areas where ordinary people can express themselves fully and also stand out, is looked down on by some people,' he said. 'Money is an interesting subject. When it comes to football, some journalists give me the impression that the players don't deserve to earn lots of money, that they believe players are earning too much. Some journalists have a kind of contempt towards professional footballers: they don't consider them to be doing a dignified job. They're not taken seriously. They're denigrated because they come from ordinary backgrounds.

'What's more, some journalists even give the impression that they could have become footballers, that they think this job is easy. When a player earns a lot of money, I'm sure lots of people are thinking: *How can people from poor backgrounds, most of whom dropped out of school at a very young age, earn so much money?* What they don't realise is that the vast majority of footballers started playing simply because they liked football. No kid thinks about money when he spends hours and hours playing in the school playground, on makeshift pitches or for a local club.

'I'd play for nothing at all. Football is my passion. We only start thinking about money when we get that first contract, that first big transfer. Money has never been important in my career. I think most footballers think about the ball before the wallet. Of course, at some point in your career the question of money will come up and become an issue that concerns you. But it's the system that brings that about. Who decides on the monetary value of a player? Who decides to transfer players? Who decides what salary to pay a certain player? These issues are rarely decided by the players. It is the club presidents who decide. We, the players, are just the product of a capitalist system that benefits many other people.

'The players are not always winners in this world of sharks. Journalists and public opinion always focus on the earnings of the very best footballers, but they forget that the majority of players don't play for rich clubs. Football is not just about the

World Cup or the Champions League, it's also about playing in the street, about Sunday morning games on bumpy pitches, about playing in unheated halls in winter. As someone who knows football from the inside, you should write about this. People don't really know what it means to be a professional footballer. They pick up a lot of false impressions that are bandied about in the press. Footballers earn good money because football gets so much coverage in the media. The odd thing is the media will criticise footballers for earning too much despite being primarily responsible for a system that gives players such a high profile.'

I listened to him without saying or promising anything.

The other thing that caught my eye that month was the media coverage of African players. Unlike France and other former colonial powers, Britain hadn't looked towards its former empire for talented footballers. In early January, the newspapers picked on the news that Leeds United were signing Anthony 'Tony' Yeboah, the fearsome centre-forward of the Black Stars, as Ghana's national team is nicknamed, and a former player with Asante Kotoko of Kumasi. Leeds signed him from German club Eintracht Frankfurt for a record fee of £3.4 million.

All the talk about a Black Stars player brought back happy childhood memories. The Ghanaian team has always been one of the best on the African continent. In Ivory Coast, which is a crossroads for people from all over West Africa, we were fascinated by the talent our neighbours in Ghana produced. I lived in a neighbourhood with several Ghanaian families, and my friends used to tell me about the exploits of the teams from the capital, Accra (Hearts of Oak) and Ghana's second city (Asante Kotoko of Kumasi). I can remember my amazement at the exploits of legendary players: goalkeeper Robert Mensah, brilliant midfielders such as Osei Kofi and Karim Abdul Razak, and talented centre-forwards like Opoku Afriyié and Mohammed Polo.

My passion for the Black Stars has endured over the years. In 1982, they won the African Cup of Nations with a team of extraordinary footballers, including Opoku Nti, who was dubbed Zico, and Abedi Pelé, an 18-year-old kid who a few years later would become one of my brother Basile's close friends at Olympique de Marseille. In 1992, Ivory Coast and Ghana met in the final of the African Cup of Nations. The whole of Ivory Coast was ecstatic when Anthony Yeboah failed to give his country a first continental success. When I heard that he was signing for Leeds, I was delighted that England would finally get to see a great player from Africa.

However, the 'Graham affair' and the joyful prospect of seeing the 'Kumasi Gunner' arrive on English soil were soon forgotten, as another story broke and began to dominate the headlines, one that I was going to experience in intense close-up. When I think back to that day, to Wednesday, 25 January 1995, it all seems incredibly vivid. It was a regular day that suddenly became a nightmare and then, strangely, returned almost to normality again. It split into three separate parts that, when put together, produced a scenario that mixed the ordinary with the extraordinary. It began with the usual morning routine, continued with an afternoon of hard studying and concluded with an evening of bizarre torment.

The morning was like any other – uneventful. I'd set the afternoon aside to study. I'd decided to immerse myself in some of the historical events that had marked Manchester out as one of the nerve centres of popular protest. As I refreshed my mind about the Peterloo Massacre, the Chartist movement and the emancipation of women, I carefully noted some relevant locations on a map of the city, barely noticing that my phone kept ringing. So absorbed was I that I let some time go by before I eventually picked up the phone.

'Hello! It's Eric!' (His tone revealed he was in a hurry.) 'Let's meet at the Cornerhouse after the game tonight.'

'Okay, see you soon. *Merde pour le match*,' I told him. Good luck in French slang.

Manchester United were heading to London to play Crystal Palace at Selhurst Park, and after the game Eric and I planned to stick to the routine that had become our ritual after away games and meet up in town or at the Four Seasons near the airport for a drink, supped slowly and with great appreciation. Eric usually opted for a lager, while I'd have a Guinness, a throwback to the Irish pubs I'd discovered during my early days in Manchester.

Back to my research, and I was soon wrapped up again in Manchester's revolutionary history, happily poring over my papers while Britain and the nascent Premier League were being shaken by the bewildering actions of King Eric.

At half nine in the evening, my reverie was suddenly interrupted by a stream of phone calls. The first was from a university friend. 'Put on the television, fast,' was all they said. 'It's incredible.'

Watching like millions of others, I was hypnotised by this ultra-violent act that lasted just a few seconds. Seeing Eric carry out his kung fu kick on a fan, I felt shocked, but at the same time extremely calm and serene.

I turned the TV off, overwhelmed by the images of my

friend's distress and the disbelief of Manchester United players, staff and fans. I discussed what I'd just seen for a little while with Anne, who was in tears.

The phone rang again. This time it was Basile, calling to see if I had any news on what was happening. He was worried about his old friend, and his questions came in a rush. 'How's Eric? Have you seen him? Has Isabelle got any news? Do you know why Eric lost his cool? How did Alex Ferguson react? Were you at the ground? Let me know when you have some news, and tell Eric that I'm right behind him.'

His was the first of several calls from friends in England, France and the Ivory Coast. Then I got a call from Eric's wife, Isabelle, whose tone was both tongue-in-cheek and deadly serious: 'Claudio, we're packing our bags and heading back to France.'

The only words I managed to get out were: 'But what's happened?'

The phone rang again. This time it was Gary King, the former Leeds United fan who had broken his link with the club he supported to follow Eric. Gary asked me if he could come to Manchester to see his 'god'. Do, I said. Amid a torrent of calls, I tried to avoid requests from journalists for a comment, an explanation, a justification, a word, a sentence that could express the incredible. I decided to go out for a few moments to try to clear my head. My thoughts were confused. I thought of the many goals Eric had scored, the games where he'd endured every kind of provocation, of the referees who had almost revelled in the 'trophy' they'd earned by showing him a yellow or red card, of his performances with France and, going back so many years to the very start of his career, with Auxerre. It was a terribly sad night.

After walking around the local streets for a few minutes, I headed home. No sooner was I back into my living room than the phone rang yet again. I recognised Eric's voice instantly. 'Can we meet at the Cornerhouse? Right away?'

I wasn't surprised. The man whose 'rush of blood' had become the biggest talking point in the country had asked me to meet him as normal, even though him doing so was a little unexpected.

'Okay.'

I headed off with Anne and Gary to the Cornerhouse arts complex, which sits almost directly opposite the BBC's Manchester base on Oxford Road. Eric walked in without showing the slightest desire to hide from or avoid any impromptu comments. I waved him over to our table. He approached with a smile and sat down without paying the slightest attention to the multitude of looks and murmurs his arrival had provoked. Eric was calm. He spoke with his eyes fixed on the three of us, giving us his side of events, smiling occasionally, breaking the incident down with precision. He wasn't upset by the emotional impact of what had taken place, and spoke without ever raising his voice. 'What's happened has happened,' he said. 'Life goes on.'

I noticed the little smile he gave at the end of each sentence, reminiscent of Robert De Niro. As bizarre as it might seem, I felt he was displaying an almost monastic calm. In this moment of extreme tension, he was both humorous and serene, reminding me, it suddenly struck me, of the moment we'd first met during his time at Auxerre, our paths crossing at somewhere close to two in the morning after he'd returned from playing in an away match in the French third division, when he'd told me the team had won, but omitted to mention that he'd scored the two goals that had turned the game.

The Selhurst Park incident was dealt with as though no more than an unexpected dish served up in a restaurant where we all knew the menu by heart. He knew I wouldn't badger him for more details, and that we were sufficiently comfortable with each other to allow silence to fill the gaps in his explanation. After all, what was the use of telling the story when the violence of the scene had become so firmly lodged in the mind?

Then Eric said, 'You know, what annoyed me most is that when I kicked out I almost fell over. Did you see that? Did you?'

What could I say? I just shook my head to signal my understanding and empathy. Gary sat silently, listening to the flow of words. The foreigner in our little group, not understanding anything in French, he had quickly realised that these were the first angry words Eric had uttered. But I had no desire to hear any justification of what had happened.

Just then, an admirer both affected and courageously buoyed by too much alcohol approached our table and stretched out his right hand to Eric. 'We love you, Eric. We love you . . .'

A little embarrassed, Eric turned to the man, almost certainly a United supporter, and thanked him twice for his politeness and appreciation. I fully expected the supporter's reaction to give the same idea to everyone else in the bar, and had the feeling we'd soon be welcoming a flood of fans to our table. But I was wrong. Although smiles of understanding were more evident, we were left to ourselves.

After half an hour, we decided to move on. But where? How would people react? Would we manage to make our way safely through the mass of people waiting outside? I decided to take the initiative and made for the door, and the crowd outside let us pass without any hassle.

'Do you have any idea where we could go?' said Eric as we were heading for the car. 'A place where we can listen to music,' he added. I suggested a bar frequented by my friends from Manchester University and off we set, determined to turn our attention to lighter things ...

The place was called the Fantasy Bar, on Deansgate. Anne went on ahead and asked two guys who looked like students if they knew the Fantasy Bar. One of them gave a slightly surprised smile. 'Are you going to work there?'

'No, I just want to go there for a drink,' Anne said.

'Are you sure you want to go there?' said the student, with a quizzical and slightly doubtful look. 'I don't think you're going to like it!'

At number 140 we saw a large sign for the Fantasy Bar, and the doorman greeted us with a broad smile. We descended the steep staircase to find ourselves in a darkened room with rhythmic music pounding out. The place was almost empty. In the gloom, I spotted a few customers sitting around, mostly men. And then we realised ...

Without any of us saying anything, we suddenly understood what kind of club this was. To my right, a scantily clad lady was gyrating on a raised dance floor, and another was sitting in the lap of a man who was apparently delighted by her company. We were in a strip club! But what could we do? It would have been rude to get up and head for the exit. How could I have let myself be tricked by the word 'fantasy', which clearly meant something quite different to the French word '*fantaisie*'? As is often the case in life's most difficult moments, the urge to laugh out loud was irresistible. My student friend, I realised, had made a fool of the *Frenchy*.

Eric burst out laughing and said, 'Claudio, do you come here often?' The three of us couldn't stop: the fatigue and tension were being released through laughter. But Gary, poor Gary, who still looked stunned, just stared at the floor with an embarrassed expression muttering, 'I can't let my wife know I was here.' He probably knew exactly what kind of place the Fantasy Bar would be but, having hot-footed it all the way from Coventry for the sake of his 'idol', hadn't dared say anything.

How could we end up in such a place after what had happened at Selhurst Park just a few hours ago? I was thinking. *How could I have brought the person who's the talk of all of England to a strip club?* Everything seemed unreal.

There was one person who was delighted, of course: the manager – surprised, but delighted to have such a prestigious customer. We ordered soft drinks and talked about anything other than Selhurst Park, and mostly about what Anne had been up to, like her work at the Museum of Science and Industry close to Granada Studios, where *Coronation Street* was filmed.

Eric drove us home around midnight. 'I'll call you tomorrow,' he said. I watched his car disappear into the silence, looked up at the sky and shook my head.

I had a suspicion the following day would be rather memorable. I deliberately avoided turning on the TV and decided to go and buy the newspapers. I had a good idea what I was going to find, but you can never be sure. This time I was right. Eric was on every front page. At the newsagent's in the Manchester University Student Union the photo of Eric's right leg in the chest of a spectator in the stand, taken by a photographer called Graham Stuart, was on every newspaper in the rack.

I picked up the lot and took them to the till, watching as they were all rung up until I was £2.50 poorer. The cashier was a little surprised at someone buying so many papers. 'For him to do something like that,' she remarked, 'I'm sure the Crystal Palace fan must have said some things that weren't very polite. Whatever happens, we love Eric, and I hope he doesn't decide to end his career after an incident like this. I'm a United supporter, you know, and we love him.'

Back home, I read through everything that was being said as quickly as possible. Every headline interested me, every word used to describe Eric riveted me. The prominence given to the 'kung fu kick' on all the front pages fascinated me. I read for hours, taking notes, stopping to look up words in the Collins dictionary and my Harrap's French dictionary. When it came to the tabloids I'd never come across so many swear words. Thanks to Eric, my vocabulary had expanded to include words like 'thug', 'madman', 'hot-tempered'. The broadsheets were more measured in their comments. The overall theme that emerged was the unprecedented nature of the incident, as well as a preoccupation with the eventual outcome of the 'Cantona affair'. All were agreed on one point: didn't this signal the end of Eric in the English game?

The episode gave me a better insight into several things I'd been aware of in 1990s England: the fear of hooliganism, the anti-French sentiment, the sanctity of the supporter, the pact of good conduct between players and supporters, the fear of a return to the violence of the 1980s. Indeed, the incident crystallised many, many issues besetting the Premier League, which had undertaken to bring about a profound change in the image of English football. And now, all of a sudden, an outsider, someone from the continent, had come along and resurrected the demons of the past. Eric represented a dark side of the Premier League that no one wanted to see or acknowledge.

My friend was in the midst of a furore that went beyond the sporting arena. He was at the heart of a debate that went much further than an account of a match featuring an 'extraordinary event'. To my surprise, however, no one mentioned our visit to the Fantasy Bar, which was exactly the kind of thing to titillate the tabloids!

In the end, Eric was severely punished: placed on 'enforced rest' by Manchester United and the FA for nine months, until 30 September 1995. He decided to leave Manchester and go and stay with his parents in the south of France.

When he came back, we soon dropped into our routine of meeting in our usual haunts again, and never received a hurtful word from anyone. As part of Eric's defence for the scheduled court case where he would be facing a charge of common assault, Manchester United's lawyer, Maurice Watkins, asked him to get some testimonials from people he trusted. I really liked Maurice: he was one of the first directors to give me considerable interview time for my thesis. The epitome of the Manchester elite, he'd been educated at Manchester Grammar School, had a successful career as a lawyer and been Manchester United's legal representative since 1984. Eric asked me to write some words:

no precise instructions, just: 'Claudio, write something from your heart.'

I went to meet Maurice Watkins in his office on Chepstow Street, which is close to the place where Manchester United was founded in 1902, and he laid out, in his perfect diction, what he wanted from me. I left his office feeling very moved by this vote of confidence and went home to wait for the evening to arrive, as that's the period when I always feel most inspired. I picked out a piece of music we used to listen to a lot in Auxerre: Peter Gabriel's live album *Shock the Monkey*. Then I began to write, without hesitating, a simple and sincere testimonial. Here are a few lines from it:

My name is Claude Boli. I was born on 20 December 1968 in Gagnoa (Ivory Coast). I have been a French citizen since 1986.

I'm currently doing my PhD at the University of Leicester (De Montfort) and at the University of Nantes (France). I belong to a European research group dedicated to comparative studies in the field of sport within the European Community. Within the framework of my research project ('Comparative study of professional football in England and France'), I decided to come to England, and more specifically to Manchester. I chose Manchester for two reasons. One, because football is very important there and, two, because I was thrilled by the idea of getting back in touch with my 'big brother' Eric Cantona. It's difficult for me to go back over how Eric became such an important influence in my life, but current circumstances have led me to pick out three instances that sum up his character particularly well . . .

On three typewritten pages, I set down the story of my relationship with Eric, from my adolescence in Auxerre to my
arrival in Manchester, careful to give specific examples of the
times when he'd turned out to be more like family to me,
and avoiding my usual academic style in order to make the
testimonial seem more personal and heartfelt.

On 23 March 1995, Eric was summoned to Croydon
Magistrates' Court for the verdict. He asked me to accom-
pany him, and naturally I accepted. Jean-Jacques Bertrand,
Eric's lawyer, came over from Paris. That afternoon we were
picked up by one of the club's drivers in Manchester and taken
straight to the Croydon Park Hotel, clearly chosen because it
was just around the corner from the court. Paul Ince, who was
also due to appear to face charges, later dismissed, of using
threatening behaviour against a fan, was staying there too.

When we arrived at the hotel, the meaningful stares from
the guests surprised me. Suddenly I felt far away from my city
of Manchester. I followed Eric to his room on the twelfth
floor, and looked out over the forest of huge skyscrapers
dominating the town centre.

'Tonight we're invited to a private concert by Prince,' Eric
informed me.

We got a taxi to an Italian restaurant where nobody was
in the least bit bothered about Eric's presence, and ate and
chatted without ever mentioning what was going to happen
the next day. Around 1 a.m. we made our way to the nightclub where Prince was going to perform in front of a small
audience after his concert earlier in the evening at Wembley
Arena. When we arrived, the doorman led us to the stage.
I've rarely been so happy in my life. I was about to meet one
of my favourite singers – following the success of *Purple Rain*,

I'd bought every Prince CD. I was a massive fan: I knew all about his various changes of musical direction, and his film work.

After a few moments, one of the venue's managers brought him over and introduced us. We both said hello and then fell silent. Prince looked at us shyly. I didn't dare to tell him that I adored him. I was terrified – hardly dared look at him, couldn't get my thoughts straight. Eventually I managed to mutter: 'You know, I also love your saxophonist, Eric Leeds.'

'He's here – go say those kind words to him,' Prince replied. 'It'll make him very happy.' In fact, after Prince, Eric Leeds was the musician I revered in his band, my idol. How could I not tell Prince I loved his saxophonist? Then, for several minutes, I stared at Eric Leeds, not having the courage to go up and tell him that I liked him.

The mini-concert was magical. We loved hearing the *New Power Generation Live* tracks. At about three o'clock we decided to head back to the hotel and, not surprisingly, there were several photographers waiting for Eric to come out to get some paparazzi shots of him.

The next morning Eric went to court with Maurice Watkins and his personal legal representative Jean-Jacques Bertand. I stayed at the hotel, thinking I wouldn't be allowed in the court room. At about 10.30, Paul Ince came to my room and gave me the news from the courtroom. 'They've decided to come down hard on Eric. The sentence has been announced: two weeks in prison. He's appealed. I have to go, I'll see you later.' Hearing these words was like a high-voltage charge through my whole body.

It had never occurred to me that the court case would turn

out this way. When I woke up, I walked over to the window below and saw a huge crowd of people and hundreds of photographers surrounding the hotel. I realised that some of them were pointing their lenses at my room, and I instantly closed the curtains. Panicking a little, I turned on the TV to find out more about the decision. It seemed every channel had a news crew here in Croydon. I realised what a big story this was.

A few hours went by, then Eric himself suddenly knocked on my door. He recounted the time he'd spent in the cells, putting a funny spin on it. 'As soon as I met the other prisoners, I started to piece together my team. That one I'll put at the back – he looks tough. The tall one will be a centre-forward, as he's got good heading skills. This one is quite slight: he'll be my midfielder wearing number six, a very technical player like Redondo [the Argentine footballer from Real Madrid]. This one will be my Keane . . .'

We couldn't stop laughing, the tears rolling down my cheeks, and it relieved the tension.

The legal process ended on 31 March when Eric's appeal was heard. The judge imposed a sentence of 120 hours' community service. I couldn't imagine things turning out any other way.

CHAPTER 14

Eight Months and One Life

One day the *Manchester Evening News* journalist David Meek asked me a question he said he'd been pondering: 'What did you do while Eric was suspended?'

That was easy: 'We spent a lot of time walking around the city,' I said, 'talked passionately about football, sailed on the Bridgewater Canal, travelled, went to the theatre and the cinema, listened to and played music ... We embraced life, David – we just got on with it. This could have the makings of a film entitled *Eight Months and One Life*! What do you reckon?'

David looked at me for a few moments, smiled, and cocked his head. *These French guys,* I imagined him thinking: *they're really nuts!*

Throughout the months we spent away from the excitement of match days, life rolled on. I continued to work on my thesis and reached significant milestones with it. After many long days of research, I was able to map out the contours that marked the dizzying rise of the industrial bourgeoisie.

I became fascinated by the people who had contributed to Manchester's glorious emergence as 'the Pride of the North', and also to the foundation of important local sporting institutions. When these were established – the Old Manchester Golf Club and the Manchester Cricket Club in 1818, the Clarence Club for rowing in 1828, and Manchester Rugby Club in 1860 – most of the important personalities in the city of Manchester had made their fortunes during the Industrial Revolution. Thanks to the wealth emanating from the cotton industry and the railways, the development of the city and its institutions was shaped by a new ethos based essentially on financial power. The prestige of the local aristocracy, embodied by the De Trafford, Egerton and Wilton families, was undermined by the likes of the Heywood, Philips, Potter, Crossley and Houldsworth families, who had control over the cotton industry and regional trade. Old money was being challenged by new, derived not from long-established prestige and standing, but from economic capital.

The influence these businessmen wielded gave them access to almost every social universe. Even the aristocratic Manchester Grammar School, an establishment renowned for its teaching of classics, was threatened: such was the sway of an elite group of merchants that the school began to re-orient its priorities towards economic specialisms. The industrial bourgeoisie gained exceptional notoriety, and effectively became the leaders of the rising urban elite. Their names became familiar: every time I walked down a street, I couldn't help but think of *my* businessmen. Every time I noticed a name on a building, I paid special attention. I was gradually becoming something of a tour guide for Eric. I loved this feeling of getting to know the city through its historical figures. Walking, which was principally how we got about, allowed me to meet time and again the personalities who were a substantial focus of my academic work.

Eric, of course, used his club car to ferry us about, but often he would park it somewhere so we could just roam. We were walkers, strollers in the true sense of the word: we had no preconceived ideas about where we were going. Nowadays it seems incredible that a star of his stature was so accessible: it was almost impossible for a fan not to stumble across the King if they happened to be passing between Piccadilly Gardens and the Whitworth Art Galleries, an important centre of student life. We walked all the time, by day and by night, and met so many people who were surprised to see Eric out and about in the heart of the city. There weren't many streets we didn't know.

In the afternoons we sometimes went to the Night and Day Café on Oldham Street for a beer. The route was hardwired in our brains: Thomas Street, down Oak Street, across Tib Street and arrive in less than ten minutes. We loved spending time talking about everything and anything – football in particular – at the café in the Royal Exchange Theatre. If we were going there, we'd park somewhere near King Street West and then walk around St Ann's Square to this magnificent building that epitomised Manchester's former economic power and had been recently transformed into a wonderful cultural space.

As a result of coming across us regularly in the street and in certain civic buildings, people got to know our regular walking routes, which is how we came to encounter a homeless man who sold the *Big Issue*. He had spotted us having lunch at Atlas on Deansgate, then at the Cornerhouse on Oxford

Street one afternoon, and another time at Café Renoir in Fallowfield. He knew he could count on us buying a copy of the magazine and leaving him a handsome tip on top. We used to bump into him regularly. One day we passed him three times, and he was quick to offer us the magazine on each occasion as a bit of fun. We played along and had a laugh with him.

We felt perfectly at liberty to wander around these squares and piazzas frequented by office workers or students. Sometimes we'd stop to chat, perhaps in Albert Square opposite the town hall, or in Whitworth Park in the student quarter, or just on a bench that caught our eye. One day we were sitting in Chinatown, not far from the City Art Gallery, when two people came up to us. One of them asked Eric if he was Eric Cantona, the Manchester United player. Eric, of course, said yes. To which the other man retorted, 'Can't you see he's talking nonsense? Can you really imagine Cantona sitting on a bench here, talking like a homeless person? Can't you see? It's someone who looks like him just having us on.'

We were speechless. Once they'd gone we burst out laughing.

Another time, on Cambridge Street, not far from Oxford Road Station, a motorist wound his window down: 'Excuse me, which way's Piccadilly Station?' Eric pointed the way for him, and he thanked us and drove off. A few seconds later, he reversed back and asked if he'd just spoken to Eric Cantona. His friends wouldn't believe him, he said, when he told them he'd met Eric. He drove off without asking for an autograph and apparently in something of a tizzy, as he headed off in the opposite direction to the one we'd indicated. This kind of encounter was typical, although more often people were

surprised to see Eric in places not usually frequented by footballers, and didn't dare approach us, assuming it was a case
of mistaken identity.

Football was the subject of long discussions during these
months of his suspension: every aspect of the game. In the
café at the Royal Exchange Theatre, over an excellent piece
of cheesecake and an equally delicious cup of tea, we debated
how football might be played to different rules. Eric thought
throw-ins could be done away with to speed up the game
and replaced with a kick from the touchline. To promote
attacking play, bonus points could be awarded to the team
that showed a willingness to attack. 'Draws should be abol-
ished,' he pronounced. 'At training grounds, priority should
be given to ball control, and sessions using the ball. At youth
level the importance of the result should be downplayed, so
children start off wanting to play for pleasure rather being
obsessed with winning at all costs. The emphasis should be
on the pleasure of playing, of improvising, on playing bare-
foot to develop a feeling for the ball. And they should learn
to play in every position – after all, just like in chess, you get
to grips with tactics by learning all the moves . . .'
    Sometimes Joël, Eric's younger brother, joined our dis-
cussions, and he also came up with some surprising ideas:
getting rid of offside, reorganising playing time, and remov-
ing goalkeeping as a dedicated position . . . Our desire for a
game where technique would take precedence over phys-
icality led us to redefine the meaning of football and, by
extension, dream up new ways to love the game. We knew
our ideas were crazy, but there was plenty of sense in them
too. We weren't football scholars, just people who loved the

game to bits. In our disjointed way, we analysed football from every angle.

One day we were discussing the game's great strategists. Eric pointed to the work done by Johan Cruyff when he was Barcelona's coach: 'He made the club in the image of Catalonia: rebellious, proud, different from Madrid. It's beautiful to watch this team: it exudes technical beauty, the art of the beautiful game, the art of the pass. There's an artistic side to it – it's one of the only teams in the world where a love of the game is a prerequisite for being part of the club. This club is unique because Cruyff wanted to create a masterpiece. Cruyff's Barça is the football I love. It's the epitome of the football I aspire to when I go out on the pitch.'

As the son of a Catalan (on his mother's side), Eric had a penchant for the *blau grana* of FC Barcelona, but he could also admire the Real Madrid of Butragueño and Michel and Martín Vásquez. He eulogised about the elegance of Italian players, in particular Giancarlo Antognoni, 'the Prince of Fiorentina', Alessandro Altobelli, 'the *fuoriclasse* of Inter Milan', the Juventus centre-forward Paolo Rossi's eye for goal and the sobriety of his teammate, defender Gaetano Scirea. Our references were mainly players from the 1980s, and our ideas derived from memories of European Cup matches, games that had taken place during the 1982 World Cup in Spain and the 1986 World Cup in Mexico, as well as domestic encounters. Our players, our coaches, even our kit references, were all from the 1980s.

I would talk about Valeriy Lobanovskyi, the coach of Dynamo Kiev and for me a mesmerising personality: always the epitome of concentration, his expression impassive, never a smile on his lips, never letting the slightest emotion cross his face, no matter what the result, and he put together a team that was feared across Europe. Not only did the Ukrainian team win the Soviet championship several times, but at a European level they also won two Cup Winners' Cups (1975 and 1986). I would pick out the names of the talented players from that 1986 team: Blokhin, Belanov, Zavarov . . . They'd crushed Atlético Madrid in the final, winning 3-0 – we could remember watching when we were in Auxerre. It was a real footballing lesson: the Spaniards had been over-whelmed by the technique, speed and power of the Soviets. The game made a real impact on all the youngsters at the Auxerre training centre. Yet, as our minds travelled on our footballing odyssey around Europe, we never gave a thought to the French championship or so much as mentioned the national team.

We got on to the 1982 World Cup, and I said I'd been impressed by the Brazilian team, which had real artists in its ranks. I recalled the emotion of their first match against the USSR: the Brazilians being pressed and hustled throughout but, with fifteen minutes remaining, making the break-through with goals from Sócrates and Eder. There was real magic in the moves that led to each goal: fascinating. After the game my brothers Roger and Basile and I went out into the street to celebrate. The Brazilians went on to play a near-perfect tournament until they were beaten 3-2 by an Italian side featuring Giancarlo Antognoni, Paolo Rossi, Marco Tardelli, Bruno Conti, Claudio Gentile and Dino Zoff. The hero of the day was Paolo Rossi, which is where Eric's nick-name of 'Paolo' at the Auxerre training centre came from.

We got carried away discussing the Brazilians' defeat. 'They were certainly better than the Italians,' said Eric, 'but they lacked realism. The Italians knew the Brazilians had defensive weaknesses and they took advantage of them. The Brazilians were too sure of themselves, and you know that unpredictability is an essential part of the beauty of football. The Italians played in the way they'd got used to: playing on the counter and being very clinical in front of goal. You remember Paolo Rossi didn't need many chances to score his hat-trick. Maybe the Brazilians saw themselves as too superior. Also, there's a tendency to depict that Italian team as being very defensive, but it had some very technically gifted players – Antognoni and Conti come to mind. The Italians were very well organised, and knew all about Brazil's weaknesses in defence.'

'But "Paolo"', I responded, 'you have to admit the Brazilian team was marvellous with all those artists in it: Sócrates, Zico, Tonihno Cerezo, Falcão, Junior. They deserved to go through. The problem was their centre-forward, because Serginho wasn't a great finisher. I would like to have seen France and Brazil in the final.'

We were on common ground when we talked about Diego Maradona. We both called him Diego, as though he were a member of our family. We loved to talk about him, and never tired of discussing his career and performances. The Argentinian was very often 'with us' when we discussed football. One afternoon, as the clouds disappeared and the sun shone in through the windows, I recounted the time I'd first heard of Maradona. We were talking about the decision that had been made by the Argentine coach, César Luis Menotti, not to pick the 18-year-old for the 1978 World Cup in Argentina. Why, we wondered? How could he leave out this prodigy from the Argentinos Juniors club, who later became Boca Juniors' golden-footed boy, '*El Pibe de Oro*' as he was nicknamed? We'd get upset about his career's dark moments, such as the odious tackle by an Athletic Bilbao defender when Diego was playing for Barcelona, which left his ankle seriously damaged and put him out of the game for three-and-a-half months. We reflected on his brilliance during his years with Napoli: the day of his presentation in the San Paolo stadium, where he delighted everyone with his ball-juggling skills; the matches he'd won against the teams from the north of Italy, especially the Juventus team run by the Agnelli family; Napoli's first league title, and their first European trophy . . .

For us, Diego symbolised football. We never ranked players. In our minds, Diego was different. There was Diego on one side, and on the other side all the rest. He was incomparable because he was unclassifiable. We loved everything about him: the shorts that clung so tightly to his powerful legs, the body feints, the dribbling, the juggling during warm-ups, the street kid vices, the sense of teamwork, the simplicity of his passes, his free-kicks, the love he had for his family and friends, the courage he showed in choosing to play for Napoli, a club with no 'history'. We'd get angry about the treatment he received during the 1982 World Cup, when the Italian defender Claudio Gentile drew on the full arsenal of dirty tricks to destroy Argentina's number 10. Not once did Diego complain. We reflected on the 1986 World Cup when he led Argentina to victory. There's been plenty of lengthy debate about his fifty-first-minute 'Hand of God' goal against England in the quarter-finals, but we remembered the slalom he produced four minutes later to score his second goal in that famous match.

Both in Argentina, in the poor neighbourhood of Villa Fiorito in the southern suburbs of Buenos Aires where he was born and brought up, and in Italy, and especially Naples, Diego is considered an icon, a 'gift from heaven'. I told Eric that the people of Naples had elevated Diego to the status of a true saint. We looked at photos of the city where altars were dedicated to Maradona, where people from every kind of background – fans, academics, shopkeepers – adored the Argentine artist. Through his exploits on the field, Diego became the symbol of Neapolitan success, improving the image of a city dominated by and primarily associated with the Mafia. We loved Diego in the same way we loved the films of Sergio Leone, Martin Scorsese and Ken Loach, spoke of him with tenderness, love, hyperbole. It was Diego Maradona that stoked our passion for football.

Eric also liked Sócrates. This stemmed from the way he typifyed the image of the committed footballer. The play-maker, with his incredibly short shorts in relation to his height and characteristic headband across his forehead: he was one of the personalities we looked up to. When we analysed the number 10's game it was his haughty style, his vision on the pitch, his elegance that we found ourselves dwelling on. But while I was most interested in the player, Eric would zero in on his political commitment. 'Dr Sócrates' (he has a doc-torate in medicine) dared to criticise the military dictatorship of the time. In November 1981, at his club SC Corinthians in São Paulo, he was one of the leaders of a unique experi-ment: the self-management of a football club by its employees, combined with a spectacular brand of football that became known as 'Corinthian Democracy'.

'Sócrates wasn't just a great player,' said Eric: 'he was

someone who used football as a laboratory for an experiment in democracy. The club became a democratic space: everyone had a part in the lifeblood of the club. I really liked that: the idea that a football club became a management model where every voice counted. It was a beautiful political project: socialism with a footballing twist. Finally the people were represented. He showed that football could serve as a powerful political opposition.' Eric had a lot of respect for Sócrates' career, which he expressed with great enthusiasm.

We ranged from country to country, each time with a particular player, club or match as our guide. When I guided us onto the Ivory Coast I got excited talking about my father, a fervent supporter of Africa Sport d'Abidjan, one of the most popular clubs in the capital, with historic ties to people from the west of the country. Our house was painted in Africa's green and red colours. I used to talk about my childhood in this green and red setting, where my father's mood changed according to the club's results, and about the childhood promises we made to him that we would play for Africa when we grew up. I was formally forbidden from wearing the yellow and black of Asec Mimosas, the 'enemy'. As a result, almost without my thinking about it, teams anywhere in the world that wore green and red shirts became my favourites: Morocco, Hungary, Portugal, Mexico, Fluminense (Brazil), CS Maritimo (Portugal), Djoliba (Mali) . . .

We took advantage of Eric's enforced hiatus from the game to go to the cinema, the theatre and concerts in Manchester and London. The Cornerhouse was our preferred venue for films, and we were happy to watch almost anything, be it the latest releases, *films d'auteurs* or those made outside the Hollywood mainstream which had often won awards. We used to go in the middle of the afternoon, and enjoyed English, American, Spanish and even French films, or stepped back into the past to pore over the work of Sergio Leone, Martin Scorsese and Brian de Palma. When we got on to particular films that had had an impact on our lives, Eric gave Mickey Rourke glowing reviews, while I recalled the string of spaghetti Westerns I sneaked in to see at cinemas in Abidjan, the mere words evoking an America of the imagination: Lux, Magic, Arizona, Hollywood, Madison ... I remembered actors relatively unknown in Europe who are real stars in Africa: Lee Van Cleef, Giuliano Gemma, Franco Nero, Terence Hill.

Eric loved the theatre too. We flew to London to see Edward Albee's *Who's Afraid of Virginia Woolf?* and *A Streetcar Named Desire* by Tennessee Williams. In London we met one of France's most famous and respected actors, Niels Arestrup, and I felt so intimidated before this giant of theatre and cinema I could barely look at him. We had dinner in a restaurant with Moroccan decor, which was very fashionable at the time, and I listened to the footballer and the actor talk about their passion for theatre, not daring to take part. I was more at ease when Eric, noticing my silence, brought me into the conversation by steering it round to cinema and music.

As for music, this was an ideal time to go and see some concerts. The Union and Manchester Academy in the Manchester University buildings were two of our favourite venues. The period was marked by the success of Britpop, but also by acid jazz (the James Taylor Quartet, Ronny Jordan, the Brand New Heavies, Incognito, Young Disciples), the crossover involving hip hop and jazz legends (Guru's Jazzamatazz, Courtney Pine, Roy Ayers, Branford Marsalis), and a significant French influence (Daft Punk, Etienne de Crécy, Cassius, Air, Kojak, DJ Cam). We often found ourselves in a throng of students and witnessed sensational performances by the James Taylor Quartet, Massive Attack and Guru's Jazzamatazz.

Things took a different turn the day we stumbled upon Forsyth's, the instrument shop at 126 Deansgate. We'd come out of the Waterstone's bookshop, crossed the street and passed House of Fraser, when Eric paused in front of Forsyth's window. 'Look at these instruments!' he exclaimed. 'Aren't they beautiful? Look at that saxophone! The classical guitar! The trumpet! The violin, the piano! I would have loved to be a musician: it's so beautiful to be able to play an instrument.' Like children, we pointed out instruments and imagined actually being able to play these extraordinary objects. Finally we decided to go in. The shop assistant recognised Eric, calmly inclining his head in greeting and keeping his distance to allow us to browse. We looked at various instruments more closely in order to fully admire their beauty. I stared at a tenor saxophone and immediately thought of John Coltrane, Dexter Gordon, Sonny Rollins, Stan Getz, Branford Marsalis ... I moved on to a Gibson guitar, which summoned up thoughts of George Benson, Norman Brown, Lee Ritenour, Christian Escoudé, Babik Reinhardt and Philippe Catherine ... I wandered over to the Steinway pianos, the Roland synthesisers – we were in a world of wonders.

I noticed Eric was lingering by the wind instruments. He called me over. 'How about we learn the trumpet? I'll take the flugelhorn, and you can choose whichever one you like.' My gaze instantly settled on one in particular: a silver

Yamaha trumpet. We bought cases, instruction books, the tools needed to take care of the instruments: cloths, the liquid to ensure they would slide properly, a mute so we could play without disturbing the entire neighbourhood. Eric asked the shop assistant if he could recommend a teacher, and he gave us the name and address of John MacMurray, a Canadian trumpeter with the Hallé Orchestra, who lived in Wilmslow.

Every Thursday, thereafter, we had a ninety-minute lesson with John at his house. We were very diligent: we practised our scales every day. We dreamed of the lyrical passages of Miles Davis and Chet Baker. A few years earlier, I had lent Eric the *Chet* album and *Let's Get Lost,* the Bruce Weber film about Chet Baker's life, and we'd been charmed by Baker's life and sound. We often talked about this CD, which features some unforgettable compositions – 'Alone Together', 'It Never Entered my Mind', 'How High the Moon' – and the film that exposed the genius and downfall of a great musician. Secretly I wanted to learn some of his repertoire, or something by Miles Davis. We started our first lesson by learning 'Basin Street Blues', superbly performed by Ella Fitzgerald.

Learning the trumpet encouraged us to listen to trumpet players, and I made a compilation of the pieces I'd enjoyed over the years on several CDs. My 'best of' included Miles Davis, Dizzy Gillespie, Chet Baker, Wynton Marsalis, Randy Brecker, Freddie Hubbard, Donald Byrd, Terence Blanchard, Roy Hargrove, Eric Le Lann and Paolo Fresu. I wanted us to immerse ourselves in the styles of different instrumentalists. That would be a long road, but we were patient. We went over the difficulties together, in particular breath control and embouchure – in photos of trumpet players, we joked, their upper lip was always crushed by the mouthpiece. Eric admitted he'd experienced some dizziness once when he'd played for almost two hours. From now on, we agreed, we'd regard musicians with a new respect.

We were all too aware of our shortcomings, of how long it would take us to master even a straightforward piece, but we practised whenever we could: when Eric's wife Isabelle organised a little barge trip on the Bridgewater Canal, we took our trumpets aboard, and the peaceful journey and glorious sunshine presented us with the perfect opportunity to show how much progress we'd made. We left Eric's home in Worsley and joined the barge at Runcorn, from where the route was dotted with familiar and picturesque places. We left Manchester and headed for the Mersey. We passed through the Trafford neighbourhood, inevitably floated past Old Trafford stadium, then sailed through beautifully verdant landscapes like Sale Water Park and the National Trust's Dunham Massey, taking turns to steer the barge like true captains. Every so often Eric and I would play on deck, enjoying the echo of the instruments as we glided along shady waterways. We were the subject of mocking laughter from our companions when they saw our distorted faces or heard our glaring errors. Undaunted, we repeated 'Basin Street Blues' over and over, thinking all the while of how Louis Armstrong had done it.

Travel also formed an important part of Eric's life during this period of professional downtime. One day, sitting in the tiny Café Renoir, we decided to plan a trip to a nearby country where we could encounter all kinds of unfamiliar sights and sounds. Scotland we ruled out owing to its relative proximity. Paris? Too familiar to a Frenchman. In the end, we opted for a Scandinavian country.

'Why not Denmark?' suggested Eric. 'It's less than two hours from Manchester, and they seem to have a laidback mentality.' I told him I'd been there before: in secondary school, I'd travelled with two friends to Aarhus, Denmark's second city, and had fond memories. So Denmark it was, and on 12 August 1995 we boarded a plane for Copenhagen.

We spent the whole flight discussing Manchester and its urban transformation rather than what we were going to do when we got there, so we had to improvise. We walked out of the hotel and went into one of the first bars we came across, and were surprised to hear two people speaking French nearby. Eric had been spotted. In situations like this, a reflex kicks in. When one of them asked us rather brusquely, 'What on Earth are you doing here in Copenhagen?' Eric fired back with a question of his own: 'Why, what are you doing here?' They told us they were sailors; we explained that we'd come to explore the city.

Eventually we set off again, although we still didn't know where we were going. Then we saw a sign pointing towards the Christiania district. I'd heard a lot about this, and suggested to Eric we check it out. Along the way a group of French people recognised Eric and, without a hint of embarrassment, one of them said to us, 'You're going to Christiania too? Good call: you're bound to find something there to satisfy you. There are all kinds of drugs! It's not like France – you can easily find what you want, and you won't be hassled. It's proper dope!' The guy added that he could show us a good dealer. We decided we'd rather go somewhere else: 'Cantona in Christiania, the land of the forbidden', I said to Eric – that would have been the headline in the newspapers the next day if we'd carried on in that direction ...

In the evening, we went to a nightclub, which we were a little surprised to find full of Manchester United supporters. Perhaps it was only to be expected, given the remarkable careers Danish players have had with the Reds, including Arnold Muhren, Jesper Olsen, John Sivebaek and, of course, Peter Schmeichel. So we were on friendly turf. We spent hours on the dance floor. The atmosphere wasn't very different from the clubs in Manchester. Eric danced and danced, his shirt soaked as he lost himself in the DJ's sounds, the DJ delighted to see a celebrity enjoying his selection. Seeing him so present on the dance floor, so obviously happy to be there, took me back to our years in Auxerre. We spent the next day walking around and then caught the plane back to Manchester.

Amsterdam was another destination for us. Eric was invited to present the trophy for the best Dutch young player of the year to Michael Mols, who was playing for Twente Enschede. Mols had asked if he could receive the trophy from his idol. We knew the city quite well: Eric had played there and I'd been there with friends several years earlier on a Jack Kerouac road trip from Bourges to Aarhus via Lille, Antwerp and Hamburg.

We felt good as soon as we arrived at our hotel near the main station and headed straight out, ambling down streets and avenues, crossing bridges. Of course, tourists that we were, we had to keep stopping to make way for speeding cyclists. Then we heard the clamour of a crowd: a football match was being played in a square, and the obvious fervour made us approach even closer. Eric looked at me. 'You know, I'm sure they're French people playing football!'

'How can you tell?' Instantly we heard one of the players

exclaim: 'I'm going to kick your fucking arse!' We laughed and discreetly slunk away.

We found ourselves entranced by the beauty of some of the places we wandered past. The colours were what particularly struck; for me it was the multicultural character of the city. Then, halfway down another attractive street, we suddenly realised where we'd ended up: only now did my myopic eyes pick out a scantily clad lady pulling the curtains closed. It took a few moments for my mind to register what was going on. I kept walking: an elderly woman was sitting cross-legged in a shop window. I looked at Eric; he nodded. 'Yes,' he said, 'we are in exactly the place you're thinking of.' We quickened our step, our eyes fixed straight ahead.

That evening, Eric presented the award to Michael Mols, making a very brief speech. 'I'm happy to be here. But today is not about me, but about honouring a promising player. Thank you.' I could see the pride in Mols' eyes at having been able to meet his hero. He seemed really happy to exchange a few words with Eric. Among the guests I recognised two Brazilian players: the young prodigy Ronaldo, at that time a budding star at PSV Eindhoven, and Márcio Santos, an athletic defender who played for Ajax Amsterdam. After the ceremony, we had a pleasant evening in one of the city's famous nightclubs, but by now our thoughts were in France. A terrorist attack had taken place at the Saint-Michel station in Paris's Latin Quarter, a neighbourhood I was very fond of, where I often went to look at Notre-Dame and buy second-hand books.

'So, did you see him? How was he? What did he say to you? What are you going to do now? When will you see each other again? Which other players were there?'

The reason for this barrage of childish questions? I wanted to find out everything I could from Eric about his meeting in Paris with Diego Maradona. On 15 September, Eric had announced to the press that he would be present at the launch of the Argentinian's initiative to establish an international footballers' union. 'Of course I shall be there,' he'd declared. 'Even if he only has one ally on the day, it will be me.' Three days later, they had launched the International Association of Professional Footballers. Among the other internationally renowned footballers present that day were Italy's Gianluca Vialli, Brazil's Rai, the younger brother of Sócrates, Sweden's Tomas Brolin, Germany's Karl-Heinz Rummenigge, France's Laurent Blanc, Liberia's George Weah and Ghana's Abedi Pelé.

The next day, as we left training at the Cliff, I was eager for Eric to tell me about Diego, the new union and what he intended to do for it, and his impressions of the other players. After the ritual signing of autographs, he got into his car and we headed for Pizza Express. As he drove and talked, I could tell from the look in his eyes he felt he was fighting for a noble cause, and wanted to immerse himself totally in it. 'Just imagine, if all of the players were united, we would have a considerable influence on football. It would impact on the whole game: on the training of young kids, on club management, transfers, relations with the federations ... Footballers are totally absent from the decision-making process within the sport's governing bodies. Is there any player who represents the voice of the players at FIFA, at UEFA? Not one. Football is the most popular sport in the world, the one that fascinates more people across the globe than any other, and it's one that generates a lot of money. But who benefits? The players do, fortunately, but so too do an army of incompetents who know nothing about it, and are only interested in football as a way of gaining some status and making a lot of money.

'If we're united, and that's the purpose of the union, we'll be recognised, respected and feared. With Diego, we have the very essence of football speaking for footballers. I know we'll scare some people, but you've seen the kind of players who are willing to get involved, and that's really motivating. I know enough about football to know that not all players think like Diego, but that doesn't matter, because for the good of football we need to bring together both the big personalities and the unknown players. And it's for the future generations too.'

'We shall overcome,' I added.

'That's a great slogan,' Eric replied. 'But isn't it the title of a song?'

CHAPTER 15

The King is Back

The week before Eric's return to Old Trafford after his long suspension remains etched on my memory.

Sunday, 24 September

The day began with Gerry Rafferty's *Baker Street* album, followed by a second, *Snakes and Ladders*, and then a third, *The Transatlantic Years*. On a day when the weather was totally wild once again, I was in a celtic mood. I continued with U2, once more going through the CDs in chronological order, listening first to *War*, then *The Unforgettable Fire*, *The Joshua Tree*, *Rattle and Hum* and *Achtung Baby*, each one in its entirety. Full of energy and happy to be so, I invited Anne to dance with me to 'Hunting Down a Killer' by the American band Cock Robin, featuring the magnificent voice of Peter Kingsbery. Then I felt a desire for African music, so I set off on a tour of the continent with Salif Keita, Youssou N'Dour, Fela Kuti,

Johnny Clegg, Alpha Blondy ... In spite of the inclement weather, the morning was whiled away very pleasantly to all kinds of rhythms from the many CDs and cassettes that occupied a large part of our living room.

In the afternoon the sun finally came out, so Anne and I decided to go for a walk in Platt Fields Park, close to Manchester City's training facilities. We saw Pakistani, Indian and Nigerian families enjoying themselves in this huge green space and watched some students improvising a game of cricket; altogether a thoroughly relaxed atmosphere. We ended our walk by heading into Rusholme for some delicious desserts from Delhi Sweet and Sanam Sweet Centre.

That evening, I called France to check on Basile, who had suffered a head injury playing for his new club Monaco during a UEFA Cup match against Leeds United almost a fortnight earlier at the Stade Louis II. Not only did Monaco lose heavily 3-0 – all the goals scored by Ghana's Tony Yeboah – but my brother and his goalkeeper Marc Delaroche had suffered a violent clash of heads late in the game and ended the evening in hospital. I'd been very worried about him, but he'd come through without a serious head injury and we spent most of the call talking about his transfer and joking about his time at Glasgow Rangers. I spent the rest of the evening immersed in Elias Canetti's *Histoire d'une jeunesse*, in which he recalled his youth in Manchester in 1911.

Monday, 25 September

My mission for the day was clear: to read the massive pile of Sunday papers on my desk – several weeks of reading. By the early afternoon I'd managed to work my way through three issues of the *Observer*, when I was surprised to get a call from Peter Boyle, one of Man United's best-known fans, renowned for the songs he composed for matches and, above all for being a staunch supporter of Eric. We'd become friends playing table football in a pub near the Hacienda, and I'd come to like Pete a lot. He used to drop by to ask me about his favourite player and tell me about the songs he was working on. On this occasion, his main reason for coming around was 'the return of the King'. We chatted for while over a beer, and he promised me there would an incredible atmosphere for the game.

In the early evening I sat with Anne as she watched her favourite soap opera, Channel 4's *Brookside*, and as always I was amazed. 'How can you understand the Liverpool accent?' I'd ask her every time she watched it.

Tuesday, 26 September

I met Eric at Pizza Express and we went back to his meeting with Maradona. I was surprised at the relative silence from players following all the media coverage of the establishment of the International Association of Professional Footballers. Eric told me we had to wait for people to wake up, but I couldn't detect much optimism in his tone. We moved on to a news story that had made us laugh: 'the Dynamo Kiev affair', in which the Ukrainian club had been excluded from the Champions League for trying to bribe the Spanish referee Antonio López Nieto before their match against Panathinaikos. The referee had told UEFA he'd been offered 'thirty thousand dollars and two mink coats if Kiev win'.

We adjourned to Café Renoir, where we met up with Saltz Anderson, who gave us the latest news on his friend Mick Hucknall, who had become a good friend of Eric's too. We talked about music and chatted with his wife and children, and before we left I promised Eric a compilation of albums by Simply Red, the Smiths, the Style Council, Prefab Sprout, Everything But the Girl and Chris Rea.

Wednesday, 27 September

I spent the day at De Montfort University in Leicester presenting the work I'd recently been working on to my thesis supervisor, Pierre Lanfranchi. I was particularly interested in the changes that had taken place in Britain in the 1970s when the leisure industry had exploded, and I'd compiled masses of photocopies of articles and reports from various libraries. Sitting on the coach to Leicester I immersed myself in Steve Bradshaw's comments on television, the fervour triggered by the new craze for DIY, John Hall's survey of the film-going population, an article by the *Guardian*'s brilliant columnist Polly Toynbee on the vogue for horse-riding and its effects on couples, the opinions of football fans on hot topics such as refereeing or fan violence at games and the great British holiday tradition.

Thursday, 28 September

I met Eric at the Cliff, where there were, as always, lots of fans waiting patiently to get an autograph, a photo and, above all, to show their affection. Eric as usual not only made himself available but was also all smiles. I could see expressions of happiness, fascination, devotion and love on the supporters' faces. At the end of the street where the road headed towards the city centre, there was often a group of young female supporters who were the last to greet us before we'd disappear into the huge intersection.

We had lunch with Isabelle at Pizza Express before going on to the Cornerhouse, Eric pointing out along the way a member of the paparazzi who had been following us for several days. As soon as he'd parked he waited for our 'follower' to park as well, then jumped out and asked the photographer to roll down his window. 'What exactly do you want? You've been following me for days – what did you think you'd find? You must know my schedule by heart: training–Pizza Express–Prestbury [Eric's new home]. Aren't you tired of following me? You'd be better off keeping track of where your wife is right now!' Taken aback by Eric's outburst, the photographer wound his window up and drove off in a hurry. We never saw him again. The whole thing happened so quickly I didn't have time to tell Eric that it might have unfortunate consequences. He, meanwhile, was as cool as a cucumber.

In the Cornerhouse Eric asked me how Basile was getting on after that clash of heads and, putting on my best Glaswegian accent, I told him my brother had changed completely: now he would wear only kilts and thought he was Sean Connery. We sat there laughing.

Friday, 29 September

We met at J. W. Johnson's on Deansgate. I was wearing a leather Basque beret, which made Eric laugh. Inevitably we discussed the huge surprise of Manchester United's elimination from the UEFA Cup by the Russian team Volgograd, and this despite a goal from Peter Schmeichel. Then we got onto the shooting of the first film in which Eric and Joël were set to appear: *Le bonheur est dans le pré* (Happiness is in the Field) by Etienne Chatiliez. I asked him if he'd shot many scenes with the famous French singer Eddy Mitchell.

'It was a great experience,' said Eric, 'and the place was beautiful. Jo and I had a great time. You know how much I like cinema. Doing the scenes over and over again,' he added, 'it's not like a football match where you have to get every move right. When you're filming, you have the opportunity to make mistakes. Football provides me with something more intense.'

We also talked about the genius of Miles Davis's album *Kind of Blue*, and I pulled out a compilation I'd made the night before of the Style Council's best tracks. When he dropped me back in Rusholme, his expression spoke volumes about the game ahead. 'You'll see, I'm going to score on Sunday,' he said.

I didn't respond, and he headed off down Wilmslow Road. I was hoping with all my heart that his wish would come true.

Saturday, 30 September

A day of relaxation. Anne and I spent most of it in the city centre, wandering through the chic shops on King Street.

Later we went to Affleck's Palace on Church Street, the home of underground culture in Manchester.

Sunday, 1 October

After 248 days, 18 hours and 57 minutes, nearly three hours in the cells, 120 hours of community service, and around 10 hours of trumpet lessons, my friend was back at Old Trafford, 'the Theatre of Dreams'. I knew this was an historic day. Anne and I had decided to get to the stadium by two, with the game against Liverpool due to kick off at four. On the tram, I found myself a little overwhelmed by the French flags bearing Eric's image and the fans singing 'Eric the King', composed by Peter 'Boylie' Boyle. I'd never experienced such an atmosphere of shared jubilation on public transport. Eric's name was on everyone's lips – it felt like a coronation day. All the *tricolores* made it seem as though we were going to watch France.

As we left the Old Trafford tram stop, we passed the make-shift stalls all bedecked with flags that bore Eric's image, sporting a range of slogans: *The King is Back*; *Eric the King: Back with a Vengeance*; *He's back – Live 1st October: Eric Cantona versus Liverpool*; *I Am Back*; *The Return of the Magnificent 7 . . .* Children and adults of all ages, dressed in the Red Devils' colours, had 'Eric is back' written on their faces in black marker. At the stadium we could already hear fans chanting their support for Eric. I could see TV trucks from broadcasters all over the world had come to cover the game. I got a wink from Ryan Giggs, and a few moments later Nicky Butt was there too.

Once we'd got our tickets, we walked around the stadium to soak up the euphoric atmosphere. As we approached the East Stand, I looked up at the clock honouring the players who had died in the 1958 Munich crash. History had caught up with me. I had learned about the sad and happy moments this club had experienced, and now the present was offering history in the making, and I was going to be a direct witness.

In the clubhouse the Cantona clan had gathered in almost full force: apart from Eric's mother, Eléonore, they'd all come over – his father Albert, his brothers Jean-Marie and Joël, the latter looking very distinguished in suit and silk tie. There were numerous friends too, among them Richard Aujard, the photographer who had set up a meeting between Eric and Mickey Rourke. I recognised the actress Sabine Azéma and her husband, the great director Alain Resnais – she had met Eric on the set of *Le bonheur est dans le pré*. Charles Gassot, a film producer, notably of Etienne Chatiliez's films, was also there.

We all ended up in a corner of the tiny suite, Albert, bag in hand filled with gifts from the megastore, enthusing about the atmosphere around the ground. 'You saw all those French flags – it's beautiful! These English people are extraordinary; they really love the game. What a great club Manchester United is!' Then he turned to more personal matters. 'You get on so well with Eric! It's so good that you're here – he often talks about you. It's good that you two from Auxerre see each other so often.' His words touched me deeply, but I was too shy to say anything much beyond thanking him.

Joël grabbed me by the neck. 'Claudio,' he joked, 'you're an Englishman now. Eric told me you're going to run for mayor soon! He also told me you're ready to play the trumpet in a brass band!' We laughed, which defused the tension a bit.

The minutes were ticking away. We didn't want to miss the players coming out for their warm-up, and went to our seats. Just as outside the ground, the stands were filled with flags lauding Eric. I was in the middle and took some pictures, at his father's request, when the players came out of the tunnel. The applause when Eric made his appearance was thunderous.

By the time the teams were due to come out, emotions were at fever pitch. Sabine Azéma shed a few tears, while the fans in the Stretford End sang 'Eric the King', and before long this hymn of love for the *Frenchy* was ringing out on all sides of the stadium. I kept clicking away with my camera, all of us now focused on Eric, who was the last to emerge from the tunnel, Andy Cole just ahead of him. He had his usual posture: head up, chest out, direct and unruffled gaze, shirt collar up, chewing gum. Just before he set foot on the turf, he made a delicate gesture: quickly kissed his index finger. He didn't glance in our direction, not wanting to lose focus at such a significant and pressurised moment. The clamour from the 34,934 spectators was so tumultuous that the announcer's voice was completely inaudible.

The atmosphere was incredibly intense, to the extent that the eventual result was neither here nor there. The King was back and that was all that mattered. And yet the outcome of the game was crucial to the title race: Manchester United were four points behind Newcastle, who had been leading the league since the third game of the season.

We didn't have to wait long for a flash of brilliance from United's number 7. The game was fifty-four seconds old when he lit up the game with a wonderful left-footed cross to Nicky Butt, who opened the scoring. The stadium exploded with joy, and the tricolour flags bearing Eric's image waved even more frenetically. It was a moment of pure ecstasy. The Family Stand was absolutely abuzz, especially because the move had taken place on our side of the pitch. We'd followed it as it unfolded at high speed, defying the ban on standing up in order not to miss an instant. I'd watched Eric drift from the centre circle to the left wing, and when he got the ball I wondered whether he would cross with the outside of his right foot or use his left. He looked up and saw Nicky running into the box, made the perfect pass with his left foot and the shot had been just as superbly timed. We roared with delight. We couldn't have asked for a better way for the game to start. But this was only the beginning of what would be a rollercoaster ride of emotions.

The Liverpool of my friend Michael Thomas, the Reds midfielder, weren't about to give their arch rivals any favours. Their prolific young centre-forward Robbie Fowler struck twice, to equalise and then give his team the lead. Our euphoria turned to awe at the strength of this team, which included the cream of English football's new generation in players such as Jamie Redknapp, Steve McManaman, Robbie Fowler, David James and Stan Collymore, as well as the legendary Welsh striker Ian Rush, and we could only watch Liverpool's resistance in almost stunned silence. We needed another touch of magic. Could there be another stroke of providence?

As with Nicky Butt's goal, the action that led to United's equaliser unfolded with breathtaking speed. Eric received the ball in the centre circle and raced forward, Ryan Giggs and Andy Cole running just ahead of him. 'Coley' cleverly switched to the right, and Eric paused for the briefest instant, weighing up whether to pass to him or to Giggsy, who went to the left. Eric feigned a pass to Andy and then delivered the ball to Ryan, who was pushed in the back by a defender. Without hesitation, referee David Elleray awarded a penalty.

Eric was the designated penalty-taker, and no one else made a move towards the penalty spot. The crowd started chanting 'E-ric the King!' Eric calmly picked up the ball and strode into the area, placing it carefully with both hands on the spot, and took a few steps back for his run-up. The action was taking place in front of the North Stand, so we were a long way off, but, except for Isabelle, we all stood, fists clenched, faces tense, waiting impatiently. I thought I caught sight of Peter Boyle glancing across furtively at our anguish. Then came the shot. David James had dived to the right and the ball went straight into the left corner. Eric had sent the keeper the wrong way. It was in!

The joy we felt was indescribable. Eric ran towards the fans behind the goal and celebrated wildly, jumping on one of the stanchions that held the net up. There were still almost twenty minutes to play, but we'd got what we wanted.

The game petered out as the two teams settled for a draw, and we stood and applauded as the hero of the day walked off into the tunnel, briefly lit up by the glare of television lights before disappearing. As we made our way to the clubhouse, Darren, one of the security staff, called out to me, 'He showed real guts by taking that penalty. The King is definitely back!'

Once we'd got back to the clubhouse, Michael Thomas came over to say hello. When we'd seen each other at J. W. Johnson's in the run-up to the game, he'd assured me that he would show my friend no mercy. But right now he was happy for me. The range of contrasting feelings we felt at the final whistle lingered throughout the evening. There were hugs, carefully chosen words, tears held back and shed, and laughter. We felt as if we'd lived through a momentous event, shared a historic episode in the Cantona story.

Eric was delighted to see us. He thanked Sabine Azéma and Charles Gassot for coming. 'So, did you enjoy it?' he asked Sabine, who was still a little shaken up by the experience.

'It's the first time I've been to a football match,' she admitted, 'and I've never experienced such emotion in my life!'

At that early point in the 1995/96 season, I never imagined that the title would be decided in such thrilling fashion, with a finale to the season that was like the plot of a Hollywood movie. That game against Liverpool proved to be the start of a glorious chapter in the Cantona legend, a mythical narrative built up with every game that I only became aware of gradually. We lived those days very much in the present, enjoying and relishing it, giving little thought to the past or the future. I was no more than an observer; Eric was the principal actor. However, in my role of historian I was aware of the importance of paying witness to a story that needed to be recorded. As a result, I followed the remaining matches that season with a yearning for football and historical knowledge alike.

The battle for the title between Man United and Newcastle was utterly absorbing. Following the draw against Liverpool, United had beaten my secret love Manchester City by the narrowest of margins: 1–0. Eric hadn't played. He returned against Chelsea, his first away game since the kung fu kick at Selhurst Park. The Reds, led by a superb Paul Scholes, won the game 4–1, with Eric putting in an excellent performance in what was effectively the number 10 position in midfield.

Despite this victory, Newcastle still led the Premier League by four points with ten games played. After fifteen games, the gap between had increased to five points, and Eric hadn't scored again since the Liverpool game.

He finally broke that barren run when he equalised seven minutes from time in a game at Old Trafford that smelt of defeat, Chris Waddle's Sheffield Wednesday leaving Manchester with a 2–2 draw. At the same time, the Newcastle team were impressing me with their consistency. After United's defeat at Leeds on Christmas Eve, the Reds were ten points behind. I always dreaded games against Leeds, and I was right to be concerned: that day Eric was injured in a clash with their centre-half David Wetherall and ended up having six stitches in his head. The title race was at a critical juncture. The media kept saying that the team that was top of the league in December had a strong chance of being crowned champions.

We spent the holiday season without our partners, who had returned to France to be with their families. Eric and I spent Christmas Day together, then met again the next day at the Cliff as we settled back into our usual routine. My spirits were lifted by the news of the imminent arrival of one of our friends from Auxerre, William Prunier, who was having a trial at Manchester United. 'Prune' had been one of my mates at the training centre. We were both Parisians. He'd started his career with Paris FC at the Porte de Montreuil, near the Porte des Lilas, where we lived, and now I was delighted with the idea of having another *Auxerrois* to spend time with in Manchester.

The match between Man United and Newcastle on 27 December was crucial. If United lost, David Ginola and his teammates would be thirteen points ahead of the Red Devils. Two things stood out for me: first, the absence from the United team sheet of three experienced defenders: Steve Bruce, Gary Pallister and Paul Parker; secondly, this meant that Eric was wearing the captain's armband for the first time. The Manchester United team, clearly hungrier than their opponents, won the game quite easily, 2–0. I'd expected the Magpies to provide keener opposition, but they were quite lacklustre. After the game, Kevin Keegan, visibly annoyed by the performance of his players, told reporters, 'We brought our circus to town, but we forgot to bring any tigers.'

On 30 December William Prunier made his debut at centre-back against Queens Park Rangers, when a crowd of 41,890 watched the Red Devils win. I was very happy for Prune. Unfortunately, though, the next match went very differently for him: he struggled as United suffered a heavy defeat at White Hart Lane, losing 4–1 with Tottenham's centre-forward Chris Armstrong enjoying one of his best games of the season. Eric felt very sad for Prune, because he knew that William's adventure at United could end abruptly.

United's 1–0 win at West Ham on Monday, 22 January kept the Reds nine points behind Newcastle, Eric scoring the only goal. Yet, while Alex Ferguson's side were being overshadowed in the league, they were brilliant in the FA Cup. Manchester City were their victims in the fifth round, Eric and Lee Sharpe helping United to continue their run. Then came the clash of the two title contenders, this time at St James' Park on Monday, 4 March. Newcastle had recently signed the Colombian striker Faustino Asprilla, while Eric's former Leeds teammate David Batty was also set to make his debut for the league leaders, whose lead was now a mere four points. Manchester United did well to win the game, Eric scoring the only goal to put United just a single point behind the leaders. The next day, still feeling quite fired up by the match, I told him it had been one of the best games in the league that season.

'For us it was really important not to lose,' he told me. 'Now the pressure's on them. We won't let up. We're going for the double!'

On 16 March, United became the league leaders for the first time that season, thanks to a last-minute goal from Eric that earned them a draw against Queens Park Rangers. Yet it was far from plain sailing for United. In April, they travelled to Southampton and fell to a 3–1 defeat in which Saints' striker Matthew Le Tissier, one of England's most French players, produced a very classy performance. This was largely forgotten the day after, though, when an unusual controversy erupted, as United's kit supplier Umbro was labelled the culprit for this humiliating defeat. The company, based in the suburbs of Manchester, was criticised by the Red Devils for the design of a new grey-speckled shirt, which supposedly blended in with the stands. According to Alex Ferguson, the players complained at half-time that they couldn't pick each other out clearly enough. The Reds had played the second half in blue shirts, but as they'd already conceded three first-half goals the damage had already been done. The two of us joked about this incident in the days that followed, although Eric remained adamant that the shirts had been a problem. Victory against Leeds at Old Trafford a few days later confirmed the Red Devils as the league leaders, albeit with just a three-point gap over Newcastle.

Soon after, 21 April proved to be a kind of redemption

day for Eric, thanks to a vote of confidence delivered by a very significant section of public opinion. Eric was voted Player of the Year by the Football Writers' Association, eight months after his return to the game. Eric attended the event in evening dress with his bow tie slightly unbuttoned. Two years on from being voted the players' player of the year, he stood on stage with the trophy beaming, visibly happy to be honoured now by the footballing press. I knew this award meant a lot to him, but his happiness wasn't unalloyed: the English press that had so often praised him had also reviled, insulted and demolished him. Yet ultimately they were showing their respect for him and his talent.

Eric also accepted the award to show his appreciation for British sports journalists, which was not matched by his feelings for their French counterparts. Since the publication of an article headlined 'Indefensible' in *L'Équipe* in January 1995, Eric had completely distanced himself from the French press. Apart from the pay TV channel Canal +, he systematically refused any interviews with a number of French journalists, notably those on the powerful daily *L'Équipe* and the weekly *France-Football*. Like the whole Cantona family, I'd been affected by the flood of hurtful articles about Eric, and whenever we met a French journalist at Old Trafford or anywhere else, Eric tended to turn down their requests. *L'Équipe*'s Erik Bielderman, a regular at Old Trafford, continued to make them, but Eric was determined never to change his mind. I also met journalists who, in an attempt to curry favour with me, said they were friends with one of my brothers, Basile or Roger, in the hope that this might give them a route to Eric.

I never tried to make Eric change his mind. However, almost since I'd learned to read I'd been addicted to the sports press, particularly *L'Équipe*, *France-Football*, *Onze* and *Mondial*. Like many kids from poor backgrounds, I used to go to the markets of Abidjan to try to find copies of sports papers that had been shipped from France by second-hand newspaper dealers and were often weeks or even months old. My cultural understanding was forged by reading newspapers, my knowledge of the countries and cities of Europe and Latin America accumulated that way. In my mind, Tuesday has always remained *France-Football*'s publication day, just as later on Saturday afternoons at 3 p.m. would belong to Premier League matches kicking off.

Coming back to the Footballer of the Year award, we were especially touched and even overwhelmed by the attention it generated, largely because as time went by we felt more and more English. The memories we now had increasingly made us feel better off in England than we had been in France. There was a growing sensation of being much more connected to England and, at the same time, of gradually moving away from our home country. We felt estranged from France and strangely English. This shared sense of Englishness manifested itself quite surprisingly one Boxing Day when we were, as usual, without our respective families. We were having dinner at the Four Seasons Hotel when Eric floated the idea of applying for British nationality. Without hesitation, I said yes. Afterwards we joked about it, but deep down the idea was not so crazy.

On Sunday, 5 May, at Middlesbrough's brand new Riverside Stadium, Manchester United claimed a stunning 3-0 win. Coached by former United players Bryan Robson and Viv Anderson, Middlesbrough were outclassed by the interplay orchestrated by Eric. The Reds were the champions. I watched the game in a pub close to Manchester Central Library, with an army of United fans celebrating the result around me, singing songs proclaiming Eric's glory. I watched without saying anything, without revealing my French identity. I was an anonymous member of the King's ardent army. Just one challenge remained: the FA Cup Final against Liverpool at Wembley.

That morning, we all met in a hotel near London's Euston Station: the Cantonas (father Albert, Joël, Jean-Marie, Isabelle, Raphaël), old and recent friends (Richard Aujard, Bernard Morlino, a writer from Nice, Gérard Gelas, the playwright and director of the Chêne noir theatre in Avignon, and Gary King, to name but a few). I spent a long time talking to Bernard: following our first meeting at the Four Seasons Hotel at Manchester Airport, we'd developed a firm friendship. We both had huge passions for three masterpieces of human genius: Diego Maradona, Miles Davis and literature. Bernard would travel to Manchester regularly, and during his stays there would enlighten Eric, Isabelle and me with his deep thinking and, above all, his humour. After interviewing Eric in May 1994 for *Globe Hebdo* magazine, Bernard had entered Eric's tight circle of close friends. He also used to call on me as his Manchester eye when it came to reporting on matches he couldn't attend. Bernard had been there, though, during the critical moments of the 1995/96 season; he was there to 'smell', as he used to say, to savour a passion for football. Having been an OGC Nice supporter, he became a United and Eric fan. Our friendship never wavered, and together we became the 'memory keepers' of that thrilling 1995/96 season. We were there for the moment that would cement the fabulous finale to Eric's season. There was a sense of history in the air, and we hoped to cross paths with it, to touch it, to relish and love it.

It was Saturday, 11 May, the day of the Cup Final, the 115th edition of the prestigious competition established in 1871. The clash was symbolic, pitting Liverpool, the dominant force of the 1980s, against Manchester United, the best team of the 1990s. It would, of course, take place in the mythical Wembley Stadium, whose very name makes all football lovers' spines tingle. So many important events that had contributed to football's legend had taken place in this stadium. When I conjure up images of Wembley, which was opened in 1923, my love of history and football come together. I think of the Twin Towers, a remarkable symbol of imperial architecture, built by architects John Simpson and Maxwell Ayrton; of the humiliating defeat of the English 'masters' by Hungary's 'magicians' in 1953, the result causing an earthquake in international football. Wembley was also the venue for two significant home successes: England's victory in the 1966 World Cup and the 1968 European Cup victory of Manchester United, coached by Matt Busby and featuring the inimitable George Best. As far as Eric was concerned, thoughts of Wembley sent me straight back to the 1994 Cup Final when Man United had beaten Chelsea 4-0, the King scoring two penalties.

As soon as I was inside the stadium, I started looking around at its obvious details – the architecture, the ceremonial entrance of the players and their pre-match attire, the match ticket – as well as more esoteric ones: the names of the supporters' associations, the number of security staff, the division of seating between the two sets of supporters. The excitement peaked first when the players came out to inspect the pitch and greet the fans. The outfits chosen by each team set the tone: Liverpool's players wore a three-button linen suit in ivory by the Italian designer Giorgio Armani, complemented with white shoes by another Italian designer, Gucci. It was Italian class with a Scouse touch. United's players went for sobriety, with a black suit by the German designer Hugo Boss. A few days before the final I'd gone with Eric to a shop in St Ann's Square to try his on, all the while repeating Paul Whitehouse and Mark Williams' unforgettable catchphrase from *The Fast Show!*, 'Ooh! Suits you, sir . . .'

I rather admired the Liverpool outfits: I thought the young midfielder Jamie Redknapp, with his dark glasses, would have been perfect in a Martin Scorsese film. From a distance, I could also see my friend Michael Thomas, a bag over his left shoulder, chatting to Andy Cole, the two of them graduates of the academy set-up at Arsenal.

Finally the moment arrived for the teams to come out. A Football Association official led the way. Behind him were the two managers, Roy Evans of Liverpool and Alex Ferguson of Manchester United, followed by their respective captains, John Barnes and Eric, with the other players in a line behind them. The two captains were in tracksuit tops and shorts, each holding a club pennant to exchange before kick-off. As is the custom, the players lined up in front of the VIP area and the captains introduced each teammate to a member of the royal family, in this case the Duchess of Kent, as well as to the FA's officials. United were set to play in their usual colours: red shirts, white shorts, black socks. Liverpool wore less familiar colours: green-and-white shirts, green shorts, white socks.

As so often on these very hyped occasions, the match was

unspectacular. United had the best opportunities to score. A pass from Ryan Giggs to David Beckham led to a great shot from the edge of the box by the young Englishman that was superbly saved by Liverpool goalkeeper David James, who diverted it behind for a corner. Later, Beckham picked out Eric for a volley that was once again saved well by James. The game was getting tighter and tighter, but United couldn't find a way through. I was worried about Liverpool's centre-forward Robbie Fowler, who was more than capable of scoring from nothing, but he seemed to be out of form. On the United side, I noticed that Andy Cole wasn't having his finest hour either, and he ended up being substituted. For his part, Eric was having a good game, playing a part in United's best openings and encouraging his teammates, but Roy Keane was their best player. He covered miles and miles on the famous Wembley turf, and was prominent in defence and attack.

Settled in block forty-four, row thirty-four, we spoke very little to each other, too caught up in the action and overawed by how much was at stake. The match was slowly heading towards a draw. Then, with four minutes to go, the ball was poorly cleared by the Liverpool defence following a corner taken by Becks and, from sixteen yards, Eric volleyed the ball through four players and into the corner of the Liverpool goal. We exploded with joy. The stands at the Manchester United end of the ground were ablaze with ecstasy. Fate had chosen its man: it was the King. Later, I would remember the words of Martin Tyler, commentating for Sky Sports: 'It comes for Cantona. *I don't believe it!* You just couldn't write the script.'

Manchester United had achieved something unique. It was

the first time a club had won a double double of the league and cup, United repeating the feat they'd managed only two years earlier. At the end of the match, all the players gathered around the King-captain to congratulate him and each other. We replayed the goal over and over, dozens of times, dissecting every phase of that decisive piece of action. A few minutes later we were exultant once again as captain Eric received the Cup from the smiling Duchess of Kent. A long night of celebration lay ahead.

On the way back to the hotel, we noticed that Gérard Gelas's mood was a little flat. He was both devastated and elated. It turned out that someone had stolen his match ticket when he was a few steps away from the turnstiles. 'I watched the match in a pub,' he told us. We all felt sorry for him. 'I didn't miss anything,' he added. 'What a great game!'

CHAPTER 16

Iconic Footballer

When I was studying at the University of Montpellier, I researched the process of 'starification' within the film world. While talent is essential to success, the public persona of an actor, whether real or imagined, can be just as decisive in their achieving leading roles, as well as raising their profile and status enormously both in the hearts of filmgoers and among those who aren't necessarily movie fans. In the same way, the Cantona legend was forged both on the pitch and through his persona, enigmatic and singular, off it. During his five-year career at Manchester United, Eric went from being something of an enigma to an iconic player, and finally to a true hero. The way we lived our daily lives and the way we interacted with the players or the fans we met contrasted with what people imagined of Eric the icon. Despite the fact that many people saw him as a star, Eric never saw himself as exceptional. He just wanted to strive for excellence by being constantly creative, unexpected and innovative.

The British press played a large part in the deification of

Manchester United's number 7, while the media as a whole contributed to the construction of a fascinating, multi-faceted character. Yet, at the same time, I spotted all kinds of completely inaccurate statements in articles and biographies about him. For instance, I've read in several books, and even ones you'd expect to be more reliable like *The Official Manchester United Illustrated Encyclopedia*, that Eric was born in Paris. I've seen articles talking about him coming from a bohemian family! He's described as an outstanding pianist, a writer from the age of five. He was said to have been married to a famous Italian model, to have owned a Rolls-Royce convertible filled with rose petals, and be the owner of a magnificent château in France ... At university, friends even asked me about his Gypsy family!

Eric intrigued and fascinated me because he never gave interviews, or at least very few. This deficit undoubtedly fostered this imaginary version of him. Eric spoke to the media a few times in his early days, but between 1995 and 1997 his relationship with the press became almost non-existent. 'I don't expect a journalist to tell me that I had a good or bad game,' he told me. 'I'm hard enough on myself to be a perfect critic of my performances. And, to tell the truth, I think journalists need us footballers more than the other way around. I don't like talking about myself – it's pointless. I prefer to talk about my movement, my passes, my interactions with a teammate who's scored a beautiful goal rather than talking about myself.'

We had very little, if any, contact with English or French journalists. Several times I was asked to facilitate an interview with Eric or to provide information 'post-Selhurst Park', but I always refused, though I made an exception for my friend

Adam Brown, a sociologist at Manchester Metropolitan University, a Man United supporter and a member of an organisation that fought against racial discrimination, who approached me about an article entitled 'Marked Man' that appeared in the *Big Issue* in February 1995.

Eric never read anything written about him, and I didn't talk to him about what was said about him in the press. I knew and liked some journalists who had written excellent articles about him, but I never tried to act as an intermediary to arrange an interview. I liked the writing of Hugh McIlvanney in the *Sunday Times*, Ian Ridley in the *Guardian* and Jim White in the *Independent*. The last two took a serious interest in Eric's career, in each case without ever being able to interview Eric. In 1995 Ian Ridley published an extremely well-researched book entitled *Cantona: The Red and the Black*. In April 1995, Jim White wrote a remarkable article in the *Independent* magazine about the economic exploitation of Eric's image by Nike, Manchester United and the street traders around Old Trafford. Other articles, such as those written by Richard Kurt, an English academic with a perfect command of French and also a Manchester United supporter and Eric fanatic, who became a friend, enabled English-speaking readers to get to know the Frenchman in different ways. In association with the offbeat football magazine *Four Four Two*, in 1996 Richard published *Cantona*, an A to Z of Eric's sporting and intellectual journey featuring thematic entries as varied as 'Decisive Goals', 'Diego Maradona', 'Existentialism', 'Provincialism' and 'Rimbaud'.

In the months following his crucial goal at Wembley in the 1996 FA Cup Final, the King's image was exploited intensely. He no longer belonged solely to the world of football, but became a commercial commodity, both with and without his consent. The evidence of this transformation first became apparent in Manchester United's official publications: the match programme *United Review*, the monthly magazine *Manchester United*, the annual report, and in *Cantona on Cantona*, the book about Eric that was written by the journalist Alex Fynn.

In September 1996, Eric was featured on the cover of *Manchester United* for the first time. The issue carried the subtitle 'Official Magazine of the Double Double Winners' and, further down the cover, claimed the distinction of being Britain's bestselling sports monthly. It featured a long and exclusive interview with Eric by James Freedman, who founded the magazine in 1993, originally as *United Magazine*. The interview covered most of Eric's sporting career: the French national team, the Premier League, the European Cup, the Wembley goal, his relationship with the press, his style of play and his post-retirement plans. The most striking aspects of the article, which ran to six pages, were the photographs in which Eric posed as though a supermodel, and another picture showing him returning to Marseille, surrounded by lots of children. The mass of Man Utd fans around the world would have relished these little-known facets of the King. I was dying to talk to him about the photo shoot around Marseille.

Eric told me he had enjoyed the time with the children. He has always loved kids, '*les minots*' ('the little ones'), as he calls them. He has the qualities of an educator and trainer: children seemed fascinated and awed by him. I accompanied him on the first day of his 120 hours of community service coaching kids, and can still recall the faces of the youngsters that day. When he spoke to the children, who were aged between nine and eleven, they looked at him as if he were a superhero: they listened attentively and applied themselves fully to every task. They seemed determined to excel in whatever exercise he set them. These scenes of children meeting their idol were fascinating to behold. After shaking Eric's hand, one child burst into tears, crying that he had met his 'god'.

The press had crowded onto this peaceful hillside in Salford. Those journalists barred from entering had realised they could get photos of 'Coach Cantona's' training session by standing on car roofs, snapping away as he taught the basics of football to kids drawn from around Salford. Eric took the role seriously, giving bits of advice and encouraging them no matter whether they got the exercises right or wrong. The sessions were serious but very good fun. 'I'm going to ask him how to take a penalty,' I heard one child say to his friend: 'he's never missed one.' Another confided to me that he was a City fan and asked if Eric would take offence if he found out. Then, at the end of the sessions, came the most eagerly awaited moment, as Eric signed autographs. Every kid wanted to remember the day by getting the King's signature. I remember one kid crying with joy after he'd got an autographed photo.

Elsewhere in Manchester we often met kids who'd surprise us with their audacity and repartee. One day, a shaven-headed teenager with a very strong Mancunian accent chased us to the entrance of the Cornerhouse, and we were surprised when he called out: 'Eric, you're the best. And you have to keep crushing City because I make a lot of money winning all my bets!' Then he went on his way singing, 'We'll drink, a drink, a drink to Eric the King . . .'

*

Eric featured either overtly or implicitly in every issue of the *United Review*. 'It goes without saying that Eric Cantona was the most popular player last season,' I read in one article, 'with our members who voted for him in the "Sir Matt Busby Player of the Year" telephone voting system. In fact, Eric was so far ahead that he received almost twice as many votes as his closest rival, Ryan Giggs.'

Marquee ads also used to take advantage of the King's popularity. I noticed, for example, the slogan 'Ooh R' that was used in an advertisement to announce the opening of the Red Café restaurant in the North Stand, which was scheduled to open in October 1996. Another advert for it read: 'Here, Eric!' A few days before the opening, it was hard to miss the interrogative 'Where's Eric? 2nd October' in the match-day programme and on huge billboards around the stadium.

Eric was clear-headed enough to realise the club was making extensive use of his image, but as long as he was kept informed and the usage was within the scope of his contract, it was acceptable. In the club's official merchandising catalogues, I spotted items specifically targeting the growth of 'Cantonamania': a football bearing Eric's signature, a duvet cover with his portrait, a metal plaque showing Eric holding up the Premier League trophy, a mug, a signed drawing in pencil, a video on Eric Cantona's career, a '100 per cent Eric Cantona' calendar. I was also aware of an explosion in Eric-related merchandise at the United ground and in the city, especially at the pop-up stalls around the centre, including in the Arndale arcade and outside Debenhams. These Cantona items were often produced by individuals, some of them Manchester United supporters. The bigger problem was businesses that profited greatly from the King's seductive selling power. In July 1996 Eric decided to take legal action to stop the unauthorised exploitation of his image. The case was an important one.

He announced through his lawyer that he would sue anyone who used his name and image without his permission, and that if this exploitation continued he was even prepared to give up football. I knew my friend well enough to know his words should be taken seriously. During one conversation, he told me that he was indeed deadly serious. The thought of the King departing prematurely got fans worried. Pete Boyle called me to ask if what was being said in the press was true. I told him it was spot on. The July 1996 issue of *United* magazine reported one fan's anxieties:

> I was really alarmed to read a newspaper report saying Eric Cantona will quit football if English companies continue misusing his name to sell rip-off merchandise. It can be difficult to tell at first glance what is or isn't official United merchandise. Of course, Eric is at the height of his fame following his magnificent efforts this season, and thousands of United fans want to pay homage to our hero. Equally, unscrupulous manufacturers are eager to jump on the bandwagon.

My university friends, especially those who specialised in sports law, were appalled by this abusive commercialisation, and urged me to encourage Eric in his courageous stand. Finally, he got what he wanted. *United* ran an insert in their August issue announcing a decision that lots of fans had been waiting for:

Eric Cantona has won a high court battle to stop a wine company using his name. The Cheshire-based firm had included the United club crest and a Cantona No. 7 shirt on the labels of some of its bottles, without permission. Eric hopes that this will be the last time he has to take unofficial traders to task for abusing his good name just to sell some shoddy product.

Eric was a household name not only locally, but also nationally. His name even started to figure among the most popular choices for baby boys: a new and unusual level of fame for a footballer.

The proliferation of products featuring Eric's face or a real or invented quote were indicators of his growing fame. Through these incredibly diverse products, I was able to measure the degree of celebrity Eric had attained: he appeared on jerseys, fanzine covers, T-shirts, plates, mugs, pens, bed sheets, key rings, cushions, wallpaper, magnets, walls in inner city areas, silk-screen artwork, paper shop doorways, sports shops, and was even turned into a garden gnome. I found his name on public benches, bus seats, inside public toilets ... The King was inescapable. Cantona the icon became a definitive part of popular culture. England's footballing world had created its idol and everyone was clamouring for him. When the name Eric was mentioned, a great many people would think of the *Frenchy*.

I delighted in keeping an eye out for these products, especially those that boasted the barbs directed by Manchester United fans at Liverpool and Manchester City supporters. Over the years, I spotted some very funny and creative examples. The logos of famous brands were hijacked in order to pay reverence to the King: *Genius* replaced Guinness, *Cantona* was depicted using Coca-Cola, Cadbury's and Carlsberg's graphics; Budweiser's 'King of Beers' was replaced by 'King of Football'; the slogan of local beer Boddingtons became 'Cantona, the Cream of Manchester'. All manner of mockery was directed at rival fans. Eric's image was used to ridicule Manchester City fans: 'Eric, the King of Manchester'; 'God is red in Manchester'; 'Where is Maine Road on Earth?'; 'Oh, no, he's back'; 'Eric: the King of Manchester City'; 'Eric: the Light of the City' . . . The mockery was also dished out to Liverpool fans. Both the city's symbols and the Beatles' songs were adapted to goad the club's supporters: 'Mercy, mercy, Eric's back'; 'We'll never win again'; 'Liverpoor': 'Eric in the sky with trophies'; 'Here comes the King' . . . I also remember seeing Eric's trademark phrases, the most famous of which was certainly the one he uttered in the 1995 press conference after his court case: 'When seagulls follow the trawler, it is because they think sardines will be thrown into the sea.' I didn't have the slightest idea what he was going to say that day – we hadn't discussed what he was planning to say – but as it turned out, he pulled off a major media coup, as all the journalists present pondered the meaning of this enigmatic statement as much as they did the verdict. Eric never revealed the mystery.

The iconic Cantona also became a huge success story during his Manchester United years for the sports equipment manufacturer Nike. After signing with the American brand in the early 1990s, he became one of its most prominent figureheads. Several advertising campaigns illustrate how the brand managed to exploit both sides of his image as genius and bad boy. In early May 1994, ten days before the FA

Cup Final and a few days after Eric had been voted player of the year by his professional peers, Nike launched a major campaign in the British and French press. It had a humorous and very offbeat tone, very innovative for the time and a far cry from the classic sports ads. The following chronology appeared in an ad in *L'Équipe*:

1992: Eric Cantona goes to Leeds United. Leeds United win the Championship.

1993: Eric Cantona goes to Manchester United. Manchester United win the Championship.

1994: Eric Cantona stays at Manchester United. Manchester United win the Championship.

1995: Eric Cantona goes to the Little Sisters of the Poor. The Sisters win the Championship.

1996: Eric Cantona goes fishing. The Association of Fly Fishers wins the Championship.

1997: Eric goes to the Louvre. The Mona Lisa wins the Championship.

Nike's intention was to cross cultural genres (football, classical art, street art, caricature, cinema), and Eric was pleased by the way they did it. His artistic sensibilities had found a powerful echo in Nike's advertising campaigns. The period from 1995 to 1997 was the most prolific in terms of advertisements that made an impression on a whole generation. Thanks to United's victories (the league and cup titles), controversies (his ban) and individual performances (player of the season awards), Eric became one of Nike's best ambassadors. One particular advert saw his fame explode: ''66 was a great year for English football. Eric was born'. It appeared in 1996.

I shared my enthusiasm for it with Eric, who reminded me that one of the reasons he had signed with Nike was their creativity. The ad appeared on 4m × 3m billboards around the stadium and on some of the city's main streets. I also remember a giant image of him appearing on the front of a building near the Museum of Science and Industry: his face was stretched about five storeys high. When we drove by it one day I was really taken aback. 'Wow! Have you seen your Nike ad? It's amazing! It must be weird to see your face so large.'

'That's the first time I've seen myself that big!' Eric replied. 'But it's beautiful! I really like things that are over the top like that. The people at Nike are artists!' Eric always seemed happy with the tone and impact of Nike's advertising campaigns. The commercials they made were also a big hit with the public.

Nineteen ninety-six was a turning point. Two commercials with Nike and the Japanese electronics company Sharp elevated Eric into a new realm as a sporting idol and flamboyant actor wonderfully capable of self-deprecation. One commercial featured an extraordinary football match, with a close-up of Eric muttering 'Goodbye!' as he pulled up the collar of his shirt. It was a great moment in the sports advertising of the 1990s. When he returned from the shoot he told me about some of the scenes. I was hugely impressed by all aspects of it: the selection of players, including Brazil's Ronaldo, Italy's Paolo Maldini, Portugal's Figo, Sweden's Tomas Brolin, England's Ian Wright, Holland's Patrick Kluivert; the shoot's location in an ancient theatre in Tunisia; the violence of some of the scenes; the director ... I didn't say so to Eric, but I was extremely proud and happy with the status he was given in relation to the other players. The implication was clear: he was the leader of the group. The people at Nike had chosen Eric as the star. It was a great mark of respect, because these were players with staggering records. Maldini was the best full-back of the time and had won several Champions League titles; Figo had won titles with Barça and then Real Madrid; Kluivert was a brilliant young centre-forward for Ajax and a recent winner of the Champions League. Eric was now being promoted by Nike's executives as nothing less than the embodiment of a certain vision of football.

Another advert further revealed a new talent: Eric's acting skills. It was a long – two minutes! – commercial for the Japanese household appliances and electronics company Sharp, Manchester United's principal sponsor. The main theme of the ad was self-deprecation. Eric Cantona made fun of Eric Cantona by referring to seagulls. The filming took place in France, in Finistère, at Cap Sizun, Plogoff, Esquibien and at the Raoulic lighthouse in Audienne, to be precise. Eric was dressed as a fisherman, first on the deck of a trawler, then below decks with the boat caught in the waves of a storm, dispensing his expertise on sardines. The ad was a masterpiece of humour, futility and irony. He talked about sardines, seagulls, fish, the sea, freedom ... and there was almost no reference to football. It revealed a side to him the general public was unaware of: his talent for self-mockery. Eric the actor took the place of Eric the footballer.

Eric invited me to his house in Prestbury for a preview. 'Sit down and watch this,' he told me. 'You'll really like it.' He put the video tape into the VCR and I watched it once, twice, three times, four times. I couldn't believe it: the writing, the production standards, the locations, and, above all, Eric's performance.

I looked at him. 'It's great! I love it! It's *really* great! What I like is the lightness of tone – it's crazy. But who wrote the script? It's really good. Plus, what I really like is that people will see you don't take yourself too seriously. It's very funny.' Eric just smiled.

On Tuesday, 15 April 1997, the local artist Michael Browne's monumental work *The Art of the Game* was unveiled inside Manchester Art Gallery. The huge 3m x 2m painting was inspired by *The Resurrection* by the Italian Renaissance painter Piero della Francesca. In Michael Browne's composition, Eric occupies a central, majestic position, facing the viewer, holding a banner similar to the Cross of St George. Below him are some of Manchester United's promising young players: David Beckham, the Neville brothers and Nicky Butt. Manager Alex Ferguson appears in the background looking patriarchal as he sits in a chariot, his pose inspired by a painting by Andrea Mantegna depicting Julius Caesar's triumphant return to Rome after a victorious campaign.

When it was first presented to the general public, the painting made an immediate impression. The Anglican Church cried blasphemy, although the Bishop of Manchester, the Right Reverend Christopher Mayfield, who appreciated the artist's offbeat approach, told *The Times*, 'This is a humorous painting which should be taken at face value.' The press focused on the almost Christ-like representation of the team's captain, while the public recognised the charisma of a personality who had been transformed into an idol.

Eric, his son Raphaël and I went to see the painting a few

days after the opening to avoid the crowds, and especially the journalists. We were happy with Michael's work because we were actually the first to have seen it taking shape. For several months we'd been following its creation as Michael worked on it. Although Michael did a lot of the work using photographs, Eric did pose for him, without the slightest hint of annoyance. Michael would ask him to sit down, stand up, show him his hands, reveal his torso, stand in profile, stare at him, look to the right and to the left ... As the days passed, we got the measure of each other, got to know and like each other, and later became firm friends. Knowing the demands of painting, Eric had a high regard for the artist. We were both impressed by Mike's patience and application. Eric and Mike discussed art in general, their respective tastes, their artistic sensibilities, their passion for football. Eric loved Mike's brush strokes, and I was amazed at how much time Mike spent looking at the painting, touching and re-touching. We used to joke that Mike would only finish the work when we'd left England, as it seemed he spent more time looking at his work than adding to it.

Mike seemed happy that we came so often. We'd have a laugh, and Mike would tell us about when he'd lived in Moss Side, one of the city's rougher neighbourhoods, about London, where he'd studied painting at the Chelsea School of Art, about his first exhibition at the age of nineteen, about meeting the Italian tenor Luciano Pavarotti. Gradually he and I became close friends and began to meet socially. I got to know his family and friends, and he used to come round for dinner. At weekends we'd meet for a drink in town, and Mike and his partner would show me their salsa dancing skills at La Tasca on Deansgate. We'd also meet up regularly to play football in different Soccer Domes. Subsequently he asked me to be godfather to his son, Junior.

The Art of the Game became Mike's masterpiece, and is now one of the most emblematic representations of Eric's iconic status in the England of the 1990s as a hero of the times. In 2000, it was selected and exhibited at the National Portrait Gallery in London as one of the defining paintings of the twentieth century.

We were in a bar opposite House of Fraser when Eric told me that he had an appointment with some people from Madame Tussauds, the London waxwork museum, to take his handprints. We headed off to the Jarvis Piccadilly Hotel nearby where the final touches were going to be made to Eric's waxwork. I watched the delicate task of getting prints of his hands: another sign of his consecration. Alongside Mel Gibson and Naomi Campbell, Eric Cantona took his place at Madame Tussauds in 1996. Truly he had conquered England.

CHAPTER 17

Au Revoir

The final image I have of that fabulous end to the 1995/96 season is of a souvenir of the FA Cup Final. I'd asked Eric if he could provide a memento for the European football exhibition I was working on at the People's History Museum in Manchester. He gave me his shirt from that final.

It had considerable historical value for several reasons. With their logos of betting company Littlewoods the sleeves illustrated the rapidly increasing importance of the business end of football – their sponsorship of the Cup had begun with the 1994 final. The shirt was also made in England, increasingly rare now that globalisation was impacting on all sectors of the sports equipment market. Much of the manufacturing had shifted to Asia, notably China, Thailand and Indonesia, but Manchester United stood out because their kit was still supplied by a local equipment manufacturer, Umbro, founded in 1924 and based in the Cheshire town of Wilmslow. The club's crest also underlined the sense of tradition, of the club being a sporting institution with long-standing values. As had been the case since the 1960s, the crest bore the club's full title, Manchester United Football Club. Two years later, when the crest received its first redesign for more than three decades, the last two words disappeared, symbolising a fundamental transformation of the institution itself. Manchester United had become, as the cover slogan of an annual report from the 2000s emphasised: *More Than a Club*. On the front of the shirt was embroidered 'FA Cup Final 1996'; on the back was 'Cantona' and the number '7'. I was very happy with this piece of history.

'You know,' said Eric, when he handed it over to me, 'you've never asked me for a shirt as long as we've known each other, and I'm not sure if there's even a photo of the two of us together.'

'True. But, I guess, in the same way, you don't always have photographs taken with your parents, or ask for things from people who've already given you so much.'

Eric said nothing; just smiled at me as we parted.

Strange as it might seem, I never felt the urge to ask for anything – jersey, tracksuit, boots, shin guards – from my footballing brothers, from Eric or from any of my other friends who were players. I had no interest in objects for their celebrity attachment, because these people were an everyday part of my life. I interacted with them in a very ordinary way. I never dreamed of being a footballer or a star: I was rather shy, and preferred to stay out of the limelight. My credo was: Let people know me for who I am, and not for who I know. I also had a personal motto: Your life with the King is extraordinary, but your everyday life is ordinary. Throughout my years in Manchester I repeated this to myself frequently.

At the same time, I had one friend who was always on the look-out for 'holy' items: Gary King. He collected all sorts of

Eric-related memorabilia, anything and everything, in fact: the bottle of champagne Eric had been given when he'd been selected as man of the match, Manchester United and France team shirts, Manchester United players' shirts, merchandise with Eric's signature on it, including caps, posters, T-shirts, match tickets, programmes ... The three of us used to joke that Gary would one day build a Cantona museum. Gary never stopped buying, collecting and preserving. He was, first and foremost, an Eric fan, always ready to drive hundreds of miles to see Eric play in a United or a France shirt. We respected and appreciated his dedication and loyalty. But I never felt the need to own anything of Eric's as a confirmation of our strong bond. Material considerations never came into our friendship. For me, all that mattered was being able to talk football with him, share our passion for music, chat about cinema, literature, the 1,001 projects planned by his brother Joël, reminisce about our friends from Auxerre, and simply have a good time together in Manchester.

Anne and I decided to spend the summer of 1996 in Manchester. A reduction in the rent over the holiday period presented us with a good reason to get to know the surrounding region a little better. We travelled around the north, to Bolton, Glasgow, Liverpool, Preston, Lancaster, Sheffield and York, and I used the time to dig up the history of the local clubs in their libraries.

The new football season began on 11 August with the traditional Charity Shield match at Wembley, played in glorious sunshine, and featuring the previous season's champions, Manchester United, against the runners-up, Newcastle United, as the Red Devils had also won the FA Cup, of course. As was the case with many of Manchester United's away games, I decided to watch the game in a city centre pub known to be red. The place was packed, the atmosphere excellent, and the terrace outside was also full of fans enjoying the summer heat.

The Red Devils crushed Newcastle, winning 4-0 at a canter. Eric opened the scoring in the twenty-fourth minute, showing great composure after a wonderful pass from David Beckham, just a few minutes after he'd been thwarted in a one-on-one with Czech goalkeeper Pavel Srníček. But it was David Beckham who really impressed me. He was now having a more significant impact on the team, his confidence growing all the time. His vision, the accuracy of his passing and his stamina were becoming a great asset for United. His on-field relationship with Eric was developing nicely.

Eric liked 'Becks'. He also really admired the young mid-fielder for his application during training, the close attention that he paid to the team's leaders, the precision of his passing and his teamwork. 'All the youngsters we have at United listen to the experienced players like Steve Bruce and Brian McClair,' Eric told me. 'He watches me because he wants to learn and progress. He may not give the impression of being a hard worker, but he definitely is. He works a lot on his free-kicks in training, and I can tell you he can strike the ball as well as almost anyone in the league. You can see how far he runs, too. He also plays the game in the right way, never cheats, and he does a lot of work for the team. The press often has a go at him because he pays so much attention to his looks, but that's normal – he's young, and he's a handsome guy. On the pitch, he's a great player. In Paul Scholes, Nicky Butt and David Beckham, United undoubtedly have three of the best youngsters in the Premier League.'

The Charity Shield provided a demonstration of the qualities of this promising new generation. Nicky Butt and David Beckham each scored a superb goal as the season got off to a good start for United. Eric felt particularly comfortable within this set-up that provided the team's youngsters with increasingly important roles. I could tell he was very happy with these budding stars from the way he celebrated with them after a goal, from his complimentary remarks about Paul Scholes and David Beckham, and from the pleasure he gained from 'guiding' such a promising generation of players. I left the pub feeling that it would be another great season. Manchester United's 'winning machine' looked set to dominate the domestic competitions again, and I was confident they would excel in the Champions League as well, although I had some reservations. Winning this was now Manchester United's major objective, and to some extent it was Eric's too.

I felt Manchester United could have a great season by drawing on the talent of Roy Keane and Ryan Giggs, the experience of Peter Schmeichel, Denis Irwin and Eric, their new signings (Karel Poborsky, Jordi Cruyff, Ronny Johnsen) and the talented young players. I saw Eric during the week after the Charity Shield victory and he not only seemed to be in tremendous shape but also told me that the Champions League would offer an ideal measure of the progress United had made. 'You'll see, Claudio: we'll do something good in the Champions League. I don't know why, but I just sense it. We've got a good team.' Then, however, he qualified his words a little. 'We're maybe missing one or two big international players to be really strong on the European stage . . .'

The presence of Dutch (Jordi Cruyff, Raimond van der Gouw), Norwegian (Ole Gunnar Solskjaer, Ronny Johnsen) and Czech players (Karel Poborsky) provided the United squad with a more continental flavour. I got the feeling that a new era was taking shape. But was this down to Manchester United wanting to demonstrate that their focus was now definitely on success in Europe? Or was it simply a result of the Bosman ruling, and the repercussions it had had in allowing the unlimited recruitment of players from the European Community?

The Premier League campaign kicked off on Saturday, 17 August. Man United met Wimbledon at Selhurst Park. Any team that took on the club nicknamed the Crazy Gang knew it was in for a tricky afternoon. That Eric was returning to the scene of his nightmare experience against Crystal Palace hadn't really occurred to me: what had happened on 25 January 1995 was long forgotten, and put even further out of mind when, in front of 25,786 fans, United completely dominated Wimbledon as they won 3-0.

I particularly remember two things about the game. It was Jordi Cruyff's first match following his move from Barcelona, and I'd seen how difficult the first training sessions at United had been for him: some of the players had wanted to show him how intense English football was by trying to rough him up. But Jordi had quickly adapted to the English mentality. Eric introduced me to him and we quickly struck up a friendship. He invited Anne and me over, and she also got on well with his girlfriend. He knew a few French words, which is always a nice touch, and I liked listening to him talk about Barcelona, a city I'd visited when I was in secondary school, and especially about the Camp Nou stadium and the atmosphere inside it on match days, about Iniesta and Xavi, two players who were graduates of the club's La Masia training centre, about the Barça–Real Madrid rivalry, the Sagrada Familia cathedral, the Parc Güel, and the El Corte Inglés department store.

The other memory of that first league match of the season was the extraordinary goal David Beckham scored in the last few minutes. After scoring the first goal and getting a yellow card, Eric had been substituted by Alex Ferguson, so he was watching from the bench when the young Englishman scored a goal from just inside his own half. He enthused about the skill that had beaten Wimbledon keeper Neil Sullivan, who was clearly surprised by Beckham's audacity. The TV commentator described it as a phenomenal goal, and it proved a pivotal point for this talented young player, who began to receive a lot more attention.

United's season continued in the same brilliant vein. In early September, they travelled to Elland Road to take on Leeds United in the fifth game of the league campaign. I was determined to see the game without letting Eric know: I was afraid he would talk me out of going because of the antagonism between the two teams. I asked a friend from Manchester University who was a Leeds supporter and also an Eric fan to get me a ticket, and he got me a great seat in among the Leeds fans. As I made my way to the ground, dressed in an outfit that didn't feature a stitch of red to avoid any indication of allegiance to the Red Devils, I couldn't stop myself smiling at the T-shirts on sale that mocked Eric. The Leeds fans were very clever and witty in expressing their hatred of Man United and Eric in particular.

I found the situation inside the ground fascinating on what was a beautiful afternoon. From a distance I was able to watch the brave Man United supporters who had dared to make the trip across the Pennines. All around me the fans were singing, clapping, laughing and in some cases insulting the Man United fans. I loved those moments when you can see an overwhelming passion for football in the eyes of every fan, and especially for their own club. I was convinced that these fans who now hated Eric had adored him four years ago when he'd been a Leeds player.

Elland Road was buzzing. It was packed, with 39,694 spectators all but filling the ground's capacity, all of them hoping to see their team humiliate their rivals and win this War of the Roses. When the stadium announcer read out the name Cantona there were more whistles and shouts of hatred directed at my friend than I'd heard at any of the Manchester United away games I'd previously attended. To some of the Leeds fans he was a demon, a traitor, the devil in red. Elland Road still hadn't come to terms with Eric leaving for the club they hated above all others. Just four years earlier, celebrating Leeds's capture of the League Championship title, they'd adored him and sung, 'I don't know why, but I love you.' Now he was despised. It gave the match a peculiar edge. How could anyone love and then hate an idol?

Eric never felt any particular pressure in the run-up to games against Leeds, and it soon became clear that the rest of the team were in a good groove too, as Manchester United made it a one-sided contest. They opened the scoring in the third minute. Following a corner, Ronny Johnsen shot at goal, a defender tried to clear but, unfortunately for Leeds, the ball rebounded off the back of goalkeeper Nigel Martyn and into the net. While Man United fans jumped for joy, the Leeds fans were stunned by the own goal. A few minutes later, a move between Eric and Ryan Giggs led to the

Welshman passing the ball to Denis Irwin, who ran into the box and passed to Jordi Cruyff, who was being held by a defender. Penalty.

As always, Eric was designated to take it. He carefully put the ball down, walked back a few metres, then ran up in his usual style. The keeper was beaten, sent the wrong way – but the ball ended up going wide of the post! Eric had missed a penalty in a Premier League match for only the second time – the first had been against Blackburn Rovers the previous season. The unimaginable had happened, right before my eyes! There was an explosion of joy and mockery among the Leeds fans on three sides of the ground, even though their team was losing. It was a strange moment, and I wondered if there would be any more surprises.

Early in the second half, a Karel Poborsky run led to an opening for Nicky Butt, who put Man United two ahead. In the seventy-sixth minute, a lightning counter-attack led by Beckham and Eric led to Poborsky scoring a third goal. In the last minute, after a brilliant cross from Beckham, Eric closed the game out by scoring a beautiful goal with the outside of his right foot. Leeds had been humiliated.

The match ended without incident and I quietly headed for the exit, not really paying attention to the downcast expressions of the Leeds fans, but relishing from afar the happiness at the Man United end, where the fans were forced to stay in the stand for a few minutes before being escorted by mounted police to the railway station. United had produced a performance worthy of the champions. I was also happy to have made a first visit to Elland Road, the ground where Eric had first captured the hearts of thousands of English fans.

The next few games went quite well, as United's unbeaten

run continued. However, between 20 October and 2 November I experienced something totally unprecedented in the time I'd been watching Eric at Man United: a run of three straight defeats. The setbacks occurred in the north, the south and then at home, and it all felt very strange.

The first defeat was to Newcastle at St James' Park, where United suffered a real beating, losing 5-0. I watched the highlights on *Match of the Day* speechless, amazed at the passivity of the United players as Newcastle attacked. The next day I met Eric. 'In a long season, you can't be a hundred per cent in every game,' was his perspective on it. I agreed, though I was aware that the Man United team was looking less dominant than in the past. Eric's performance had also intrigued me a little, because for the first time he appeared to me to be off his game. I felt this was largely down to a Newcastle team determined to avenge the rivals who had dominated them in recent seasons. David Ginola, Alan Shearer and Peter Beardsley had been the architects in the Magpies' sparkling victory.

Six days later, United suffered a second heavy defeat, this time at Southampton. The Saints thrashed the Red Devils 6-3. Wearing blue and white shirts bearing the names of the club's historic players, United were unable to blunt the Southampton attack, in which the excellent Eyal Berkovic stood out, the Israeli striker taking the United defence apart to score two wonderful goals. On the upside, Eric looked much more himself, and was involved in United's dangerous moves and their goals. Even so, a year on from the famous defeat caused by the 'oddly designed shirts', United had lost again at the Dell, and this time there were no extenuating circumstances. The following Saturday, in front of 55,198 fans at Old Trafford, the Dutch manager Ruud Gullit's Chelsea team stunned Manchester United, winning 2-1. After the match, we didn't talk much about the game when we went into town for dinner, but the mood was still quite upbeat. 'We didn't play well today, but the championship is very long and we always finish very strongly,' Eric reassured me. 'I'm not worried.' I was thinking much the same thing: Manchester United had lost three games, but there were still thirty or so to play before the end of the season. There was still plenty of reason for optimism.

The arrival of winter brought with it a shift in United's fortunes, as well as a sumptuous goal to celebrate. Just before Christmas, United played Sunderland, and Eric was reunited with an old teammate, goalkeeper Lionel Perez: they had played together in France at Nîmes Olympique. Before the kick-off, Eric approached him to shake hands but, incredibly, Perez looked away and snubbed this courteous gesture. Though surprised, Eric didn't react, and walked back towards the centre circle.

United easily won 5-0, and Eric scored a brilliant goal. It began with a dribble, then a pass to Brian 'Choccy' McClair. Eric got a return pass and delivered a masterful lob from the edge of the box that surprised Perez. His celebration of the goal was just as memorable. Head held high, collar raised, Eric spun slowly around, eyeing the fans in the stands, then raised his arms ... Dazzling. Everyone in the Family Stand was bowled over by this moment of genius, and we all stood up to applaud his class. For a long time afterwards, the fans sang their songs to the glory of the King. Eric's reaction to the goal was as unexpected as Lionel Perez's behaviour before kick-off.

United had regained the momentum needed to challenge for the title. Eric was proving very effective at scoring crucial goals and in playing the role of Alex Ferguson's conduit on the pitch. During games, I often noticed him approaching the United bench to receive instructions from the manager. The leader who had hitherto spoken very little had now become a leader in both gestures and words, fully assuming his role as captain. Eric was listened to and respected by his teammates and feared by opponents. At some home games, I would stand in the tunnel near the exit from the clubhouse and watch the other team's players as Eric appeared with his captain's armband on his right arm. The awe that some of them felt before walking onto the pitch at Old Trafford was plain to see.

At the end of January, United moved to the top of the league table and maintained that position to the end of season, defending their Premier League title. But their progress wasn't as serene in the Champions League. United's campaign started in September with a 1-0 defeat at the Stadio Delle Alpi against Juventus of Turin, whose team featured plenty of household names, notably Zinedine Zidane and the Croatian Alen Boksic, who played for Olympique de Marseille with my brother Basile. Eric had played in a new position of centre-forward, but the experiment didn't work at all. I preferred to see him in a hybrid role as a playmaker and striker.

'We lacked experience,' was Eric's verdict. 'The Champions League is very different. It's good for the youngsters to see how demanding these European games are, especially against a team like Juventus.' In the return match at Old Trafford in late November, the Italians won again by the same score.

A few days before the match, the relationship between Eric and Didier Deschamps, which had been strained for a few years, partly as a result of critical comments made about Eric by some of France's players, worsened even further as a consequence of a comment Eric made to the press about the positional and footballing qualities of the France and Juventus defensive midfielder. 'Deschamps?' Cantona had said. 'He gets by because he gives a hundred per cent of himself, but he'll always be a water-carrier. Players like that are to be found on every street corner.'

Deschamps had responded by return: 'First of all, you need water-carriers, and if Eric wants to judge others, he can do what he wants. Now, I'm not so sure that, as he says, there are players on every corner who have won the Champions League twice.' The war of words was on and has never ended.

After the game, we decided to go for a drink at the Mottram Hall Hotel, not far from where Eric lived. We'd been sitting at the bar for a few minutes when we saw the Juventus team arrive. Both they and we – the three Cantona brothers, some friends and me – were surprised to see each other. Zidane was the only one to offer any sign of friendliness, offering us a smile and giving a friendly wink to Eric, his fellow *Marseillais*.

Those two defeats didn't prevent United from reaching the semi-final of the Champions League, though. After fine victories over Austria's SK Rapid, Turkey's Fenerbahçe and Portugal's FC Porto, United were just one step away from the final of Europe's most coveted competition, facing Germany's Borussia Dortmund. Since we'd been kids, we'd been drawn to the big European Cup nights, lost in admiration for the players in the legendary teams: Real Madrid, FC Barcelona,

Bayern Munich, Benfica, Liverpool, Juventus, Dynamo Kiev, Red Star Belgrade, AS Saint Etienne, Anderlecht ... We loved European Cup matches, and I knew during that 1996/97 season that Eric was particularly preoccupied with Europe's most prestigious tournament. That isn't to say he was obsessed with it, but he wanted that Champions League trophy in Manchester United's trophy cabinet. Conquering Europe after winning multiple Premier League titles was both a personal and a collective ambition.

The first leg the Germans won by the narrowest of margins: 1-0. Several players, including Eric, had had opportunities to score, but they'd all been passed up. Every member of the United staff was bewildered by the number of chances they'd missed, but they were optimistic for the return match. 'We had a lot of chances in Dortmund,' Eric told me. 'I'm sure we'll create just as many chances to score. The crowd will really get behind us. We're going to win.'

The second leg at Old Trafford proved to be one of extreme psychological intensity. In the week leading up to it, Eric and I never spoke about the game directly, but I could sense the high expectations he had for it. The things we did talk about offered a clue to how much victory in the Champions League was on his mind: players like Romario, Ronaldo, Zinedine Zidane, Patrick Kluivert, Luis Figo, Laurent Blanc, Matthias Sammer – all of whom had shone in this elite competition. 'If you had a Romario, a Zidane, a Laurent Blanc, together with some youngsters like Keane, Giggs, Scholes and Beckham, I'm sure you'd go a long way in the Champions League,' Eric told me one evening. 'A few years ago I spoke to the boss about the possibility of getting Lolo [Laurent Blanc] or Zidane – they were available on the transfer market – but I don't think he was too keen. He had other plans for developing the team. I think he's got a lot of faith in the youngsters, but I'm convinced they would improve much more quickly if they were playing with great players.' Eric's list of players looked like the perfect team. However, we all know that the league championship has immense prestige in England, and if it came to choosing between a win against old rivals Liverpool or beating the well-respected Juventus, I was pretty sure Alex Ferguson would prefer to see his team win against the Merseysiders.

All of Eric's entourage in the Family Stand were in a highly stressed state as kick-off against Dortmund neared. We were all caught up – perhaps too much so – in how high the stakes were. When I looked at Isabelle, I could see the deep anxiety in her face. As for me, instead of soaking up the pre-match atmosphere outside the ground as I usually did, I wanted to get to my seat as quickly as possible: I couldn't wait for the game to start. I was oblivious to the laughter of the fans on the way to Old Trafford; I didn't notice the smell of the onions, the fish and chips and the pork pies that used to delight me. Instead, I weaved quickly through the crowds, desperate to take my place in the stands, desperate to see United qualify for the final. There I cracked a few jokes with Isabelle to relieve the stress for a moment, but deep down I was racked by nerves. This match had taken on a staggering importance, to the point where it seemed to have become a turning point in Eric's career. It was a test not only of United's standing among the European greats, but also of his position among the best players on the continent.

A few minutes before the match got under way, we were all chatting as we always did, our conversation without nuance, our opinions on how it would pan out betraying our feelings, and therefore very subjective. We were playing the game out before it had even started. All of a sudden, sitting here in the Family Stand's comfortable seats, we were acting as though we were Man United players or members of the coaching staff. This game had changed us: we'd become strangers to ourselves, obsessed with a positive outcome – we couldn't imagine an unhappy ending. We'd forgotten that no spectator, no matter how sincere or passionate, has ever changed the course of a match by scoring a goal.

The match itself was one of complete frustration. The Germans opened the scoring in the eighth minute thanks to full-back Lars Ricken. United now needed to score at least three to qualify. The mission didn't seem insurmountable, but as the minutes passed there weren't any glimmers of hope. And yet still we believed in a miracle. Eric got a great chance from an Andy Cole cross, but the centre-back Kohler, although flat out on the ground, somehow managed to get a touch on the ball and send it away from the empty net. Then Eric had a second chance. Ole broke down the left, crossed, Cole deflected the ball to Eric, who cushioned it and shot. The ball appeared to hit the arm of a Dortmund player. Eric raised his arm for a penalty. We roared in protest. Even though we hadn't seen the incident clearly, we still bawled at the injustice. But the Swiss referee Urs Meier decided there hadn't been a hand involved.

As the match wore on, the anxiety levels continued to rise. Dortmund's Swiss striker Stéphane Chapuisat had a chance to score a second goal, but missed. At the other end, with just the keeper to beat, Gary Pallister rose to head a cross from Andy Cole and sent the ball wide. It was United's last chance: soon afterwards the referee blew his whistle. United had lost. They wouldn't be appearing in the final in Munich to enjoy a date with history. It would have been a nice tribute to the Busby Babes. Fate had decided this wasn't to be United's moment.

Eric got changed quickly, then spent a few moments at the clubhouse until the security staff signalled that his car was ready. He signed a few autographs and there were shouts of encouragement from supporters, and then we left the Theatre of Dreams in a hurry, feeling unfulfilled. In the car the frustration was palpable; disappointment hung heavy. 'The tie was decided in the first leg,' Eric said calmly. 'That's where we should have made the difference. That's where we should have won the game – we had the chances to win in Dortmund. Here, the stakes were too high for us. We need to get more experience, especially in the Champions League.'

He was visibly affected by the defeat, but not as devastated as he might have been. Without even telling him how we were feeling, he knew we were much sadder for him than we were for Manchester United. I kept my disappointment to myself; I was alone in a grief that wasn't my own, because it was Manchester United who had been defeated, not Eric. But I couldn't get the thought out of my head that this was a defeat for Eric's crazy ambition: to win the Champions League. The thought that it was just a football match didn't make me feel any better: the game was about more than just sport. For everyone close to him, Eric's success was a question of pride, of courage, of humility, a meaning given to life, a love of a city, a love of English football, a mad desire to link our lives to England forever, a desire to be loved, an appeal to the France that had let us go.

We returned to Old Trafford on Monday, 5 May, when 54,489 spectators came out in a show of loyalty. In the match programme I read Alex Ferguson's comments on the team's Champions League failure.

At the end, the question I wanted answering above all others came back loud and clear ... we are good enough to play at this level, and I promise you that next season we will be competing on even better terms. We have youth on our side in our team, and so many of them are going to get better that I have no doubts that we will be a force when we try again in Europe.

The game between United and Middlesbrough ended with a rather strange scoreline: 3–3. Ole's equaliser, with around fifteen minutes to go, saved United from another home defeat. But they were almost certain to win the title. The official coronation was set to take place on 11 May, when they were due to play West Ham at Old Trafford. And so it proved, as Ole and Jordi Cruyff helped United win the final league game in style and lift the FA Carling Premiership trophy.

After the match there was a festive feel. The dozens of photographers from the national and international press wanted a photo of the players and the whole coaching staff, and the exultation was evident on the faces of the players and Alex Ferguson's key assistants: assistant manager Brian Kidd, physio David Fevre and kit manager Albert Morgan. Eric had won another major trophy, his fourth league title with Man United in five years! Over the course of the season, he'd made more appearances than any other player (forty-nine games) and was second in the scoring chart (fourteen goals). He had continued to make his mark on the history of the club and of English football.

These statistics should have filled me with delight, but a few small details had made me rather subdued. The day after United had claimed the title, I scanned the celebratory pictures and noticed Eric's apparent restraint. In every photo he appeared in the background. When he lifted the impressive championship trophy towards the fans, his look was not one of unbridled happiness. Eric's expression was neutral: there was no evidence of heartfelt joy. I knew him well enough to suspect he was holding something back. To confirm my theory that there was something brewing, I compared these photos with those taken on the three other occasions when he'd lifted the league trophy. No doubt about it: in May 1997 there wasn't the same ebullience.

A few days before he went on holiday, Eric took part in a charity match with Manchester United in aid of David Busst, the Coventry footballer whose career had been cut short by a serious injury sustained in a match against United in April 1996. Later, we went to the Four Seasons. As we sat there, Eric looked me in the eye, put his right arm on my shoulder and told me, 'Claudio, I'm stopping. I've decided to quit football, but keep it to yourself. Not many people know yet.'

This was a shock, but at the same time I wasn't actually that surprised. I let him continue without interrupting: 'You know, when I told Ferguson, he was stunned. He told me to take a few days off. "You'll come back with a clearer head," he said. "The end of the season was painful with the defeat in the Champions League. Take some time off, spend it with your family. It's an important decision."'

As he spoke to me, Eric sounded tired, exhausted from years of playing football at the highest level. He seemed both deeply disappointed by the way the end of the season had played out and relieved to be ending his career after winning another prestigious title.

I had little to say to him, except that I was very happy to have had such an extraordinary time with him here in Manchester. 'You can be proud of what you have done here,' I told him. 'Thanks to you, the English have changed their view of foreign footballers, of French footballers.'

He didn't respond, and our conversation switched to other things. He asked me how I was getting on with my thesis, and how well I knew Barcelona, the city where he was probably going to settle with his family. We talked about an acquaintance from Auxerre, Miguel Pineda, who played for the Espanyol club in Barcelona, his grandparents' home city, which they'd fled after fighting against Franco. Eric said he planned to continue with his fledgling film career and would immerse himself in theatre, as well as help his brother Joël develop beach football.

Fundamentally, though, it was a sad evening. I thought of all the good times we'd shared since Auxerre, and also about the things that had led Eric to take this decision.

On Sunday, 18 May, at 12.30 p.m., a newsflash went out to the media warning of a press conference that was due to take place at Old Trafford at around 3 p.m. that same afternoon. Inside the Europa Suite, a grim-faced Manchester United chairman Martin Edwards, with Alex Ferguson sitting alongside, stated concisely: 'Good afternoon, ladies and gentlemen. Thank you for attending at such short notice. We have been asked to come along today so that we may announce that Eric

Cantona has indicated his wish to retire from football with immediate effect.' This was followed by a statement from Eric that Martin Edwards read out:

> I have played professional football for thirteen years, which is a long time. I now wish to do other things. I always planned to retire when I was at the top, and at Manchester United I have reached the pinnacle of my career. In the last four and a half years I have enjoyed my best football and a wonderful time. I have had a marvellous relationship with the manager, coach, staff and players and not least the fans. I wish Manchester United even more success in the future.

A part of a life was over. At the age of thirty, Eric Cantona was no longer a professional footballer.

The announcement caused shock waves in Manchester and beyond. I received lots of phone calls but decided to maintain my silence. The next day, I went to Old Trafford. Lots of fans were there, stunned by the news of the King's abdication. Most were wearing shirts with 'Cantona' and the number 7 on them. The emotion around the ground was palpable: I saw several people sobbing, as though we were in national mourning. I heard people asking each other why he had left, others suggesting reasons for his retirement. I was caught up in these feelings of grief myself. I saw a child crying and being comforted by his parents, a couple embracing in tears. Faced with this outpouring of grief, I didn't have the courage to stay and, in tears, I walked home.

On 18 August 1998, Eric returned to Old Trafford for a match commemorating the fortieth anniversary of the Munich Air Disaster. The game was an enticing one:

Manchester United vs Eric Cantona's European XI. Eric's team featured the likes of Jean-Pierre Papin, Laurent Blanc, Paul Gascoigne, Joël Cantona, William Prunier, Christophe Galtier and Bernard Ferrer. All the guests stayed at the Mottram Hall Hotel and we were happy to see each other again. On the morning of the match, a small game had been planned. I was playing in a team with Joël Cantona and French goalkeeper Pascal Olmeta against Eric's team. It was the friendliest of friendlies. After it, I dashed away to teach French at the Open University in one of Manchester Metropolitan University's campuses. Once the class was over, I headed for the ground for the 8 p.m. kick-off.

The fans had come out in droves to see their idol again. We were back in the Family Stand like the year before. There was one small surprise, as Eric's son Raphaël came onto the pitch holding his father's hand, but otherwise nothing had really changed. The ritual of a quick trip to the clubhouse before taking our seats had been maintained. Once we got there, the fans were singing 'Eric the King' as they had been doing all season. I could see the enthusiasm and joy on Peter Boyle's face as he sang the anthem once again in front of Eric the King.

The tribute proved to be a happy reunion between Eric and the Man United fans. The pre-game ceremony began with Mick Hucknall performing an a cappella version of Ella Fitzgerald's wonderful song 'Every Time We Say Goodbye'. I felt moved and joyful, the more so as events unfolded. Eric walked around the stadium with Raphaël, waving goodbye to the fans. The King had retaken his place in the hearts of the Red Devils, and would never be forgotten. He left for Barcelona the next day, but I remained in Manchester. My own story with Manchester United still had some time to run . . .

Epilogue

Nantes, 2003: my life as a student ended. I submitted my PhD on the history of English football, concentrating specifically on Manchester United and the city of Manchester. It was the culmination of a period of research lasting almost ten years, during which I'd talked to all kinds of people in the football world. I'd travelled to the grounds of elite clubs and those in lower divisions and burrowed through all sorts of esoteric archives. All the seconds, minutes, months and years I'd shared with Eric in Manchester were very much part of that long period of study. Now I was about to finish my student life a long way from my home in Manchester, at the University of Nantes, with an oral viva on my thesis before a jury of academics, and felt it was time.

The rules allowed for the student to be accompanied by an impartial observer of their choice, and I immediately thought of Eric, who was as well acquainted as anyone with my work. He made the trip from Barcelona, where he now lived, without hesitation. All those who had followed and supported my research were present: Anne, Basile, Roger, my sister-in-law Françoise (Roger's wife), even the former minister of sport, Roger Bambuck, who had approved my research grant. The viva went very well, the jury not only commending me on my presentation but also offering the further honour of listing my thesis

274

as among the best to have been produced on sport at an English university. Amid the formal congratulations from my family and friends, and their joshing, tears, relief and joy, Eric quietly said 'Bravo, Claudio', and smiled. 'Good work!' As we walked through the streets of Nantes to a restaurant to celebrate my doctorate in history, we fell to reminiscing about Manchester.

In 2004 I moved to Vincennes, near Paris. I found myself missing Manchester terribly. I was a Mancunian in Paris, and I had lost my bearings. I didn't even know which way to look before crossing the road, which for someone who had worked as a lollipop man near Maine Road was the final straw! I was surprised by how dry the weather was – such a difference from the north of England. I longed to hear English being spoken around me, to make me feel I was still in Rusholme, Moss Side, Victoria Park, Oxford Road. I used to go to the British Council library, and hung out in WH Smith on Rue Rivoli. I shopped at Marks & Spencer, wore my Clarks shoes all the time, listened to the Stone Roses. I got a real kick from watching over and over again all the second-hand comedy DVDs I'd bought – I relished those evenings with *The Fast Show, Little Britain, Absolutely Fabulous, That Peter Kay Thing* and *The Lenny Henry Show.* Instantly, I'd be transported back to my terrace house, and more precisely to my flowery sofa in Rawcliffe Street, M14.

Every Saturday at 3 p.m., especially, I was overcome with melancholy. Paris life seemed dull without the match-day buzz of my old street facing Manchester City's ground. I followed games on BBC Radio, but it couldn't compare with the noise and atmosphere of a live Premier League match. I had a new life and new routines, however, and in due course football and music became secondary pursuits. Eric and I kept in touch, but not to the same extent we had done in

Manchester. Every year there was a Christmas card, a phone call or two out of the blue, perhaps a hastily arranged meet-up when he came to Paris that helped us maintain our friendship.

Eventually I got used to France, but I didn't forget Manchester. As luck would have it, in 2007 Eric moved to Nogent-sur-Marne with his new wife, the actress Rachida Brakni, which meant he wasn't very far from where I lived. We still didn't see much of one another, though, because our lives were so busy. I was teaching history and sociology at the University of Evry and at a business school in Tours, and was then recruited to be scientific director at the National Museum of Sport. Anne and I also had our first son, Clément. Student life was in the distant past. Eric was very busy too with his various commitments in football, cinema and theatre. But when we did manage to get together, there was always plenty of laughter. That hadn't changed.

Eric never lost the passion and pleasure he'd always got from playing football. With his brothers Joël and Jean-Marie he helped to promote beach football in France, and was an immediate success in this branch of the game. In 2005, he was the player-coach of the French team that won the world championship against the Portuguese, who themselves had eliminated the Brazilians, the kings of the beach.

In 2011, however, he stepped away from the game to devote himself entirely to film. I've followed his career closely since his first films, *Le bonheur est dans le pré* in 1995 and *Elizabeth* in 1998. I was thrilled by the success he had in this new world, the more so as I noticed how the roles he was taking on moved him away from being typecast as a former footballer. The transformation was complete when in 2003 he played the role of a police commissioner in *L'Outremangeur*. From then on, I saw him as an actor. The footballer had disappeared.

During one of our get-togethers, he told me about his new life, about this completely different adventure, and as he talked I could hear the passion come through. When I thought back to all the conversations we'd had about directors, cult films, cinema icons, though, I wasn't at all surprised to see how much he was enjoying his new role, however far from the football pitch.

As well as cinema, he also entered the world of theatre. In 2010, Anne and I attended the play *Face au Paradis* at one of Paris's most famous venues, the Théâtre Marigny just off the Champs Elysées. It was directed by Rachida and also starred the distinguished actor Lorant Deutsch. Sitting in the front row with my two young children, I watched my friend closely, terrified of catching his eye in case somehow this might put him off, and was both delighted and very moved by his performance. Unlike with a football match, though, I refrained from judgement: I didn't go to the theatre much, which made me feel unqualified to have an opinion. My two very young children, used to the more interactive atmosphere of children's shows, kept asking me which one of the actors was my friend and why won't he come over to us? At the end of the performance we went to Eric's dressing room, and he jokingly remarked that we'd certainly got ourselves noticed. Perhaps going with the children hadn't been the best way to get an insight into his new profession . . .

Eric and I continued to see each other occasionally. Once, in Marseille, on the eve of a conference I was attending, I got a phone call from him to say he was in the city too. We met at a hotel near the Vieux Port, and he told me about a documentary project he was working on, which he would be directing, about the links between football and immigration.

'Claudio', he said, 'we have to tell our story, and that of our parents, who came from elsewhere and built our destiny.' I was delighted: in France immigration is an issue that interests me greatly, to the extent that in 2010 I had curated an exhibition on the impact of immigration on French football at the Cité Nationale de l'Histoire de l'Immigration in Paris.

I was thrilled when Eric asked me to write the script. The film featured some memorable moments, especially a bit where Zinedine Zidane was brought to tears as he talked about his father, who was of Algerian origin and had worked on the Stade de France where 'Zizou' had scored the goals that helped win the 1998 World Cup Final. In another striking sequence, Eric's mother recalled her parents fleeing the Spanish Civil War and the atrocities perpetrated by Franco's regime in the mid-1930s, and migrating to the south of France.

In December 2014, we were invited by the French president, François Hollande, to present Eric's film, *Foot et Immigration*, at the Elysée Palace, and Eric and his brothers, together with my brother Basile, went along to represent France's immigrant community. I wanted to be there too to express the pride we felt in our heritage and pay tribute to our parents, but unfortunately I'd already planned a trip to the Ivory Coast to see my mother. It was a good call, as it turned out to be the last time we were together: she died a few months later (we lost my father in 2002). During the aftermath my friendship with Eric was one of the things that got me through.

In 2016, Rachida organised a surprise birthday party for Eric's fiftieth near the Centre Pompidou, and on my way there I noticed a youngster on the Métro wearing a T-shirt that read 'Manchester, City of United'. On the back was a picture of Eric Cantona. I smiled to myself: my extraordinary, ordinary friend . . .

Acknowledgements

This book owes its existence to one person: Eric.

I was also fortunate to have been accompanied by a team of outstanding supporters. Leading the way was Anne, my ocean of happiness and the first to read my words. Then there are my stars of joy: Isabelle, Joël, Bernard, Raphaël, Joséphine, Basile, Roger, Laurent, Patricia, Geneviève, Bérangère, Déjo, Elisabeth, Clément, Thomas, Lilian and Paul.

Following them are the visible and invisible actors in this piece: the Reds, notably Sir Alex Ferguson and his staff, with a nod to 'Albi', plus the players of the 1992 generation. I'd like to give specific mention to Ryan Giggs, Ole Gunnar Solskjaer, Jordi Cruyff, Paul Ince, Steve Bruce, Terry Cooke, Danny Higginbotham, Leon Mills, Wilf and Paul McGuinness, Paddy Crerand (the King's staunch supporter), Tony Whelan, Mark Wylie and 'The Supremes' (Nicola Struthers and Gillian Moors), Ruth Hobson, Barry Moorhouse, Maurice Watkins, David Gill.

Thanks to the International Centre for Sport History and Culture at De Montfort University, Leicester, notably Pierre Lanfranchi, Matt Taylor, Richard Holt, Tony Mason, Charles Korr, Jean Williams, John Williams of Leicester

University (thank you for your precious advice and availability), Jean-Michel Faure and Harry Mephon (University of Nantes).

To my Mancunian friends: Saltz Anderson, Michael Brown and his son Junior (you are always on my mind), Mick Hucknall, David Latchimy, Catharine Rew, Rodney Watson, John and Chris Lee, Andy Holding, Mohammed Abdullah, Phil, Alana, Joshua and Dany.

To footballers Michael Thomas, Chris Waddle and Georgiou Kinkladze.

To Peter Boyle, Andy Walsh, Adam Brown, Richard Kurt and Andy Mitten in United's Red Army.

Finally, my thanks go to the whole team at Simon and Schuster, particularly Frances Jessop. I would also like to express my gratitude to Peter Cossins, the *'maillot jaune'* at all stages of the writing process, the ideal team member and the most French of the English, and to my agent and 'Messi', David Luxton. Thanks to you I've realised my dream by writing about football, music, literature and my city, Manchester.